ASTRONOMY DATA BOOK

ASTRONOMY DATA BOOK

J. Hedley Robinson

A HALSTED PRESS BOOK

JOHN WILEY & SONS

NEW YORK

Published in the USA
by Halsted Press, a Division
of John Wiley & Sons, Inc.
New York

ISBN 0 470 72801–9

Library of Congress Catalog Card No 72–9496

Printed in Great Britain
by Latimer Trend & Company Limited Plymouth

INTRODUCTION

This book is intended as a reference tool for the student and amateur astronomer and for those interested in the earth sciences. Over forty years of practical observation and teaching astronomy has shown the need for one, single book that brings together basic data and information that is at present scattered throughout numerous publications, and in a way that is easy to refer to.

To include all known astronomical information, even just tabular data, would result in one or more very bulky volumes in which it would be difficult to find quickly the most commonly needed information. It would also defeat one purpose of this book, which is that it should be kept at hand for both reference and the insertion of new discoveries and personal notes and observations. The wide margins and blank areas and pages are for the reader to insert notes on his or her own special interests, making the book up-to-date and as useful as possible for each person concerned.

It is intended that the observer shall use this book in conjunction with a Star Atlas. In some cases the positions of interesting objects on the celestial sphere are quoted in Right Ascension and Declination, while in others, no positions are quoted. This applies to the long lists of classified objects which can be traced in a good Star Atlas if the observer wishes. The positions of the most interesting objects, however, are given.

CONTENTS

Contents

Contents

Contents

LIST OF ILLUSTRATIONS

15

GLOSSARY OF ASTRONOMICAL TERMS

ABERRATION Apparent displacement due to the movement of the Earth at an angle to the path of the light from a star. Also one of several types of distortion produced by optical instruments.

ABSOLUTE MAGNITUDE Magnitude of a star if it were seen from a standard distance of ten parsecs (32·6 light years).

ABSORPTION LINES Dark lines in solar or stellar spectrum caused by intervening gas of lower density than source.

ACHROMAT Lens made of two different glass elements designed to cancel each other's chromatic aberrations.

AEROLITE Stony meteorite.

AIRGLOW Faint luminosity of the night sky.

ALBEDO Reflecting power of a non-luminous body.

ALTAZIMUTH Type of telescope mounting with movement in altitude and azimuth.

ALTITUDE Angular elevation above the horizon.

ÅNGSTRÖM UNIT   Unit of measure of the wavelength of light equivalent to one ten millionth of a millimetre.

APHELION   Position of a planet or similar body when furthest from its primary body, the Sun.

APOCHROMAT   Triple-lens system designed to remove residual chromatic aberration of an achromat.

APSIDES, LINE OF   The major axis of an orbit.

ASHEN LIGHT   Faint visibility of the night side of Venus.

ASTEROID   Small solid body orbiting Sun between orbits of Mars and Jupiter.

ASTRONOMICAL UNIT   The distance between the Sun and Earth —149,600,000km (93,000,000 miles).

ASTROPHYSICS   The physics and chemistry of stars.

AZIMUTH   Angular bearing of an object measured parallel to the horizon.

BARYCENTRE   Centre of gravity of the Earth-Moon system.

BINARY STAR   Star having two components.

BLINK MICROSCOPE   Instrument for examining two photographs in rapid succession.

BOLIDE   A brilliant meteor.

BUTTERFLY DIAGRAM   Plotting sunspots on a chart of heliographic latitude against time gives an effect resembling butterfly wings.

CEPHEID   Type of variable star, short period (50 days and less) and pulsating.

CHROMATIC ABERRATION   Colour produced by a lens.

CHROMOSPHERE   Part of the Sun.

CHRONOMETER   Accurate timekeeper or clock.

CLINOMETER   Instrument for measuring altitude angles.

COELOSTAT   Mirror instrument for maintaining the direction of light constant, as in solar observation.

COLOUR INDEX   Measure of a star's colour.

COLURE   Great circle on the celestial sphere, through the equinoctial or solstitial points.

COMA   The fuzzy part of a comet's head. Also an aberration in off-axis images produced by lenses and mirrors.

COMES   Faint member of a binary star.

CONJUNCTION   Apparent close approach of two celestial objects. In the case of Mercury and Venus inferior conjunction is when the planet is between Earth and Sun, while superior conjunction occurs when the planet is on the far side of the Sun. All three bodies—Earth, Sun and planet—are in a straight line.

CONSTELLATION   Group of stars.

CORONA   Outermost envelope of the Sun's atmosphere, or similar feature of a star or planet's atmosphere.

CORONAGRAPH   Instrument for examining the corona of the Sun.

COSMIC RAYS   High-energy corpuscular radiation, probably from supernovae or similar objects.

COSMOGONY   Study of the origin of the Universe and Solar System.

COUNTERGLOW   Another name for the Gegenschein.

CRESCENT   Phase of the Moon or planet between new and half.

DAWES' LIMIT   Practical limit of resolution of a telescope.

DECLINATION   Angular distance North or South of the celestial equator.

DICHOTOMY   Exact half phase of a planet or Moon.

DIURNAL MOTION   Apparent motion of the celestial objects due to the rotation of the Earth.

DOPPLER EFFECT   Apparent change in wavelength of light or sound caused by the motion of either the source or the observer, or both.

DOUBLE STAR   Star made up of two components; some are optical doubles merely because they happen to lie closely in line of sight without having any real physical connection.

DRIVING CLOCK   Device for moving a telescope to follow the object under observation.

EARTHSHINE   Light reflected on to the Moon by the Earth causing the dark part of the Moon to be made visible.

ECLIPSE, LUNAR   When the Moon passes through the shadow of the Earth.

ECLIPSE, SOLAR   When the Sun is hidden by the body of the Moon.

ECLIPSING VARIABLE   Star whose light varies because it is a binary, the components of which eclipse each other.

ECLIPTIC   Projection of the Earth's orbit on to the celestial sphere.

ELECTROMAGNETIC SPECTRUM   The whole range of radiation.

ELECTRON   Part of an atom carrying a negative charge.

ELEMENT   Substance that cannot be split into simpler chemical substances.

ELONGATION   Apparent angular distance of a planet or other body from the Sun.

EMISSION SPECTRUM   Spectrum produced by an incandescent gas, consisting of separate lines characteristic of each element.

EPHEMERIS   Table showing the predicted motions of a moving celestial body, eg a comet.

EPOCH   Date chosen for reference in quoting apparent positions of stars etc.

EQUATION OF TIME   Difference in time by which the mean Sun differs in position from the true Sun.

EQUATOR, CELESTIAL   Projection of the Earth's equator on the celestial sphere.

EQUATORIAL MOUNT   Mounting of a telescope or other instrument so that its motion sweeps parallel to the plane of the Earth's equator.

EQUINOX   Time of equal day and night, also the two points on the celestial sphere where the ecliptic cuts the celestial equator.

ESCAPE VELOCITY   Minimum speed at which an object must move to escape from the gravitational pull of a planet or other body.

EVECTION   An inequality in the Moon's motion, caused by the pull of the Sun.

EXOSPHERE   Outermost part of the Earth's atmosphere.

FACULAE   Bright temporary patches on the Sun.

FINDER   Small telescope of low magnification used for sighting a larger instrument.

FIREBALL   Exceptionally bright meteor.

FIRST POINT OF ARIES   Point on the ecliptic at which the Sun crosses the equator from South to North. This is now in the constellation Pisces because of precession.

FLARES   Bright outbursts on the Sun or a star.

FLARE STARS   Faint stars that may brighten suddenly.

FREE FALL   Normal state of an object in space as the Earth is in free fall around the Sun.

FRAUNHOFER LINES   Absorption lines in Solar spectrum, first mapped by Fraunhofer.

GALAXY OR GALAXIES   Separate star systems, of which some 1,000 million have been photographed.

GALAXY, THE   The system of stars to which our Sun belongs.

GAMMA RAYS   Short wavelength radiations.

GAUSS   Standard unit for measuring magnetic field.

GEGENSCHEIN   Faint glow in the sky opposite to the Sun.

GHOST   Spurious image caused by internal reflection in optical instruments.

GIBBOUS PHASE   Phase of the Moon or planet between half and full.

GLOBULAR CLUSTERS   Spherical concentrations of stars surrounding a galaxy, especially our own.

GLOBULES   Dark patches in gaseous nebulae.

GNOMON   The pointer of a sundial.

GOULD'S BELT   System of stars inclined to the plane of the Galaxy at about 20 degrees.

GRANULES   Granular structure of the Sun's surface.

GREAT CIRCLE   Circle on a sphere whose plane passes through the centre of the sphere.

GREENWICH MEAN TIME   Time at Greenwich reckoned according to the Mean Sun.

H-REGIONS Clouds of hydrogen. In H-I regions the hydrogen is neutral; in H-II regions it is ionised.

HARVEST MOON Full Moon nearest autumnal equinox as seen in the Northern Hemisphere.

HELIACAL RISING Rising at the same time as the Sun.

HERTZSPRUNG-RUSSELL DIAGRAM Diagram with stars shown relative to their spectra and luminosity.

HORIZON Great circle on the celestial sphere 90 degrees from the observer's over-head point or Zenith.

HOUR ANGLE Angle measured in hours etc by which a celestial object is removed from the meridian of the observer's position, measured westward.

HOUR CIRCLE Great circle passing through both North and South poles of the sky.

HUBBLE'S CONSTANT Increase of apparent recessional velocity of galaxies and quasars with distance from the observer.

HUNTER'S MOON Full moon following Harvest moon.

INFERIOR CONJUNCTION See Conjunction.

INFRA-RED RADIATION Radiation at wavelength longer than that of red light but shorter than radio waves.

INTERFEROMETER Instrument for measuring by the interference principle of light or radio waves.

INTERSTELLAR MATTER Material between stars.

ION An atom having lost or gained one or more electrons, so gaining a positive or negative charge respectively.

IONISATION   Process of driving off one or more electrons from an atom.

IONOSPHERE   Ionized region of Earth's atmosphere above the stratosphere.

JULIAN DAY   Count of days reckoning from 1 January 4713BC.

KEPLER'S LAWS   Three laws of planetary motion.

KILOPARSEC   One thousand parsecs.

KIRKWOOD GAPS   Regions in the belt of asteroids where almost no minor planets are found.

LATITUDE, CELESTIAL   Angular distance from the nearest point on the ecliptic, measured at 90° to the ecliptic.

LIBRATION   Wobble of the Moon in longitude and latitude; diurnal by rotation of the Earth moving the observer.

LIGHT YEAR   Distance travelled by light in one year.

LONGITUDE, CELESTIAL   Angular distance from the First Point of Aries, measured along the ecliptic.

LUNATION   Interval between successive new moons.

MAGELLANIC CLOUDS   Nearest external star systems separate from the Galaxy.

MAGNETIC STORM   Sudden disturbance of the Earth's magnetic field.

MAGNETOSPHERE   The area of the Earth's magnetic field.

MAGNITUDE, ABSOLUTE   See Absolute Magnitude.

MAGNITUDE, APPARENT   Apparent brightness of a celestial body.

MAGNITUDE, BOLOMETRIC   Brightness measured by all wavelengths emitted.

MAGNITUDE, PHOTOGRAPHIC   Apparent brightness on photographic plates, which are blue-sensitive.

MAIN SEQUENCE   Main band of stars on the Hertzsprung-Russell Diagram.

MASS   Quantity of matter contained in a body.

MEAN SUN   Imaginary body travelling along the celestial equator with regular motion, completing one revolution in the same time as the real Sun.

MEGAPARSEC   A million parsecs.

MERIDIAN   Great circle passing through the zenith and both celestial poles.

METEOR   Small particle moving round the Sun which appears as a 'shooting star' on collision with the Earth's atmosphere.

METEORITE   Solid body which survives collision and reaches the Earth's surface without being destroyed.

MICROMETEORITES   Very small particles which do not produce luminous effects.

MICRON   Unit of wavelength equal to 10,000 Ångström units (1/1000 of a millimetre).

MIDNIGHT SUN   The Sun seen above the horizon at midnight.

MILKY WAY   Luminous band in the sky formed by the Galaxy as seen from Earth.

MINOR PLANETS   See Asteroid.

MOLECULE   A stable association of atoms.

MULTIPLE STAR   A star made up of more than two components.

NADIR   Point on the celestial sphere below the observer's feet.

NEBULA   Mass of tenuous gas and dust in space.

NEUTRINO   Fundamental atomic particle with no mass nor charge.

NEUTRON   Particles in the nuclei of atoms other than the hydrogen atom having unit mass but no charge.

NEUTRON STAR   Very compact, very dense star composed mainly of neutrons, diameter about equal to that of Earth. Thought to be supernova remnants.

NOCTILUCENT CLOUDS   Clouds in the ionosphere seen at night.

NODES   Points at which an orbit cuts the plane of the ecliptic.

NORTH POLAR DISTANCE   Angular distance from the North Pole.

NORTH POLAR SEQUENCE   List of stars whose photographic magnitudes have been accurately measured.

NOVA   Star which experiences a sudden outburst and then fades to its normal faintness.

NUTATION   The slow 'nodding' of the Earth's axis.

OBJECT GLASS   Large lens at the front of a telescope.

OBLIQUITY OF THE ECLIPTIC   Angle between the ecliptic and the equator.

OCCULTATION   The apparent covering of one celestial object by another, as seen from Earth.

OCULAR Eyepiece for a telescope or similar instrument.

OPPOSITION Position of an object exactly opposite the Sun in the sky.

ORBIT Path of a celestial object.

ORRERY Model of the Solar System.

PARALLAX Apparent shift of an object when viewed from two separate directions.

PARSEC The distance at which an object would show a parallax of one second of arc, equal to 3·26 light years or 206,265 astronomical units in length.

PENUMBRA Area of partial shadow.

PERIASTRON Position in an orbit nearest a star.

PERIGEE Position in an orbit nearest Earth.

PERIHELION Position in an orbit nearest the Sun.

PERTURBATION The disturbance of an orbit.

PHASES Apparent changes of shape as of the Moon, due to changing angles of view and illumination.

PHOTOMETER Instrument for measuring the intensity of light.

PHOTOMETRY Study of the intensity of light and its measurement.

PHOTOMULTIPLIER Piece of apparatus for intensifying the current induced by light.

PHOTON The smallest unit of electromagnetic radiation, especially light.

PHOTOSPHERE   The visible surface of the Sun.

PLANETARY NEBULA   A hot star exciting a surrounding gaseous shell to shine.

PLANETS   Non-luminous bodies travelling round a luminous primary body.

POLES   North and South points of the celestial sphere, defined by the Earth's axis of rotation.

POPULATIONS, STAR   Two main types of stars are Population I and Population II. See section on Stars for details.

POSITION ANGLE   Apparent direction of one object from another, measured from the primary through East from North.

PRECESSION   Apparent slow circular motion of the celestial poles on the celestial sphere, taking 25,800 years to complete its revolution, due to the pull of the Sun and Moon on the Earth's equatorial bulge.

PRIME MERIDIAN   The meridian passing through Greenwich.

PROMINENCES   Masses of glowing gas rising from the Sun's surface.

PROPER MOTION   Individual motion of a star through space.

PROTON   Fundamental particle of the atom with a positive charge.

PULSAR   Rapidly spinning neutron star with strong magnetic field emitting regular pulses of radio energy.

QUADRATURE   When two bodies are seen at right angles to each other from Earth.

QUANTUM   Energy possessed by one photon of light.

QUASAR   A very remote highly luminous object emitting radio waves.

RADAR (ASTRONOMY)   Pulse energy emitted and bounced back from a distant object by a radio telescope.

RADIAL VELOCITY   Movement of a body measured by the Doppler effect.

RADIANT   Point from which meteors appear to radiate.

RADIO ASTRONOMY   The study of the sky at radio frequencies.

RADIO STARS   Radio sources, not stars. An obsolete term.

RADIO TELESCOPES   Radio receivers designed to detect faint astronomical radio waves.

RADIUS VECTOR   Line joining centre of a planet to centre of Sun.

RED SHIFT   The Doppler Effect towards the red.

REFLECTION   The turning back of light at the interface between two different media.

REFRACTION   The bending of light upon passing through media of different densities.

REGRESSION   The movement of the nodes of the Moon's orbit slowly westwards due to the gravitational pull of the Sun.

RETARDATION   Difference between the time of moonrise on two successive nights.

RETROGRADE MOTION   Movement of a body in the Solar System in the opposite direction from that of Earth.

REVERSING LAYER   Part of the Sun's atmosphere lying immediately above the photosphere.

RIGHT ASCENSION   Angular distance from the First Point of Aries measured eastwards, usually expressed in hours, minutes and seconds. It is also the sidereal time of the meridian passage of an object.

ROCHE LIMIT   Distance from the centre of a planet within which a second body would be broken up.

ROCKET ASTRONOMY   The science in which rockets are used to explore the celestial bodies.

RUSSELL DIAGRAM   See Hertzsprung-Russell Diagram.

SAROS   Period of 18 years 11·3 days after which the Earth, Moon and Sun return to almost the same relative positions.

SATELLITES   Minor bodies moving round some planets.

SCHRÖTER EFFECT   The discrepancy between theoretical and observed dichotomy.

SCINTILLATION   Twinkling of stars due to Earth's atmosphere.

SECULAR ACCELERATION   Slowing of the rotation of the Earth through the tides. The Moon recedes from Earth at about 9cm (four inches) per month, due to the same effect.

SEEING   Quality of steadiness and clarity of the image of a celestial body in a telescope, etc., due to the Earth's atmosphere.

SELENOGRAPHY   Study of the Moon's surface.

SHELL STARS   Hot stars surrounded by shells of gas.

SHOOTING STARS   Common name for Meteors.

SIDEREAL PERIOD   Time taken for a planet or similar body to make one journey round the Sun, or a satellite round a planet, with respect to the stars.

SIDEREAL TIME   Local time reckoned according to the apparent rotation of the celestial sphere.

SIDERITE   Iron meteorite, usually with some nickel.

SIDEROLITE   Stony iron meteorite.

SOLAR CONSTANT   Unit for measuring the energy received from the Sun on the Earth's surface.

SOLAR PARALLAX   The parallax of the Sun, measured from the Earth's equatorial radius, value 8·79 seconds of arc giving mean distance of 149,600,000km (92,957,209 miles).

SOLAR SYSTEM   System of the Sun and planets, satellites, comets, minor planets etc.

SOLAR TIME   Local time by the actual Sun.

SOLAR WIND   Steady flow of atomic particles from the Sun.

SOLSTICES   Times when the Sun is at its most northerly or southerly point, summer and winter.

SOLSTITIAL COLURE   The colure passing through the solstitial points on the celestial sphere.

SOLSTITIAL POINTS   Points on the ecliptic where the Sun is at maximum declination North or South.

SPECIFIC GRAVITY   Density of a substance relative to water.

SPECTROHELIOGRAPH   Instrument for photographing the Sun in light of one particular wavelength.

SPECTROSCOPE   Instrument for studying the spectrum.

SPECTROSCOPIC BINARY   Star with the components too close to be observed visually, shown as binary by changes in its spectrum.

SPECTROSCOPIC PARALLAX   Distance of a star obtained by spectroscopic observation.

SPECULUM   The main mirror of a reflecting telescope.

SPHERICAL ABERRATION   Difference in the focal length from the centre to the edge of a lens or mirror.

SPICULES   Jets in the solar atmosphere.

SPORER'S LAW   The appearance of the first spots on the Sun in the new cycle in high latitudes while last ones of the old cycle die away in low latitudes, giving rise to the 'butterfly diagram'.

STAR   A self-luminous body like the Sun.

STRATOSPHERE   Layer in the Earth's atmosphere.

SUN   Star nearest to Earth, the centre of the Solar System.

SUNDIAL   Instrument for telling the time by the shadow cast by the Sun.

SUPERGIANTS   Very large luminous stars.

SUPERIOR PLANETS   Planets beyond the orbit of Earth.

SUPERNOVA   Exploding star expelling much of its material.

SYNODIC PERIOD   Interval between oppositions of a superior planet, or conjunctions of an inferior one, as seen from Earth.

SYZYGY   Position of the Moon at new or full, also applicable to other bodies when three are in a straight line as in the case of the Moon, Earth and Sun at full or new moon.

TEKTITES   Small glassy bodies found in some areas of the Earth.

TELESCOPE   Instrument for observing objects at a distance.

TEMPORARY STAR   The old name for a Nova.

TERMINATOR   Boundary between day and night on the surface of a planet or satellite.

THERMOCOUPLE   Instrument for measuring small quantities of heat.

TIDES   Daily rise and fall of the oceans due to gravitational pull of the Moon and the Sun. There are also tides in the Earth's crust and atmosphere from the same causes, and in the bodies of some binary stars.

TIME   A measure of change described in hours, minutes and seconds at a constant rate.

TORR   Unit of pressure equal to 1mm of mercury.

TRANSIT   Passage of an object across an observer's meridian, or across the disk of another object, eg the Sun or Jupiter.

TRANSIT INSTRUMENT   Instrument for measuring the time of meridian transit of an object.

TROJANS   A group of asteroids associated with Jupiter.

TROPICAL YEAR   See Year.

TROPOSPHERE   Lowest layer of the Earth's atmosphere.

TWILIGHT, ASTRONOMICAL   State of illumination when the Sun is below the horizon by less than 18 degrees.

TWINKLING   See Scintillation.

ULTRA-VIOLET   Radiation shorter than violet light in wavelength.

UMBRA   Main dark part of a shadow.

UNIVERSAL TIME   Same as Greenwich Mean Time.

UNIVERSE   The whole of everything that exists.

VAN ALLEN ZONES (BELTS)   Zones around Earth in which electrically charged particles are trapped by the Earth's magnetic field.

VARIABLE STARS   Stars that vary in brightness.

VARIATION   An inequality of the Moon's motion, caused by the Sun.

WHITE DWARF   Small star with great density.

WIDMANSTÄTTEN PATTERN   Figures found when an iron meteorite is cut and polished.

WOLF RAYET STARS   Very hot type of star showing emission lines in the spectrum.

X-RAY ASTRONOMY   Study of astronomy at X-ray frequency.

YEAR, ANOMALISTIC   Interval between perihelion passages of the Earth (365·25964 days).

YEAR, SIDEREAL   True period of revolution of Earth round the Sun as related to a fixed point in space (365·25636 days).

YEAR, TROPICAL   Interval between successive passages of the Sun through the First Point of Aries (365·24219 days).

ZENITH   Celestial point above an observer's head.

ZENITH DISTANCE   Angular distance from the Zenith.

ZENITH HOURLY RATE   Number of meteors per hour as would be recorded if the shower were overhead.

ZODIAC   Band of twelve constellations along the ecliptic, in which the Sun, Moon and planets appear to move.

ZODIACAL CONSTELLATIONS   Constellations of Aries, Taurus, Gemini, Cancer, Leo, Virgo, Libra, Scorpio, Sagittarius, Capricornus, Aquarius, and Pisces. A small part of Ophiuchus should also be included.

ZODIACAL LIGHT   Cone of light along the ecliptic probably caused by small particles in the plane of the Solar System reflecting sunlight, seen at dawn or dusk.

IMPORTANT DATES IN THE HISTORY OF ASTRONOMY

BC
2000 The constellations were drawn up around this time.
 580 Pythagoras considers the motion of Earth and planets.
 395 Herakleides teaches the Earth's diurnal rotation.
 300 Aristillus and Timocharis determine the Zodiacal stars.
 280 Aristarchus suggests the Earth moves round the Sun.
 270 Eratosthenes measures the size of the Earth.
 230 Apollonius devises the system of eccentrics and epicycles.
 130 Hipparchus makes his star catalogue.

AD
 140 Ptolemy writes his *Almagest*.
 813 *Almagest* translated into Arabic.
 850 Albategnius makes observations and compiles tables.
 903 Al-Sufi revises the Alexandrian list of stars.
1000 Abul Wefa discovers the Moon's variation.
1038 Alhazen discovers the law of refraction.
1054 Supernova in Taurus recorded by Chinese.
1080 Arzachel publishes the *Toletan Tables*.
1230 The *Almagest* translated into Latin.
1270 *Alphonsine Tables* published.
1433 Ulugh Beigh's observatory at Samarkand.

1440 Nikolaus Krebs speculates on the motion of the Earth.
1474 Regiomontanus proposes lunar method of determining longitude.
1543 Copernicus publishes his *De Revolutionibus Orbium Caelestium*.
1572 Tycho Brahe observes Supernova in Cassiopeia.
1576 Tycho Brahe founds observatory at Uraniborg.
1595 Mira Ceti observed by Fabricus.
1596 Uraniborg observatory abandoned as Tycho leaves Denmark.
1600 Bruno burned at the stake.
1603 Publication of Bayer's Star Catalogue *Uranometria*.
1604 Kepler's supernova in Ophiuchus.
1608 Lippershey develops the telescope.
1609 Galileo uses the telescope for observation.
1611 Sunspots observed by Galileo and others.
1612 Orion Nebula first reported by Peiresc.
1618 Kepler's Third Law of Planetary Motion published.
1627 Publication of the *Rudolphine Tables* by Kepler.
1631 Transit of Mercury predicted by Kepler, observed by Gassendi.
1632 Publication of Galileo's *Dialogue*.
1633 Galileo before the Inquisition.
1638 Variability of Mira Ceti discovered by Holwarda.
1639 Transit of Venus observed by Horrocks.
1647 Hevelius' map of the Moon.
1651 Riccioli's map of the Moon.
1655 Titan discovered and true form of Saturn's rings determined.
1659 Huygens first sees the markings on Mars.
1663 James Gregory suggests reflecting telescopes.
1665 Newton's experiments on light.
1666 Polar caps of Mars observed by Cassini.
1668 Newton builds his reflecting telescope.
1669 Variability of Algol discovered.
1671 Paris Observatory founded. Cassini discovers Iapetus.
1675 Royal Greenwich Observatory founded. Cassini dis-

AD

covers the division in Saturn's rings. Rømer measures the velocity of light.

1676   Halley at St Helena catalogues southern stars.

1683   Cassini observes the Zodiacal Light.

1687   Newton publishes his *Principia*.

1704   Newton publishes his *Opticks*.

1705   Halley predicts return of Halley's Comet (see 1758).

1725   Flamsteed's star catalogue, final version, published.

1728   Bradley discovers the aberration of light.

1729   Chester More Hall discovers principle of achromatic lens.

1744   Cheseaux's six-tailed comet.

1750   Lacaille catalogues 10,000 stars at the Cape of Good Hope.

1758   Halley's Comet discovered on its foretold return. Dollond rediscovers principle of achromatic lens.

1761   Transit of Venus observed and its atmosphere discovered.

1762   Bradley completes measurements of positions of 60,000 stars.

1767   Nevil Maskelyne founds the *Nautical Almanac*.

1769   Transit of Venus observed, measuring the astronomical unit.

1772   Bode's Law published.

1774   First recorded observation by William Herschel.

1776   Tobias Mayer's lunar map published.

1779   Schröter founded his observatory at Lilienthal.

1781   *Messier's Catalogue* published. Herschel discovers Uranus.

1783   Goodricke's theory of variability of Algol.

1784   Goodricke discovers variability of Delta Cephei.

1786   Herschel puts forward his disk theory of the Galaxy.

1789   Herschel completes his 40ft reflector.

1796   Laplace publishes his Nebular Hypothesis.

1801   Ceres discovered by Piazzi. Lalande's Catalogue of 47,380 stars.

1802   Herschel announces discovery of a binary star system. Wollaston observes absorption lines in solar spectrum.

1803 L'Aigle meteorites, and nature of meteorites established.
1811 Olbers' theory of comet tails.
1813 Schröter's observatory destroyed.
1815 Fraunhöfer observes dark lines in solar spectrum.
1818 Encke's comet returns as predicted.
1819 Bessel completes reduction of Bradley's observations of stars.
1824 Great Dorpat refractor erected.
1826 Biela's comet discovered by both Biela and Gambart.
1832 John Herschel commences observation of southern stars.
1833 Great Leonid meteor shower.
1834 Bessel discovers irregular proper motion of Sirius and attributes it to presence of a companion star (see 1862).
1837 Beer & Mädler's *Der Mond* with map of the Moon published.
1838 Bessel measures parallax and thus distance of 61 Cygni.
1840 Draper's first Moon photographs.
1842 Doppler shift principle announced by Doppler.
1843 Schwabe discovers sunspot cycle.
1845 Lord Rosse's 72in reflector completed at Birr Castle. Solar photographs taken by Fizeau and Foucault. Biela's comet breaks up (see 1872).
1846 Neptune discovered by Adams and Le Verrier.
1847 15in refractor set up at Cambridge (Mass).
1848 Roche proves Saturn's rings cannot be solid.
1850 Bond discovers Saturn's crêpe ring.
1854 Brorsen (Danish astronomer) discovers the Gegenschein.
1858 Donati's Comet.
1859 Kirchhoff interprets the dark lines in solar spectrum.
1861 Spörer's law of sunspots announced.
1862 Sirius B discovered visually by Clark (see 1834).
1863 Secchi classifies stars into types. Huggins identifies elements in spectra of Betelgeux and Aldebaran.
1864 Huggins proves gaseous nature of unresolvable nebulae.
1867 Wolf-Rayet stars described by Wolf and Rayet.
1868 Ångström's map of solar spectrum. Solar prominences observed without eclipse of the Sun; Jansen and Lockyer.

AD

1872   Bielid meteor shower (see 1845).
1874   Transit of Venus observed, astronomical unit remeasured.
1877   Schiaparelli describes 'canals' of Mars. Deimos and Phobos discovered by Hall.
1878   Schmidt's map of the Moon published.
1882   Transit of Venus, astronomical unit remeasured.
1890   Lockyer's theory of stellar evolution. Vogel establishes reality of spectroscopic binaries.
1891   Spectroheliograph invented.
1894   Flagstaff Observatory founded by Lowell.
1896   Meudon 33in refractor erected.
1897   Yerkes Observatory opened.
1900   Reality of light pressure established by Lebedev.
1901   Nova Persei appears.
1903   Tsiolkovskii publishes the first paper on astronautics
1905   Mount Wilson Observatory founded.
1908   Hertzsprung describes giant and dwarf stars.
1912   Cepheid period-luminosity law discovered by Miss Leavitt.
1913   Russell's theory of stellar evolution.
1914   Goddard commences experiments with rockets.
1915   Sirius B spectrum studied by Adams leading to the discovery of white dwarf stars.
1917   100in Hooker telescope completed.
1918   First accurate idea of the shape of the Galaxy.
1919   Catalogue of dark nebulae by Barnard. Goddard's monograph *A Method of Reaching Extreme Altitudes*.
1920   Red shift in the spectra of galaxies announced by Slipher.
1922   Goddard's first tests with liquid fuel motors (see 1926).
1923   Hubble proves galaxies lie beyond the Milky Way (see 1920). Hale invents the spectrohelioscope.
1926   Goddard fires his first liquid fuel rocket (see 1922).
1927   Oort shows centre of Galaxy lies in Sagittarius.
1930   Pluto discovered by Tombaugh from Lowell's calculations.
1931   Eros close approach to Earth, astronomical unit re-

measured. Jansky discovers radio waves from Milky Way. Winkler in Germany successfully fires liquid fuel rocket.

1932 Carbon dioxide discovered in atmosphere of Venus.

1934 White spot on Saturn discovered by Will Hay. Nova Herculis discovered by Prentice.

1937 Grote Reber builds his dish radio aerial. First rocket tests at Peenemünde (see 1942 etc).

1938 New theory of stellar energy by Bethe and Von Weizsäcker.

1942 61 Cygni B is discovered to have a massive planet. Successful tests of V2 rockets at Peenemünde.

1944 H. Van de Hulst suggests interstellar hydrogen emits radio waves at 21·1cm (see 1951).

1945 Peenemünde captured by the Russians.

1946 Radar echoes from the Moon recorded by Z. Bay.

1947 Fall of large meteorite in Vladivostok region of USSR. Woomera Rocket Range established.

1948 Hale 200in telescope at Mount Palomar completed.

1949 First step-rocket fired at White Sands.

1950 First rocket launching from Cape Kennedy.

1951 Discovery of 21·1cm radiation from interstellar hydrogen (see 1944).

1952 Baade announces revision of the distance scale of galaxies.

1955 Jodrell Bank 250ft dish completed.

1957 *Sputniks I* and *II* launched by USSR.

1958 Completion of 120in reflector at Lick Observatory. *Explorer I*, first American satellite launched successfully. First successful launching of Vanguard rocket by USA. Discovery of Van Allen Zones (or belts). Outbreak in lunar crater Alphonsus observed by Kozyrev.

1959 Russian *Lunik I* passes the Moon; *Lunik II* landed on Moon; *Lunik III* sent back pictures of far side of Moon.

1960 American *Pioneer V* launched towards orbit of Venus.

1961 Russian Venus probe launched. Manned space flight by

AD

Y. Gagarin in *Vostok* vehicle. American space flight by Shepard. New measures of the astronomical unit.

1962 First American orbital flight. First active geodetic satellite. Venus probe *Mariner 2* (USA) sends back information. Russians launch, but lose contact with, Mars probe.

1963 First manoeuvrable satellite by Russians: *Polyot I*. Schmidt discovers Quasars.

1963 Valentina Tereshkova-Nikolayeva of USSR first woman in a space flight.

1964 American *Ranger VII* takes close-range Moon photographs.

1965 First space walks by Leonov (USSR) and White (USA). Close range photos of Mars by *Mariner 4* (USA). Space docking operation by *Gemini 6* and *7* (USA).

1966 First soft landing on Moon by *Luna 9* (USSR). Russian *Venera 3* lands on Venus. First American soft landing on Moon by *Surveyor I*. Improved close range photos of Moon by *Orbiters I* and *II*.

1967 *Orbiter III* photographs Moon at close range. Disaster at Cape Kennedy, deaths of three astronauts. First fatal accident in space: V. Komarov (USSR) in *Soyuz I*. First soft landing on Venus (USSR). American *Surveyor III* trenches lunar surface. *Orbiter IV* takes close-range photos of Moon. *Venera 4* (Russian) and *Mariner V* (American) to Venus. Pulsars discovered.

1968 *Apollo 8* with three-man crew, 70 miles above Earth. *Apollo 9* manned test flight.

1969 *Apollo 10* rehearsal for Moon landing. *Apollo 11* Moon landing by Armstrong and Aldrin; Collins third man in lunar module. *Apollo 12* Moon landing 200yd from *Surveyor III* (see 1967), 90lb of rock samples brought back.

1970 *Apollo 13* failure. *Luna 16* (USSR) first automatic probe to land on the Moon and return. Lunokhod vehicle on Moon. *Venera 7* (USSR) landed on planet.

1971 *Apollo 14* Moon landing and further rock samples brought back. *Mariner 9* and *Mars 2* and *3* launched towards Mars by USA and USSR. *Salyut* (USSR) vehicle in space. Spaceship *Soyuz II* makes successful re-entry but crew, Dobrovolsky, Volkov and Patsayev, found dead on opening capsule. *Apollo 15* Moon landing with Lunar Rover vehicle and further rock samples brought back by Scott and Irwin with Worden as third man. *Luna 18* (USSR) launched, but landed unfortunately on the Moon. *Luna 19* (USSR) launched.

1972 *Luna 20* (USSR) to the Moon. *Venera 8* (USSR) to Venus. *Pioneer 10* (USA) to Jupiter. *Apollo 16* (USA) to Moon, north of Descartes.

TABLES

USEFUL CONVERSION FACTORS

To convert from	To	Multiply by
Kilometres	metres	1,000
	centimetres	100,000
	feet	3,280·83
	miles	0·62137
Metres	kilometres	0·001
	centimetres	100
	inches	39·37
	feet	3·2808
	miles	$6·21 \times 10^{-4}$
Centimetres	inches	0·3937
	feet	0·03281
Feet	metres	0·3048
Miles	kilometres	1·60935
	inches	63,360
	feet	5,280
Ångström Unit	centimetres	10^{-8}
Micron	centimetres	10^{-4}
Square feet	square centimetres	929·03
Cubic feet	cubic centimetres	28,316·9
Hours	minutes	60
	seconds	3,600
	degrees of arc	15
Degree of arc	minutes of time	4
Horse power	watts	746
Watts	ergs/sec	
	joules/sec	10,000,000

Light years and *parsecs*—see under Astronomical & Physical Constants, p 47.

ASTRONOMICAL AND PHYSICAL CONSTANTS

Tropical year (1900)	31,556,925·947–s
Gaussian gravitational constant	0·01720209895 = 0°·9856076686
Astronomical unit	149,600,000km = 92,957,209mi
Speed of light in vacuo	299,792·5km s⁻¹ = 186,282·6mi s⁻¹
Equatorial radius of the Earth	6,378·160km = 3,963·208mi
Dynamical form-factor J_2 for the Earth	0·0010827
Product of gravitational constant and mass of the Earth	398,603km³ s⁻² = 95,630mi³ s⁻²
Earth-Moon mass ratio	81·30
Moon's sidereal mean motion (1900)	2·661699489 × 10⁻⁶ radians s⁻¹ = 0″·5490149294s⁻¹
General precession in longitude per tropical century (1900) ..	5025″·64
Obliquity of the ecliptic (1900)	23° 27′ 08″·26
Constant of nutation in obliquity (1900)	9″·210

Solar parallax	8″·79405
Light-time for unit distance	499·012s = 0·00577560d
Constant of aberration	20″·4958
Mean distance Earth to Moon	384,400km = 238,855mi
Sine of Moon's mean equatorial horizontal parallax	3422″·451
Lunar inequality	6″·43987
Parallactic inequality	124″·986

Length of the year

Tropical (equinox to equinox)	365ᵈ·24219
Sidereal (fixed star to fixed star)	365·25636
Anomalistic (apse to apse)	365·25964
Eclipse (Moon's node to Moon's node)	346·62003
Gaussian (Kepler's law for $a = 1$)	365·25690

Length of the month

Tropical (equinox to equinox)	27ᵈ·32158
Sidereal (fixed star to fixed star)	27·32166
Anomalistic (apse to apse)	27·55455
Draconic (node to node)	27·21222
Synodic (New Moon to New Moon)	29·53059

Length of the day

Mean solar day ..	24ʰ 03ᵐ 56ˢ·555 = 1ᵈ·00273791 mean sidereal time
Mean sidereal day ..	23ʰ 56ᵐ 04ˢ·091 = 0ᵈ·99726957 mean solar time
Sidereal rotation period of the earth	23ʰ 56ᵐ 04ˢ·099 = 0ᵈ·99726966 mean solar time

Figure of the Earth

Equatorial radius	6,378·160km = 3,963·208mi
Polar radius	6,356·775km = 3,949·920mi
Reciprocal flattening	298·25

$*\rho \sin \phi' = S \sin \phi$, $\rho \cos \phi' = C \cos \phi$, where

$S = 0.99497418 - 0.00167082 \cos 2\phi + 10^{-8} (210 \cos 4\phi + 15.7h)$

$C = 1.00167997 - 0.00168208 \cos 2\phi + 10^{-8} (212 \cos 4\phi + 15.7h)$

$\rho = 0.99832707 + 0.00167644 \cos 2\phi - 10^{-8} (352 \cos 4\phi - 15.7h) +$
$\qquad\qquad 10^{-8} \cos 6\phi$

$\tan \phi' = [0.9933054 + (0.11 \times 10^{-8}h)] \tan \phi$

$\phi - \phi' = 692''.74 \sin 2\phi - 1''.16 \sin 4\phi$

$1°$ of latitude $= [111.1333 - 0.5598 \cos 2\phi + 0.0012 \cos 4\phi]$ km

$1°$ of longitude $= [111.4133 \cos \phi - 0.0935 \cos 3\phi + 0.0001 \cos 5\phi]$ km

Acceleration due to gravity

$\qquad g = 978.0310 \, [1 + 0.00530239 \sin^2\phi - 0.00000587 \sin^2 Z\phi - (31.55 \times$
$\qquad\qquad\qquad 10^{-8}) \, h]$ cm.s^{-2}

Length of seconds pendulum

$\qquad l = [99.35769 - 0.26272 \cos 2\phi + 0.00029 \cos 4\phi - (3133 \times 10^{-8}) \, h]$ cm

Constant of gravitation	..	..	6.670×10^{-8} g^{-1} cm^3 s^{-2}

Mass of the Earth	..	5.976×10^{27} g
Mass of the Moon	..	7.351×10^{25} g
Mass of the Sun	..	1.990×10^{33} g
Annual general precession	..	$p = 50''.2564 + 0''.0222 \, T*$
Annual precission in RA	..	$m = 3^s.07234 + 0^s.00186 \, T$
Annual precession in Dec	..	$n = 20''.0468 - 0''.0085 \, T$
Node of moving on fixed ecliptic	..	$\pi = 173° \, 57'.06 + 54'.77 \, T$
Speed of rotation of ecliptic	..	$\pi = 0''.4711 - 0''.0007 \, T$
Invariable plane of the solar system	..	$\Omega = 106° \, 35' \, 01'' + 3452'' \, T$
		$i = 1° \, 34' \, 59'' - 18'' \, T$

Solar radiation

Solar constant	..	..	1.99 cal cm^{-2} min^{-1}
Radiation emitted	..	..	3.90×10^{33} erg s^{-1}
Radiation emittance at surface	..	..	6.41×10^{10} erg cm^{-2} s^{-1}
Total internal radiant energy	..	..	2.8×10^{47} erg
Radiation emitted per unit mass	..	..	1.96 erg s^{-1} g^{-1}
Visual absolute magnitude (M_v)	..	..	$+4.79$
Colour indices (B–V, U–B)	..	..	$+0.62, +0.10$
Spectral type	..	..	G2V
Effective temperature	..	..	$5,800 °K$

The Galactic System

Pole of galactic plane (1950)	..	α 12^h 49^m.0, $\delta + 27° \, 24'$
Point of zero longitude (1950)	..	α 17^h 42^m.4, $\delta - 28°55'$
Galactic Longitude of North Pole	..	$123°.00$
Mass ..	..	1.1×10^{11} solar masses $= 2.2 \times 10^{44}$ g
Average density	..	0.1 solar mass pc^{-3} $= 7 \times 10^{-24}$ g cm^{-3}
Diameter	..	25,000pc
Thickness	..	4,000pc
Distance of Sun from centre	..	8,200pc

$*\phi$ = geographic or geodetic latitude.

ϕ' = geocentric latitude.

ρ = geocentric distance in equatorial radii.

h = height in metres.

Distance of Sun above galactic plane 8pc
Solar apex (1950)† .. .. α 18h 06m, δ+30°
Solar motion† .. .. 20·0km s^{-1} = 12·4mi s^{-1}
Period of revolution of Sun about centre .. .. .. 2·2 × 10^{8}yr

Conversion factors
Light-year .. 9·4607 × 10^{12}km = 5·8786 × 10^{12}mi = 63,240au = 0·30660pc
Parsec.. .. 30·857 × 10^{12}km = 19·174 × 10^{12}mi = 206,265au = 3·2616 l.y.

MISCELLANEOUS DATA

		Logarithm
π	3·14159 26536	0·497 1499
e	2·71828 18285	0·434 2945
$M = \log_{10} e$	0·43429 44819	$\bar{1}$·637 7843
$1/M = \log_e 10$	2·30258 50930	0·362 2157
$\sqrt{2}$	1·41421 35624	0·150 5150
$\sqrt{3}$	1·73205 08076	0·238 5606
1 radian	57°·29577 95131	1·758 1226
	3437'·74677 078	3·536 2739
	206264"·80625	5·314 4251
1°	0·01745 32925 radians	$\bar{2}$·241 8774
1'	0·00029 08882	$\bar{4}$·463 7261
1"	0·00000 4848137	$\bar{6}$·685 5749
1 metre	3·28084 27 feet	0·515 9855
1 foot	0·30479 973 metres	$\bar{1}$·484 0145
1 kilometre	0·62137 173 miles	$\bar{1}$·793 3516
1 mile	1·60934 26 kilometres	0·206 6485
ft s^{-1}	0·68182mi hr^{-1}	$\bar{1}$·833 67
mi hr^{-1}	1·46667ft s^{-1}	0·166 33

1 revolution = 360° = 1,296,000" = 24h = 86,400s
1 Sphere = 12·5664 steradians = 41,253 square degrees
1 Julian year = 365·25 days = 31,557,600 seconds

SYMBOLS AND ABBREVIATIONS

SUN, MOON AND PLANETS

☉ The Sun	☾ The Moon generally	♃ Jupiter
● New Moon	☿ Mercury	♄ Saturn
● Full Moon	♀ ·Venus	♅ Uranus
☽ First Quarter	⊕ Earth	♆ Neptune
☾ Last Quarter	♂ Mars	♇ Pluto

ASPECTS AND ABBREVIATIONS

☌ Conjunction, or having the same Longitude or Right Ascension.
☍ Opposition, or differing 180° in Longitude or Right Ascension.
□ Quadrature, or differing 90° in Longitude or Right Ascension.
☊ Ascending Node; ☋ Descending Node.
α or R.A., Right Ascension; δ or Dec., Declination.
h, m, s, Hours, Minutes, Seconds of Time.
° ′ ″, Degrees, Minutes, Seconds of Arc.

SIGNS OF THE ZODIAC

♈ Aries..........0°	♌ Leo..........120°	♐ Sagittarius ...240°
♉ Taurus........30°	♍ Virgo........150°	♑ Capricornus ..270°
♊ Gemini........60°	♎ Libra........180°	♒ Aquarius.....300°
♋ Cancer........90°	♏ Scorpius.....210°	♓ Pisces........330°

THE GREEK ALPHABET

A, α	Alpha	I, ι	Iota	P, ρ	Rho
B, β	Beta	K, κ	Kappa	Σ, σ	Sigma
Γ, γ	Gamma	Λ, λ	Lambda	T, τ	Tau
Δ, δ	Delta	M, μ	Mu	Υ, υ	Upsilon
E, ε	Epsilon	N, ν	Nu	Φ, φ	Phi
Z, ζ	Zeta	Ξ, ξ	Xi	X, χ	Chi
H, η	Eta	O, o	Omicron	Ψ, ψ	Psi
Θ, θ, ϑ	Theta	Π, π	Pi	Ω, ω	Omega

ATOMIC NUMBER AND WEIGHT OF ELEMENTS MOST COMMONLY FOUND IN CELESTIAL BODIES

Element	Symbol	Atomic number	Atomic weight	Log of cosmic abundances	
				number	weight
Hydrogen	H	1	1·008	12·00	12·00
Helium	He	2	4·002	11·16	11·76
Lithium	Li	3	6·939	3·00	4·00
Beryllium	Be (Gl)	4	9·013	2·40	3·40
Boron	B	5	10·812	2·80	3·80
Carbon	C	6	12·011	8·48	9·56
Nitrogen	N	7	14·007	7·96	9·11
Oxygen	O	8	16·000	8·83	10·03
Flourine	F	9	18·999	5·40	6·70
Neon	Ne	10	20·184	8·44	9·74
Sodium	Na	11	22·991	6·22	7·58
Magnesium	Mg	12	24·313	7·46	8·84
Aluminium	Al	13	26·982	6·28	7·71
Silicon	Si	14	28·090	7·47	8·92
Phosphorus	P	15	30·975	5·53	7·02
Sulphur	S	16	32·066	7·22	8·72
Chlorine	Cl	17	35·454	5·40	6·90
Argon	Ar (A)	18	39·949	6·62	8·22
Calcium	Ca	20	40·080	6·22	7·82
*Titanium	Ti	22	47·900	4·82	6·50
Vanadium	V	23	50·994	3·78	5·48
*Chromium	Cr	24	52·000	5·38	7·09
Manganese	Mn	25	54·940	5·10	6·84
Iron	Fe	26	55·849	6·90	8·65
Cobalt	Co	27	58·936	4·72	6·49
Nickel	Ni	28	58·710	5·93	7·70
Strontium	Sr	38	87·630	2·75	4·69
*Yttrium	Y	39	88·908	2·40	4·34
*Zirconium	Zr	40	91·220	2·40	4·40
†Uranium	U (Ur)	92	238·040	0·00	2·40

* Elements found in lunar rocks.
† Uranium fission is suspected in the lower solar corona.

C

SUN, MOON AND PLANETS

Name	Equatorial diameter — Unit dist "	Equatorial diameter — Mean opp'n Dist* "	Equatorial diameter — Kilometres†	Sidereal Period of Axial rotation ‡	Inclination § ° '	Reciprocal mass Sun = 1 ‖	Density water = 1	Escape velocity kms	On scale Earth = 1 — Equatorial diameter	On scale Earth = 1 — Mass	On scale Earth = 1 — Volume	On scale Earth = 1 — Surface gravity **	Mean visual opp'n mag ††	Albedo
Sun	1919·26	...	1392 000	25ᵈ·380	7 15	1·0000	1·409	617·50	109·1200	332,946	1303 600	27·9000	−26·8	...
Moon	4·79	1865·16	3 476	27·322	1 32	27 068 000	3·342	2·38	0·2725	0·0123	0·0203	0·1653	−12·7	0·07
Mercury	6·97	11·37	4 870	58·700	0	5980 000	5·500	4·27	0·3820	0·0560	0·0560	0·3810	0·0	0·06
Venus	16·69	60·32	12 100	243·000	178	408 520	5·250	10·36	0·9489	0·8150	0·8572	0·9032	−4·4	0·76
Earth	17·59	...	12 756	23ʰ 56ᵐ 04ˢ	23 27	328 900	5·517	11·18	1·0000	1·0000	1·0000	1·0000	...	0·36
Mars	9·36	17·87	6 790	24 37 23	23 59	3098 700	3·940	5·03	0·5320	0·1074	0·1504	0·3799	−2·0	0·16
Jupiter	196·95	46·86	142 800	9 50 30	3 04	1047·36	1·330	60·22	11·197	317·89	1 318·7	2·643	−2·6	0·73
Saturn	164·54	19·27	119 300	10 14	26 44	3499·60	0·706	36·25	9·355	95·14	743·6	1·159	+0·7	0·76
Uranus	65·00	3·57	47 100	10 49	97 53	22930	1·70	22·40	3·700	14·52	47·1	1·110	+5·5	0·93
Neptune	66·70	2·30	48 400	15 48	28 48	19300	1·770	23·90	3·790	17·25	53·7	1·210	+7·8	0·84
Pluto	8·20	0·21	5 900	6ᵈ·390	?	3300 000	5·50	5·10	0·470	0·10	0·10	0·470	+14·9	0·14

* The values for Mercury and Venus are those at mean inferior conjunction.

† The polar diameters of the Earth, Mars, Jupiter, Saturn, Uranus and Neptune are respectively 12 714, 6 750, 133 500, 107 700, 43 800 and 47 400 kilometres.

‡ Where there is non-solid body rotation the values given are for the equatorial regions (*ie* System I is given for Jupiter). The polar regions of the Sun rotate in a period of 29 or 30 days. For Jupiter, the rotation period of System II is 9h 55m 41s; radio methods have recently led to System III, with a period twelve seconds shorter than this. High-latitude spots have been observed on Saturn rotating in a period of 10h 40m. The rotation of Venus is *retrograde*.

§ The inclinations are those of the equators, with respect to the ecliptic for the Sun and Moon, and to their orbits for the planets.

‖ These include the mass of the satellite system, if any. The value for Pluto is little more than a guess.

** The quantities given are those of the planet's attractions, and not the resultant of gravity and centrifugal force; the latter would diminish the values by up to 9 per cent at the equator of Jupiter and up to 16 per cent at that of Saturn.

†† The values for Mercury and Venus are those at mean greatest elongation.

ORBITS OF THE PLANETS

Planet	Mean distance from the Sun		Sidereal period (days)	Mean synodic period (days)	Inclination to ecliptic ° ′ ″			Eccen-tricity	Mean orbital velocity (km/s)
	astro-nomical units	millions of km							
Mercury	0·387	57·91	87·97	115·88	7	00	15	0·206	47·87
Venus	0·723	108·21	224·70	583·92	3	23	40	0·007	35·02
Earth	1·000	149·60	365·26	—		—		0·017	29·79
Mars	1·524	227·94	686·98	779·94	1	50	59	0·093	24·13
Jupiter	5·203	778·34	4,332·59	398·88	1	18	17	0·048	13·06
Saturn	9·539	1,427·01	10,759·20	378·09	2	29	22	0·056	9·65
Uranus	19·182	2,869·60	30,685·00	369·66	0	46	23	0·047	6·80
Neptune	30·058	4,496·70	60,190·20	367·49	1	46	22	0·009	5·43

SATELLITE DATA

Satellite	Mean distance from primary			Sidereal period			Diameter (km)	Maximum magnitude
	thousands of miles	AU	thousands of km	d	h	m		
		EARTH						
Moon	239	·0026	382	27	7	43	3,476	−12·5
		MARS						
Phobos	5·8	·00006	9·3		7	39	13	10·0
Deimos	14·6	·00001	23·4	1	6	18	8	11·0
		JUPITER						
Amalthea (V)	113	·0012	181		11	57	200	13·0
Io (I)	262	·0028	419	1	18	28	3,200	5·5
Europa (II)	417	·0045	667	3	13	14	2,900	5·7
Ganymede (III)	666	·0072	1,066	7	3	43	5,000	5·1
Callisto (IV)	1,170	·0126	1,872	16	16	32	4,500	6·3
Hestia (VI)	7,120	·0767	11,392	250	16		100	13·7
Hera (VII)	7,290	·0783	11,664	259	26		30	17·0
Demeter (X)	7,300	·0785	11,680	260	23		20	18·8
Adrastea (XII)	13,000	·1420	20,800	625		R	20	18·9
Pan (XI)	14,000	·1510	22,400	700		R	20	18·4
Poseidon (VIII)	14,600	·1570	23,360	739		R	20	16·0
Hades (IX)	14,700	·1580	23,520	758		R	20	18·6
		SATURN						
Janus	98	·0010	157		17	58	300	14·0
Mimas	113	·0012	181		22	37	500	12·1
Enceladus	149	·0016	238	1	8	53	600	11·6
Tethys	183	·0020	293	1	21	18	1,000	10·6
Dione	235	·0025	376	2	17	41	1,000	10·7
Rhea	328	·0035	525	4	12	25	1,300	9·7
Titan	760	·0082	1,216	15	22	41	4,800	8·2
Hyperion	920	·0099	1,472	21	6	38	500	13·0V
Iapetus	2,200	·0238	3,520	79	7	56	1,100	9·0
Phoebe	8,050	·0866	12,880	550	10	50R	200	16·0
		URANUS						
Miranda	76	·00087	122	1	9	50R	300	17·0
Ariel	119	·0013	190	2	12	29R	800	14·0
Umbriel	166	·0018	266	4	3	28R	600	14·7
Titania	272	·0029	435	8	16	56R	1,100	14·0
Oberon	364	·0039	582	13	11	7R	1,000	14·0
		NEPTUNE						
Triton	220	·0024	352	5	21	3R	3,700	13·0
Nereid	3,500	·0372	5,600	359			300	19·5

R indicates retrograde motion.
V indicates variable.
Many of the satellite diameters are rough estimates based on brightness.

THE LAWS OF PLANETARY MOTION

The laws governing the motion of the planets were discovered by Johannes Kepler. His first and second laws were published in 1609 and the third in 1618. They may be stated thus:

1. Every planet moves in an ellipse, with the Sun in one of the foci.
2. The straight line drawn from the centre of the Sun to the centre of the planet (the planet's radius vector) sweeps out equal areas in equal times.
3. The squares of the periodic times of the several planets are proportional to the cubes of their mean distances from the Sun.

From the above laws Newton deduced the following:

1. The force on any planet varies inversely as the square of its distance from the Sun.
2. The force under which a planet describes its orbit always acts along the radius vector in the direction of the Sun's centre.
3. The forces on different planets vary directly as their masses, and inversely as the squares of their distances from the Sun.

Therefore we can say that

$$P : P' = \frac{M}{r^2} : \frac{M'}{r'^2}$$

where P is the force of attraction by the Sun on the Earth
P' is the force of attraction by the Sun on another planet
M is the mass of the Earth
M' is the mass of another planet
r is the radius of the Earth's orbit
r' is the radius of the other planet's orbit

It thus becomes possible to calculate an unknown function once the others are known, ie by relating P, M and r.

For the relationship between planets within the Solar System, travelling around the Sun as their common primary, we can say that

$$\frac{R^3}{T^2} = \frac{r^3}{t^2}$$

neglecting planetary masses, where R is the mean radius of the Earth's orbit, T the revolutionary time of Earth, r the mean radius of orbit of another Solar System planet, and t its revolutionary time.

When we apply the laws more accurately or to orbits outside the Solar System in comparison to those within it, we have to take into account the various masses involved. We get a similar equation, thus:

$$\frac{M_1 + m_1 = R_1^3 / T_1^2}{M_2 + m_2 = r_2^3 / t_2^2}$$

where we have added M_1 the mass of the Sun, m_1 the mass of the Earth, M_2 the mass of the other primary body (another star for instance in the case of binary systems) and m_2 the mass of the secondary body revolving around it.

Thus, a more accurate statement of Kepler's Third Law reads:

$$(M_1 + m_1)T^2 : (M_2 + m_2)t^2 = R^3 : r^3$$

A development of this formula as applied to stars will be found under that heading on page 199.

THE CELESTIAL SPHERE

To understand the systems of reference on the celestial sphere, imagine yourself at the centre of a hollow sphere, with the stars and other objects projected on the inside. Any plane passing through the observer is a great circle on the sphere, and the separation of objects on any such great circle is measured in degrees etc.

The *Zenith* and *Nadir* are the points respectively immediately above the observer, and below him.

The *Poles*, *Equator* and *Meridian* are projections on the celestial sphere of the terrestrial counterparts. The cardinal points East and West are the points of intersection of the equator with the horizon.

Altitude is the angular distance above the horizon, while *Zenith Distance* is the angular distance from the zenith.

Declination is the angular distance from the equator, North or South.

Right Ascension is the arc of the equator measured Eastward from the First Point of Aries, where the equator cuts the ecliptic. It is expressed in hours, etc (fifteen degrees to the hour) and is hence the sidereal time of the transit of any object across the observer's meridian.

Latitude and *Longitude* are angular distances measured at right-angles to and along the ecliptic instead of the equator. The ecliptic is inclined to the equator at an angle of 23° 27'.

Hour Angle is the interval expressed in time that has elapsed since a star or other object was last on the meridian.

Sidereal Time is the hour angle of the First Point of Aries expressed in time. It is usual to express position on the celestial sphere in Right Ascension (R.A. or the Greek letter Alpha) and Declination (Dec. or the Greek letter Delta).

Galactic Latitude and *Longitude* are occasionally used to express position in reference to the plane and poles of the Galaxy.

PRECESSION IN RIGHT ASCENSION AND DECLINATION

Owing to the regular precession of the Earth's pole, the apparent positions of the stars change from one epoch to another. It is thus necessary to give the date (or epoch) of any position when recording the places of objects on the celestial sphere. The changes are generally referred to 1925 or 1950 as the datum epoch. The following tables give the ten-year adjustments in Right Ascension and in Declination for various positions on the celestial sphere, working from an earlier date to a later one. For referring back, the signs should be reversed. Beyond 60° North or South the changes become so large that more elaborate treatment becomes necessary, but these quoted should suffice for most amateur needs.

10-YEAR PRECESSION IN RIGHT ASCENSION

RA	Declination						
	+60° m	+40° m	+20 ° m	0° m	−20° m	−40° m	−60° m
0ʰ	+0·5	+0·5	+0·5	+0·5	+0·5	+0·5	+0·5
1ʰ	+0·6	+0·6	+0·5	+0·5	+0·5	+0·5	+0·4
2ʰ	+0·7	+0·6	+0·6	+0·5	+0·5	+0·4	+0·3
3ʰ	+0·8	+0·6	+0·6	+0·5	+0·5	+0·4	+0·2
4ʰ	+0·8	+0·7	+0·6	+0·5	+0·4	+0·3	+0·2
5ʰ	+0·9	+0·7	+0·6	+0·5	+0·4	+0·3	+0·1
6ʰ	+0·9	+0·7	+0·6	+0·5	+0·4	+0·3	+0·1
7ʰ	+0·9	+0·7	+0·6	+0·5	+0·4	+0·3	+0·1
8ʰ	+0·8	+0·7	+0·6	+0·5	+0·4	+0·3	+0·2
9ʰ	+0·8	+0·6	+0·6	+0·5	+0·5	+0·4	+0·2
10ʰ	+0·7	+0·6	+0·6	+0·5	+0·5	+0·4	+0·3
11ʰ	+0·6	+0·6	+0·5	+0·5	+0·5	+0·5	+0·4
12ʰ	+0·5	+0·5	+0·5	+0·5	+0·5	+0·5	+0·5
13ʰ	+0·4	+0·5	+0·5	+0·5	+0·5	+0·6	+0·6
14ʰ	+0·3	+0·4	+0·5	+0·5	+0·6	+0·6	+0·7
15ʰ	+0·2	+0·4	+0·5	+0·5	+0·6	+0·6	+0·8
16ʰ	+0·2	+0·3	+0·4	+0·5	+0·6	+0·7	+0·8
17ʰ	+0·1	+0·3	+0·4	+0·5	+0·6	+0·7	+0·9
18ʰ	+0·1	+0·3	+0·4	+0·5	+0·6	+0·7	+0·9
19ʰ	+0·1	+0·3	+0·4	+0·5	+0·6	+0·7	+0·9
20ʰ	+0·2	+0·3	+0·4	+0·5	+0·6	+0·7	+0·8
21ʰ	+0·2	+0·4	+0·5	+0·5	+0·6	+0·6	+0·8
22ʰ	+0·3	+0·4	+0·5	+0·5	+0·6	+0·6	+0·7
23ʰ	+0·4	+0·5	+0·5	+0·5	+0·5	+0·6	+0·6
24ʰ	+0·5	+0·5	+0·5	+0·5	+0·5	+0·5	+0·5

10-YEAR PRECESSION IN DECLINATION

RA		RA	
0^h	$+3'$	12^h	$-3'$
1^h	$+3'$	13^h	$-3'$
2^h	$+3'$	14^h	$-3'$
3^h	$+2'$	15^h	$-2'$
4^h	$+2'$	16^h	$-2'$
5^h	$+1'$	17^h	$-1'$
6^h	0	18^h	0
7^h	$-1'$	19^h	$+1'$
8^h	$-2'$	20^h	$+2'$
9^h	$-2'$	21^h	$+2'$
10^h	$-3'$	22^h	$+3'$
11^h	$-3'$	23^h	$+3'$
12^h	$-3'$	24^h	$+3'$

HOUR ANGLE EXPRESSED IN DEGREES, OR HOURS, MINUTES AND SECONDS

Owing to the diurnal rotation of the Earth, all celestial objects appear to move across the sky from East to West. The apparent movement is expressed sometimes in degrees of arc and sometimes in time. The proportion is 15° per hour, or 4′ of time per degree. The following table gives the intervals in both systems:

Hours	Degrees		Minutes	Degrees	Minutes
24	360		45	11	15
23	345		30	7	30
22	330		20	5	
21	315		15	3	45
20	300		10	2	30
19	285		5	1	15
18	270		4	1	00
17	255		3	0	45
16	240		2	0	30
15	225		1	0	15
14	210				
13	195				
12	180				
11	165				
10	150				
9	135				
8	120				
7	105				
6	90				
5	75				
4	60				
3	45				
2	30				
1	15				

The above figures relating to minutes of time and degrees and minutes of arc are the same for seconds of time related to minutes and seconds of arc. Other intervals can be found by adding suitable intervals from the table.

SIDEREAL TIME

Due to the motion of the Earth around the Sun, the solar day of 24h is accomplished with reference to the stars in 23h 56m 4·09s. Thus 'Sidereal' or star time gains one whole day on Mean Solar Time during each year. This necessitates an adjustment between Mean Time and Sidereal Time for any interval expressed in one kind and required in the other. The following tables give the gain or loss between these time intervals.

FOR *Mean Time interval*	ADD *Sidereal Time gain*	FOR *Sidereal Time interval*	SUBTRACT *Mean Time loss*
1m	0·16s	1m	0·16s
3m	0·49s	3m	0·49s
4m	0·66s	4m	0·66s
5m	0·82s	5m	0·82s
15m	2·46s	15m	2·46s
30m	4·93s	30m	4·91s
1h	9·86s	1h	9·83s
2h	19·71s	2h	19·66s
3h	29·57s	3h	29·49s
4h	39·43s	4	39·32s
5h	49·28s	5h	49·15s
10h	1m 38·56s	10h	1m 38·30s
18h	2m 57·42s	18h	2m 56·93s
24h	3m 56·56s	24h	3m 55·91s

Other time intervals can be obtained by adding together those quoted above. In the case of transposing Sidereal Time to Mean Time, the losses must first be added and the sum of these subtracted from the Sidereal Time interval.

THE EQUATION OF TIME

The Equation of Time is an expression of the difference between apparent time and mean time. Mean Time is derived from the successive transits of an imaginary regularly moving Mean Sun across the meridian at Mean Noon. The apparent Sun does not move regularly in the heavens but crosses the observer's meridian sometimes early and sometimes late.

This difference is made up of two components—one due to the variation in the Earth's orbital speed because of the elliptic eccentric orbit; the other due to the difference in length of the apparent paths of the Sun as it is near the equinoxes or solstices. (See Glossary for definitions of these terms.) Both factors are constantly variable and must be computed for each transit of the apparent Sun if the Mean Sun's position or Mean Time is to be derived from it, accurately. Note that the equation of time vanishes four times each year.

To put it another way, the Sun appears to move faster during the northern winter months when the Earth is closer to the Sun, and the true Sun moves along the ecliptic and not along the equator on which time is measured; hence its projected motion along the equator will not be the same at the equinoxes as at the solstices because at the equinoxes the angle between the ecliptic and the equator is greater than at the solstices. Some examples are set out below:

Date		Minutes	Date		Minutes	Date		Minutes
January	1	− 3·2	May	1	+ 2·8	September	1	− 0·2
	16	− 9·6		16	+ 3·7		16	+ 4·8
February	1	−13·5	June	1	+ 2·4	October	1	+ 10·0
	16	−14·2		16	− 0·4		16	+ 14·2
March	1	−12·6	July	1	− 3·5	November	1	+ 16·3
	16	− 9·0		16	− 5·9		16	+ 15·3
April	1	− 4·2	August	1	− 6·3	December	1	+ 11·3
	16	0		16	− 4·4		16	+ 4·8

DECIMAL PARTS OF A DAY

(Intermediate values can be obtained by adding suitable intervals from the table)

Decimal	h	m	s		Hours	Decimal of one day	Hours	Decimal of one day
0·01		14	24					
0·02		28	48		1	·04166	13	·54166
0·03		43	12		2	·08333	14	·58333
0·04		57	36		3	·12500	15	·62500
0·05	1	12	00		4	·16666	16	·66666
0·06	1	26	24		5	·20833	17	·70833
0·07	1	40	48		6	·25000	18	·75000
0·09	2	9	36		7	·29166	19	·79166
0·10	2	24	00		8	·33333	20	·83333
0·20	4	48	00		9	·37500	21	·87500
0·30	7	12	00		10	·41666	22	·91666
0·40	9	36	00		11	·45833	23	·95833
0·50	12	00	00		12	·50000	24	1·00000
0·60	14	24	00					
0·70	16	48	00					
0·90	21	36	00					

Minutes	Decimal of one day	Minutes	Decimal of one day
1	·00069	25	·01736
2	·00139	30	·02083
3	·00208	35	·02430
4	·00277	40	·02777
5	·00347	45	·03125
10	·00694	50	·03472
15	·01042	55	·03819
20	·01389	60	·04166

CONVERSION OF DISTANCE MEASURE

Kilometres	Argument in miles or kilometres	Miles
1·609	1	0·621
3·219	2	1·243
4·828	3	1·864
6·437	4	2·485
8·047	5	3·107
9·656	6	3·728
11·266	7	4·350
12·875	8	4·971
14·484	9	5·592
16·094	10	6·214
32·187	20	12·427
48·281	30	18·641
64·375	40	24·855
80·468	50	31·068
96·562	60	37·282
112·655	70	43·495
128·750	80	49·709
144·843	90	55·923
160·936	100	62·136

Use the argument column for either unit and read left or right as required for kilometres or miles.

eg   100km equals 62·136 miles

100 miles equals 160·936km

NOTES

TELESCOPES

Telescopes are of two main types, the refractor and the reflector.

REFRACTORS

Refractors usually have an achromatic objective lens system normally made up of one crown and one flint lens, so designed that combined they destroy most of the inherent colour aberration present in the separate lenses. The crown glass lens is double convex and the flint lens concave one side and convex the other. The focal ratio is generally in the region of F/12 to F/15, that is, the focal length is some twelve to fifteen times the diameter of the objective lenses. Both red and blue light is theoretically brought to the same focal point. There is unavoidably, however, some residual colour. In a well corrected system, stars appear as yellow points with faint red-purple borders. If the lens system is under corrected, stars appear with a red fringe, and if over corrected they have a deep yellow apperance with a green-blue background. The eye tolerates the well corrected system's red-blue border.

The objective system must be square on to the light beam passing through it and in large instruments this adjustment is provided for. The lenses should be a loose fit in their cell. If the lenses are pinched, the 'out of focus image', comprising a series of diffraction rings, will show distortion and the proper 'in focus image' will suffer accordingly.

Size of the prime focus image depends on the focal length of the objective lenses. For solar work, where there is light to spare, a focal length of some twenty times (or more) the diameter of the lenses can be employed usefully. For normal work the shorter focal ratio is more useful because the exit pupil must not exceed the diameter of the iris of the eye when dark adapted—that is, about 7mm. This is to a large extent controlled by the focal ratio between the objective lenses and the eyepiece.

Rich Field telescopes are of shorter focal ratio; the lowest magnification that can be employed is in the region of three diameters' magnification per inch of objective diameter, otherwise light is spilled over the observer's face around the eye pupil.

REFLECTORS

Reflectors or reflecting telescopes are usually of shorter focal ratio than refractors, and normally have ratios between F/5 and F/9 for visual work. The main mirror is parabolic in curvature to bring all light beams to a focal point. After reflection the light may be caught by a flat mirror set at 45°, as in the case of the Newtonian telescope, or sent back on itself by a convex mirror and passed through a hole in the centre of the main mirror to form a Cassegrain type of instrument, with the focal plane behind the main mirror. An alternative is the Gregorian type, with a concave secondary mirror, but this is not so satisfactory for astronomical observation because light leaks into the eyepiece from the space surrounding the secondary mirror. The Cassegrain is a more compact instrument than the Newtonian, but has the disadvantages of the focus being below the primary mirror and so near the floor of the observatory, and that body heat radiated by the observer below the main mirror can cause trouble.

Schmidt and Maksutov as well as Ritchey-Chrétien reflectors are of very short focal lengths in comparison with the above mentioned types. They are really reflecting type cameras, whose purpose is to obtain wide-angle photographs of the sky. They are not usable visually for the observation of planets and the Moon, etc, apart from the Maksutov.

Herschelian Reflector type instruments are not now employed. The one main mirror viewed directly through the eyepiece causes left to right reversal of the image and the observer gets in the way of light received from the sky on to the mirror unless he is placed to one side, which causes coma in the image unless the mirror is ground to a spherical curve. This introduces focusing problems.

EYEPIECES

Eyepieces or oculars are of various types. Only the positive kind with the focal plane outside the optical system can be used on the shorter reflecting telescopes because the angle of convergence of the light towards the focus is wide in comparison with that of the longer refractors.

Huyghenian eyepieces are the most common, with two plano-convex lenses—the first, the field lens, and the second, the eye lens, are separated by a distance of two thirds of the focal length of the field lens. The image falls between the lenses. They are not usable on short focus instruments, such as reflectors, but are comparatively cheap to buy.

Ramsden eyepieces are composed of two plano-convex crown lenses with their convex sides facing each other. The image is a positive one. The focal length is the product of the several focal lengths of the lenses divided by the sum minus the distance between the lenses, which are of similar focal lengths. These are often used in micrometers.

Kellner eyepieces have a large field, but they have the disadvantage of the focal plane being on the face of the field lens; thus any dust is magnified by the eye lens.

Tolles, solid eyepieces are clear but have small fields of view. They work down to F/7 and are suitable for reflectors.

Orthoscopic eyepieces are made up of a triple colour corrected field lens and a viewing eye lens. They are reputed to be ghost (ie internal reflectors) free; they have large fields and are suitable for planetary observation.

Monocentric eyepieces in the achromatic form are excellent, but have smaller fields of view than the orthoscopic. They are excellent for planetary observation and work well with reflectors.

Erfle eyepieces (as illustrated) are useful for wide angle fields.

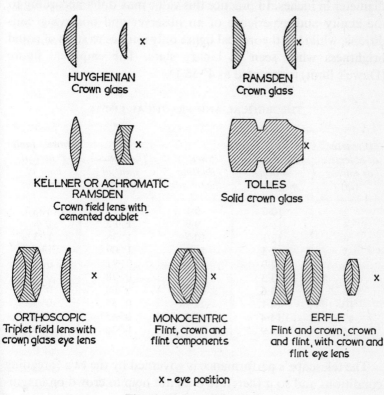

HUYGHENIAN
Crown glass

RAMSDEN
Crown glass

KELLNER OR ACHROMATIC
RAMSDEN
Crown field lens with
cemented doublet

TOLLES
Solid crown glass

ORTHOSCOPIC
Triplet field lens with
crown glass eye lens

MONOCENTRIC
Flint, crown and
flint components

ERFLE
Flint and crown, crown
and flint, with crown and
flint eye lens

x - eye position

Fig 1   Types of eyepieces

PERFORMANCE

The faintest object that can be seen with a telescope depends on the area of the objective or primary mirror. Theoretically this relationship is expressed by the formula Mag = 9·1 + 5 (log D in inches), but practically this limit is not reached. The

values for both theoretical and practical limiting magnitudes are
set out below for instruments of various sizes. Others can easily
be obtained by use of the formula, or by integration.

The resolving power of a telescope depends on the diameter
of the objective or primary mirror. This relationship is theoretically S (the limit of separation) = $5''{\cdot}45/D$, where D is the
diameter in inches. In practice this value may differ according to
the acuity and experience of an observer and observing conditions, while the theoretical figure only applies to stars of equal
brightness when seen as binary stars. The empirical figure
(Dawe's limit) is accepted as $4''{\cdot}56/D$.

THEORETICAL AND PRACTICAL LIMITS

Diameter of objective or mirror (in)	Theoretical limiting magnitude	Practical limiting magnitude	Theoretical limit of resolution	(Dawe's limit) Practical limit of resolution
2	10·6	9·1	2″·73	2″·5
3	11·4	9·9	1″·82	1″·8
4	12·1	10·7	1″·36	1″·3
5	12·5	11·2	1″·09	1″·0
6	12·9	11·6	0″·91	0″·9
7	13·3	12·0	0″·78	0″·7
8	13·6	12·3	0″·68	0″·6
10	14·1	12·8	0″·55	0″·5
12	14·4	13·2	0″·45	0″·4
15	14·9	13·8	0″·36	0″·3

The telescope's performance is governed by the two foregoing
conditions and so it therefore does not help to crowd on magnification beyond the capability of the instrument in the hope of
obtaining a better picture. Over magnification makes star images
appear woolly and planetary detail indistinct.

Theoretically, the maximum magnification is in the region of
one hundred diameters per inch of the objective diameter. A
more practical figure, when atmospheric conditions are taken
into account on an average footing, is fifty per inch diameter. In
the case of large instruments, this figure drops to about thirty

diameters per inch of objective diameter. The main object is to obtain as clear an image as possible, and this is normally realised with lower powers than is usually imagined. The foregoing assumes that the instrument is properly mounted without shake, uneven driving movement, and poor balance, any of these faults reducing performance.

MOUNTINGS

For astronomical purposes, mountings are preferably of the equatorial type, although much good work has been done with the ordinary altazimuth mounting. A steady driving clock or motor is used to move the instrument in concert with the Earth's rotation, thus keeping the object stationary in the field of view. The polar axis of the equatorial mounting is therefore arranged parallel to the Earth's axis. It is important to remember that the altitude of the pole equals the latitude of the place. The polar axis must also lie on the meridian of the place of observing, that is, due North and South. Circles are usually provided for finding objects by their right ascension and declination.

The process of setting up an equatorial mounting is as follows:
1. Approximate orientation of the polar axis in altitude and azimuth; using a plumb line shadow at local solar noon to set the azimuth, and a clinometer to set the altitude.
2. Zero setting of the declination circle by reading the declination of a star with the instrument alternately at either side of the mounting. Half the difference between the two readings should be the correct setting; adjust the reading vernier. Repeat this procedure with ever decreasing errors until the correct reading is obtained.
3. Final adjustment of the polar axis in altitude by observing a star of known declination through the telescope and adjusting the altitude of the axis to read this figure on the declination circle. Reverse the instrument and repeat the process, but on the other side of the mounting. This should be done with the star near the meridian for ease of manipulation.
4. Final adjustment of the polar axis in azimuth; select two

stars at equal distances from the meridian and of similar declination. View the eastern star with the telescope, and clamp the instrument at that declination. Swing to bring the western star into view. Decide whether any observed difference between the declinations of the stars (corrected for actual difference) shows the western star too far North or South in the instrument.

If the western star is too far South, the polar axis lies NE–SW. If the western star is too far North the polar axis lies NW–SE. Finally, check by other stars of known declination and by reading the declination circle.

It is assumed that the optical axis of the instrument has been set accurately at the right angles to the declination axis, and that polar and declination axes are truly perpendicular to each other.

AUXILIARY INSTRUMENTS

Micrometers. Instruments for measuring small angles in the field of the telescope. There are various kinds:

Ring micrometers are formed by a flat opaque ring at the focus, whose inner and outer diameters are defined with the greatest accuracy. Stars or other objects are allowed to trail across the ring and from the difference between transits times, small separation angles can be computed.

Cross bar micrometers are formed by two straight wires intersecting at an angle to each other in the focus, together with a thinner wire bisecting two of the angles. With a star travelling along the thinner wire as it is allowed to trail, the times of transits of another across the thick wires are noted and from them the differences in position in seconds of arc can be obtained, as between the two stars.

The Filar micrometers consist of a system of webs (or wires), one or more of which is adjustable, with an indicator showing the amount of movement made when the apparatus is operated. The relationship between the divisions of the indicator and the angle in seconds of arc on the celestal sphere is established by observation of known separations of stars. Once this factor is established, it is comparatively easy to convert readings of indicator units to seconds of arc in any direction when making observations.

The regular method is to set the wires to the closed position and read the indicator setting as the zero point between each measurement. The differences between zero point and observed point readings are the true separation in indicator divisions which are subsequently converted to seconds of arc. It is usual to take a mean value of a number of measurements.

In many cases micrometers are provided with position angle circles for measuring the angle's direction from North through East, South and West, from zero to 360°. To describe a binary star we say that the separation is so many seconds of arc in such and such a direction or position angle.

Transfer of a micrometer from one instrument to another involves re-establishing the value of the indicator divisions, when the micrometer is used at the different focal length of the second telescope. It will be recalled that the size of the image in a telescope is governed by its focal length; the values of the indicator divisions do not change, but remain constant in relation to the actual physical movement of the wire.

Photometers. Instruments for measuring the intensity of light. They can be of the simple wedge type, where a tinted glass wedge is progressively darker from tip to base. This is used to find the extinction point of a star or similar object, and the point's position is read off on a scale. Other types, such as the Zöllner, employ artificial stars that are adjustable in brightness and are matched to an actual star in the telescope's field of view. In use, all these types require the zero point established in terms of actual stellar magnitude because of variations in atmospheric absorption. It is sometimes convenient to measure the brightness of a known star and to compare the unknown magnitude to that by observation. To avoid the difficulties mentioned, it is often accurate enough to use two comparison stars, one brighter and one fainter than the unknown magnitude, and to interpolate visually the magnitude of the star whose brightness we wish to establish. This method is used by the British Astronomical Association's Variable Star observers.

PHOTOGRAPHY

Astronomical photography falls mainly into two distinct types. First, there is wide angle photography of comparatively large areas of the sky; second there is photography of the Sun, Moon and planets etc, demanding larger images of small angle objects. Whereas large angle cameras may take in areas of 3–4° diameter, the planet Jupiter for example subtends an angle of only 40″ arc.

Wide angle photographs. Such photographs of the sky may be obtained by using camera lenses of short focal ratio, from about F/5 downwards, with F/3 being quite usual for amateur work. Shorter than this come the Schmidt, Maksutov, and Ritchey-Chrétien reflectors. Length of exposure time is governed by liability to sky fogging, and for larger instruments employed on very long exposures, reciprocity failure is a limiting factor.

Accurate following (usually achieved by using a guiding telescope set on a bright star near the area to be photographed, on the same mounting as the camera) is essential, while a good clock drive is advisable. Lenses of short focal length do not usually give a wide field accurately focused at the circumference. It is usual in these cases to use only the central portion of the image on the plate of film. An alternative is to use the more expensive apochromat. It must be remembered that the larger the lens the more efficient it will be in recording faint objects. Objects fainter than those visible to the naked eye can be recorded by photography in a few seconds. Experiment will decide the best exposure time to use in a particular environment with a particular lens and emulsion. The most rapid emulsion, with its inherent fault of large grain, is not necessarily the best for all astro-cameras.

Solar Photography. Here there is more light than is needed, and the aim is to get an image of satisfactory size. Image size is determined by the focal length of the lens, and ratios of F/15 to F/20 may be used to advantage with a lens of only 10–15cm (4–6in) diameter. An alternative to the long focus lens is the normal type with an eyepiece to give the longer equivalent focal length. The image in either case is projected on to a focal plane behind a shutter, usually of the roller blind type, and during exposure the shutter operates allowing the image to fall momentarily on the plate or film. With exposures of 0·01–0·002s, no driving mechanism is necessary, and a fast emulsion is not recommended; better pictures are obtained with slow small grained film or plate. (See notes in section on the Sun.)

Lunar and Planetary Photography. This can well be undertaken for pleasure with moderate instruments. Reasonable pictures can be made by using the normal eyepiece used for viewing such objects. After careful focusing, the camera is placed as close to the eyepiece lens as possible, with the camera focused to infinity. It is best to use trial and error to find the most satisfactory length of exposure. Much depends on the particular eyepiece, the size of the telescope and the distance the camera has to be away from the eyepiece. Direct photography may be undertaken using only the prime focus, or a Barlow lens may be used to enlarge this image. A good drive is recommended to hold the image steady during exposure.

The size of images of the Moon's diameter for various smaller telescopes is as follows:

Focal length of objective (in)	Diameter of the Moon's image (in)
45	0·4
60	0·54
78	0·7

These are at prime focus without any eyepiece to magnify the image.

Limiting magnitude for any diameter telescope and any exposure measured in minutes relative thereto is expressed:

$$Mp = 5\log D + 2 \cdot 15\log E + 6$$

where Mp is the photographic magnitude, D the diameter in inches and E the length of exposure in minutes of time.

The use of an eyepiece cuts down the magnitude in proportion to the square of the magnification and the square of the distance of the plate or film from the eyepiece.

Plates and films of the ordinary type are sensitive from 2000Å to 5300Å. Isochromatic and orthochromatic emulsions extend into yellow at about 6000Å. Thus most of the redder light is not recorded so well as the blue end of the spectrum.

Colour photography may also be attempted and Kodak, Ektachrome-X, High Speed Ektachrome and Anscochrome films have proved successful. It should be noted that no colour film records colours as they are seen by the human eye in pictures of the stars and nebulae.

The most common faults in photography are: poor driving mechanism causing following of the object to be erratic; failure to focus the image accurately in the plane of the emulsion (this applies to the actinic focus as opposed to the visual focus); and over-enthusiasm resulting in photography being undertaken in poor conditions.

A LIST OF GREAT TELESCOPES

REFLECTORS

Place	Aperture in	Aperture cm	Date of completion
Mount Semirodniki, Zelenchukskaya, USSR	236	600	In course of erection (1971)
Mount Palomar, USA	200	508	1948
Kitt Peak, USA	158	400	Under construction (1971)
Siding Springs, Australia	150		Under construction (1971)
Lick Observatory, USA	120	305	1958
McDonald, USA	107	272	1969
Crimea, USSR	102	260	—
Mount Wilson, USA	100	254	1917
Chile	100	254	Projected 1971
Herstmonceux, England	98	249	The Isaac Newton Telescope, 1967
Kitt Peak, USA	90	228	1969
Mauna Kea, Hawaii	88	223	1970
McDonald, USA	82	208	1939
Haute-Provence, France	74	188	1958
Pretoria, S Africa	74	188	1948
Mt Stromlo, Australia	74	188	1955
Dunlap, Toronto, Canada	74	188	1935
Victoria, Canada	72	182	1919
Flagstaff, USA	72	182	The Perkins Telescope removed from Delaware in 1961
Harvard, USA	61	155	1937
Bloemfontein, S Africa	60	152	1933
Mt Wilson, USA	60	152	1908

REFRACTORS

Place	Aperture		Focal length (ft)	Date of completion
	in	cm		
Yerkes, Williams Bay, USA	40	102	63	1897
Lick, Mt Hamilton	36	91	58	1888
Paris, Meudon	33	84	53	1896
Potsdam	32P	81	$39\frac{1}{2}$	1905
Allegheny, Pittsburg	30P	76	46	1914
Bischoffsheim, Nice	30	76	59	1887
Pulkova, USSR	30	76	46	1886
Herstmonceux	28	71	28	1894
Bloemfontein	27	68	40	1928
Vienna	27	68	$34\frac{1}{2}$	1878
Johannesburg	$26\frac{1}{2}$	67	35	1926
Herstmonceux	26P	66	22	1897
McCormick, USA	26	66	$32\frac{1}{2}$	1873
Johannesburg	26P	66	36	1925
Washington, USA	26	66	$32\frac{1}{2}$	1873

P indicates a photographic instrument.

The Yerkes 102cm (40in) objective is probably the largest likely to be produced because at these large sizes the loss of light through the large lens is inefficient, and the difficulties of supporting large lenses without distortion become great. In large sizes the reflector with its mirror is more satisfactory.

A list of radio telescopes occurs in the section on radio astronomy.

NOTES

THE EARTH

The age of the Earth is roughly 4,700 million years. The orbit is elliptical, with an eccentricity of 0·0167. Its orbital speed is about 29·79km/s. The mean distance from the Sun is 149·6 million km, or 92,957,209 miles. The sidereal period of revolution round the Sun is 365·256 days. Other types of year are described in the Glossary.

The Earth may be regarded as a triple shelled planet consisting of the lithosphere together with the hydrosphere, atmosphere and magnetosphere.

LITHOSPHERE

The lithosphere or main body of the Earth is composed of a core, an outer core, the mantle and the crust.

The core is made of metallic nickel iron of which the outer 2,253km (1,400 miles) is molten; the rest is solid under great pressure, with a specific gravity of about 16. The diameter of the outer core is about 5,790km (3,600 miles); its chemical constitution is uncertain.

The mantle extends from the core up to the crust from which it is separated by the Mohorovičić Discontinuity (the Moho). The crust, in proportion to the whole body of the Earth, is as the skin is to an apple, being only about 40km (25 miles) thick. Under the continents the basement (substrata) consists of granite rocks which are exposed in many places, while under the oceans the basement is largely of basalt rock or rocks of a similar density. The continents stand some 4·8km (3 miles) above the ocean floors, and the visible mountains are in comparison trivial.

There is constant movement in the crust, which throws up mountains occasionally. Volcanoes are caused by hot magma rising from the deeper parts of the crust to the surface.

ATMOSPHERE

The atmosphere today is not the first atmosphere that has enwrapped the lithosphere of the Earth. During the Cambrian period there was much carbon dioxide and very little free oxygen. When green plants appeared, the process of photosynthesis removed much of the excess carbon dioxide and produced more oxygen. Now there is a state of balance in which plants supply oxygen which animals breathe in and expel carbon dioxide. The atmosphere surrounding the Earth is little more than the thickness of the skin surrounding an orange. The main body of the atmosphere is roughly 160km (100 miles) deep, but since the atmosphere becomes progressively more diffuse with height, it is difficult to set a boundary; very faint traces lie somewhere about 8,045km (5,000 miles) above the Earth's surface.

At lower depths the atmosphere is 78 per cent nitrogen with 21 per cent oxygen, with water vapour, argon and carbon dioxide. Above the ionosphere lies the exosphere consisting mostly of hydrogen, helium and traces of oxygen, and nitrogen. The temperature of the atmosphere differs from one layer to another as shown in the following chart.

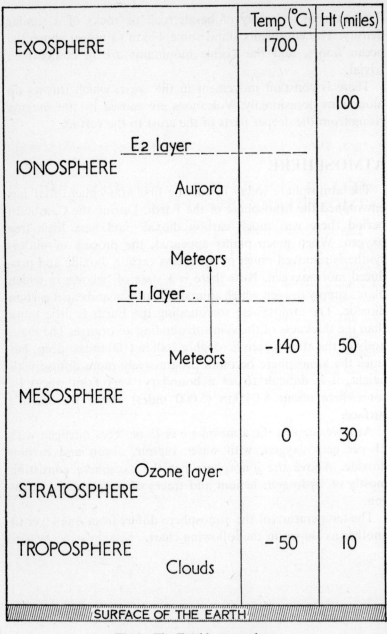

Fig 2   The Earth's atmosphere

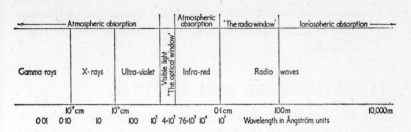

Fig 3   Electromagnetic spectrum showing optical and radio windows

STELLAR APPARENT MAGNITUDES AND ATMOSPHERIC ABSORPTION

The nearer a star is to the observer's horizon the fainter the star appears because of atmospheric absorption. While this dimming is effective from the zenith downwards in increasing amounts, for practical purposes in comparing the apparent magnitudes of stars by the naked eye, it may be neglected above an altitude of some 45°. For altitudes below this figure, the dimming in terms of magnitudes is given in the table below, which should be regarded as an average set of values because the actual dimming in terms of exact magnitudes depends on local atmospheric conditions.

Apparent altitude in degrees	Dimming in terms of magnitude
1	3·0
2	2·5
4	2·0
10	1·0
13	0·8
15	0·7
17	0·6
21	0·4
26	0·3
32	0·2
43	0·1

D

In general the absorption varies as the coefficient of the loss
of magnitude at the zenith multiplied by the secant of the star's
zenith distance.

MAGNETOSPHERE AND AURORAE

The Magnetosphere is approximately teardrop shaped, having
a frontal lobe towards the Sun and a tail streaming away behind
the Earth away from the Sun. It is the magnetic field of the Earth,
distorted at large distances from Earth by the action of the Solar
Wind. The main stronger field lies near the Earth and acts
similarly to the field surrounding a bar magnet.

The Aurorae occur in this part close to Earth and are caused
by ionisation of the particles in the air by the intrusion of solar
particles expelled from the Sun. These solar particles are posi-
tively charged, are trapped by the magnetic force and enter the
Van Allen belts, saturating them; the particles are then ac-
celerated towards the terrestrial poles, causing Aurorae to occur
in Northern and Southern skies. The Van Allen Belts; where
particles from the Sun are trapped more or less permanently,
lie within the Magnetosphere.

The magnetosphere proper extends beyond these areas and
the tail has been traced to a distance equal to thirty times the
radius of the Earth. The night side does not rotate with the
Earth but remains permanently streaming away from the Sun.
This causes considerable churning as the inner part rotates daily
with the Earth; within this churned portion is the arch opposite
the frontal lobe and on the night side of Earth. The Earth's
magnetic field is 'rigid'. We thus have a strong steady field inside
the magnetosphere and a comparatively weak field with turbulence further out towards its exterior.

The Earth-Moon system revolves around the barycentre and is
unique in the Solar System because the Moon is, in proportion
to the Earth, much larger than any other satellite in proportion
to its primary body.

AGES OF THE EARTH

	Geological time	Millions of years past	First appearance of Species
PHANEROZOIC EON · CENOZOIC ERA	Holocene (Modern) Pleistocene	1	Homo sapiens, modern Man Early Man. Glaciations caused changes
	Pliocene	13	Marine life similar to modern types
	Miocene	25	Sharks, deciduous trees
	Oligocene	36	Crabs, snails, sea urchins. Small primates, modern insects
	Eocene	58	Semi-aquatic mammals. Modern type flora
	Paleocene	65	Fishes similar to present day. Primitive birds
MESOZOIC ERA	Cretaceous Period	110 120	Tyrannosaurus, turtles, etc. Primitive birds
	Jurassic Period	135 180	Crustaceans, sauria and reptiles. Coniferous forests
	Triassic Period	190 230	Ichthyosaurs, dinosaurs. Primitive mammals and insects
PALEOZOIC ERA	Permian Period	260 280	Marine plants, amphibia. Ferns
	Carboniferous Period	290 345	Fishes. Vegetarian in swampy lowlands
	Devonian Period	350 400	Marine vertebrates, primitive sharks. Ferns, millipedes and spiders
	Silurian Period	400 425	Marine vertebrates, sea scorpions. Some vegetation
	Ordovician Period	425 500	Fossil animals, invertebrates
	Cambrian Period		Invertebrates. Seaweed

		Geological time	Mil- lions of years past	First appearance of Species
CRYPTOZOIC EON		Pre- Cambrian Period	600 3,200	This vast eon includes about five- sixths of geological time. No fossils

Four Ice Ages occurred between 11,000 and 800,000 years ago. They are (in order of increasing antiquity): The Wurm Ice Age, the Riss Ice Age, the Mindel Ice Age and the Gunz Ice Age. These are known in America as the Wisconsin Ice Age, the Illinoin Ice Age, the Kansan Ice Age and the Nebraskan Ice Age. It will be noted that they occurred predominately during the Pleistocene age.

NOTES

THE SUN

The Sun is a normal star of spectral type G2 in the Main Sequence. The nearness of the Sun means that we have the opportunity to observe in detail the behaviour and structure of a normal star.

It appears unusually bright merely because the Earth is situated near to the Sun, a matter of only 149·6 million km (93,000,000 miles). Despite the fact that the Sun's light output is steady, there are variations in its behaviour which give rise to the eleven-year sunspot period and the twenty-two-year magnetic period, which are probably closely connected. These periods can be seen also to affect the shape of the solar corona and to behave in concert with the emission of plasma and flares.

While it is usual to regard the Sun as composed of a series of skins overlying a central core, and this scheme has been adopted in this book, it must not be forgotten that there are not necessarily sharp boundaries between the layers; one gradually merges into the other, with the exception of the surface of the photosphere, with which we are familiar. But even in this case we are not sure of the position of the apparently sharp boundary to an uncertainty of 320km (200 miles) or so in depth. There is constant motion and turbulence which, together with poor definition, makes accurate observation well nigh impossible to this fine limit.

GENERAL DATA

Mass: 332,946 that of Earth.
Volume: 1,303,600 that of the Earth.
Density: 1·409 that of water at 4°C. (Density Earth = 5·517.)
Gravity at Surface: 27·9 that at the surface of the Earth.

The Core. Never visible, estimated temperature about 13,000,000°C. Atomic dissociation is prevalent.

The Photosphere. The part normally seen through dark glass filters. Diameter: 1,392,000km (864,900 miles). The Mean Rotation: Sidereal 25·38 days. Synodic period (as seen from Earth) at Solar latitude:

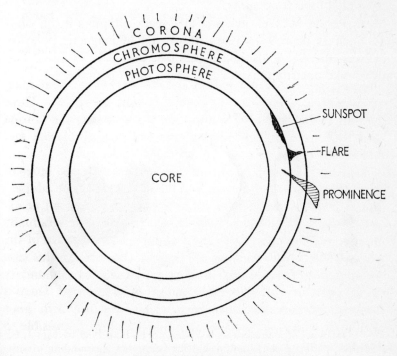

Fig 4   Section of the Sun—not to scale

20° N or S	27·27 days
40° N or S	27·5 days
80° N or S	30 days

Visible surface temperature of photosphere is 6,000°C.
Granulations or hydrogen clouds diameter 160–965km (100–600 miles); usually at higher temperature than remainder of photosphere.
Total energy output approximates to 7hp per square centimetre.

Sunspots occur on the surface of the photosphere and appear dark against photosphere bright background, and mostly as depressions.
Temperature of umbra about 4,000°C.
Temperature of penumbra in region of 5,000°C.
H alpha line in spectrum gives 3 per cent faster rotation than integrated light from spots.
Mean Period between maxima 11·1 years, although it can vary as much as from 9–14 years. Reversion of magnetic polarity between successive maxima makes true period of variation between like polarity maxima 22·2 years, mean period.

Fig 5   Drawing of a sunspot as recorded on 13 June 1969 by Mrs J. P. Merrilees. Note the dark umbra and the penumbra surrounding it with pores and bright areas, indicating strong activity

Series of spots overlap at minima. (See Fig 8.)
Spots in groups or trains have alternative magnetic polarity.

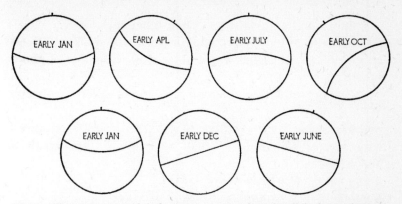

Fig 6   The apparent paths of sunspots across the solar disk change because of the apparent shift of the Sun's axis as the Earth carries the observer round the Sun annually. The apparent paths are straight lines only during early June and December.

Polarity of leading spots is reversed between N and S Hemispheres. Spots have magnetic fields over them. The decline from maximum is normally slower than the rise from minimum; normal intervals are $6\frac{1}{2}$ and $4\frac{1}{2}$ years.

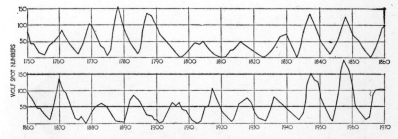

Fig 7   Sunspot activity is recorded by Wolf Numbers, which are an expression of the general activity prevailing when an observation is made. The Wolf Number is the sum of the number of groups multiplied by ten, plus the number of the individual spots. The diagram shows the maxima of 1750, 1761, 1769, 1778, 1787, 1804, 1816, 1830, 1837, 1848, 1860, 1870, 1883, 1893, 1905, 1917, 1928, 1936, 1947, 1957, 1968–70, from which the period of 11·11 years is derived

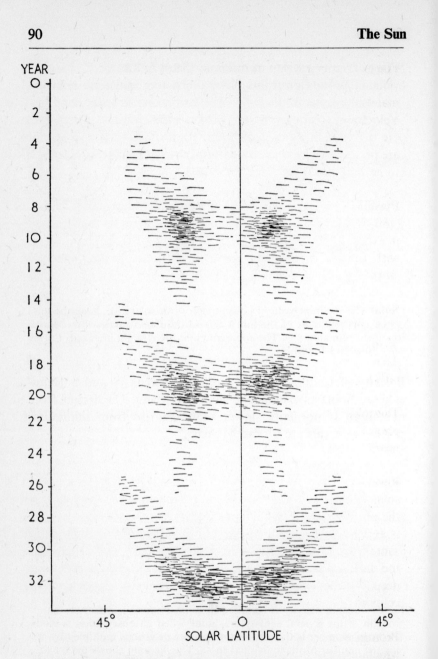

Fig 8   Typical butterfly diagrams, showing variations of spot latitude
with stage of cycle

Flares. Temperature estimated at about 5,000,000°C. Outward velocity 100–200km/s (60–120 miles/s) sometimes exceeded and material ejected in the form of solar plasma or solar wind (qv). Velocity of escape from Sun: 618km/s (380 miles/s). Small flares are detected in ultra-violet light. Radio fade-outs and aurorae are produced when ejected material reaches Earth and is trapped in its magnetic field. (See Aurorae.)

Plasma. Expelled clouds with velocity from about 300–1,250km/s (180–780 miles/s). Ionised clouds of hydrogen at temperatures in excess of 100,000,000°C with strong magnetic fields. Collision with Earth's atmosphere causes bright aurorae and magnetic storms.

Solar Wind. Continuous emission of plasma at 250–800km/s (155–495 miles/s). Nearly radial from centre of Sun. The centres of magnetic areas seem to emit plasma faster than from boundaries. Solar wind ionises cometary material and so makes comet tails visible.

Thermal Plateau occurs some 1,900km (1,180 miles) above the photosphere for some 150km. Here the temperature remains nearly constant at 20,000°C.

Reversing Layer causes absorption lines (Fraunhöfer lines) in solar spectrum. It consists of the chromosphere which overlies the photosphere. The elements in the chromospheric gas, which is at a lower density than the photosphere, absorb light at the same frequency as they would themselves emit, and hence cause the dark lines. It is about 8,000–16,000km (5,000–10,000 miles) deep; temperature 5,000+°C. Rose-coloured as seen during eclipses.

Prominences, masses of glowing gas erupting from photosphere, which occur in this level carry excess velocity, therefore chromosphere rotates more slowly than the lower regions of the Sun. Pressure thought to be between 10^{-1} and 10^{-4} Earth atmospheres.

Turbulence present through radiation pressure from photo-sphere. Prominences are of two main types: quiescent, hydrogen-type and active metallic-type. The former are longer lived than the latter.

Composition of the Sun's Atmosphere

Hydrogen	93% ⎫
Helium	5% ⎬ Total 100%
Other elements	2% ⎭

Corona. The outer envelope of the Sun, in continuous motion. Electronic Temperature 1,000,000° or more. The shape of the corona varies with intensity of solar activity. The corona is winged at solar minimum. The shape of the corona by radio measurements varies with wavelength used; the corona is more oval at long wavelengths.

The Sun's Energy. By transformation of hydrogen into helium using carbon, nitrogen and oxygen as catalysts. (See Stellar Energy.)

Energy Control

1. Radiation Pressure, radial from centre of Sun
2. Centrifugal acceleration assisting emission.
   Balanced by:
3. Opacity Brake, which raises central temperature and causes envelope to dilate.
4. Gravity Brake, which prevents total explosion of Sun.

OBSERVATION

The danger of looking at the Sun with any optical aid, how-ever small, cannot be too strongly emphasised. There is only one general rule: never, repeat never, look at the Sun through even the smallest telescope or binocular. The best way is to use a telescope to project the image of the Sun on to a screen behind a low-power eyepiece. Some arrangement must be made to shade the screen from direct sunlight, normally a sheet of card fixed to the telescope or, more sophisticated, a box with one side open to permit vision of the screen inside it can be employed.

Provided an efficient solar eyepiece comprising a Herschel prism is used, most of the heat can be discarded from the solar beams, but a further two plane surface reflections will be necessary to bring the intensity of the light within the accommodation capacity of the eye. One plane surface reflection from a Herschel prism can usually be made satisfactory by the use of dark filters in the eyepiece. If a polaroid filter is incorporated, adjustment of the intensity of the light can be accomplished by rotating it with reference to the prism. Sometimes silvered glass filters are used, but they can be expensive.

Low-powered eyepieces are best since the air is disturbed by the Sun's heat and seeing conditions are comparatively poor.

If a spectroscope is used, by widening the slit slightly and placing it at a tangent to the Sun's limb, the prominences can be seen.

It is usual to employ an image of the solar disk of 15cm (6in) diameter for drawing sunspots etc, and this screen image can be satisfactorily photographed with the camera as near to the optical axis of the telescope as possible to avoid distortion.

Direct photography of the solar disk can be effected provided the camera is capable of making the very short exposures required. The actual duration of exposure varies with the type of film or plate used and with the focal ratio of the telescope, here used as a camera, and the amount of amplification used. It will probably be found to lie somewhere between 1/100th and 1/500th of a second.

A long focus telescope is better for solar photography than a short one and a diameter of 12cm (5in) will suffice for good detail. An objective of 10–15cm (4–6in) diameter with focal length of 20·5m (68ft) will give a plate scale of 10″ of arc per millimeter, without eyepiece amplification.

In view of the short exposure involved, there is no need to

have the telescope clock driven, and an ordinary telescope of the 10–15cm (4–6in) variety may well be used in conjunction with an eyepiece giving the equivalent of longer focal length for this work.

It is usual to employ a focal plane shutter for solar photography and some means of checking the image in the camera is necessary.

For spectroscopic work to be of value, it is usual to employ a fixed horizontal, or sometimes vertical, telescope fed by a coelostat mirror, which enables long focal lengths to be employed together with a spectroscope or spectrograph of adequate proportions and capabilities.

Radio observation of the Sun indicates that the longer the wavelength, the higher and more rarified the solar levels from which it emanates. Hence metre-band radiation is detected in the corona. There is close relationship between radio and visual general level of activity. The radio sun is strongly ellipsoidal with increasing ellipticity with increased wavelength of the signals recorded.

TOTAL ECLIPSES AD 1954–2000

Date	Starting position	Duration (*min*)
1954 June 30	N America	$2\frac{1}{2}$
1955 June 20	N of Madagascar	7
1956 June 8	S of New Zealand	5
1958 October 12	E of New Guinea	5
1959 October 2	Near New York	3
1961 February 15	W of France	3
1962 February 5	Borneo	4
1963 July 20	Japan	1
1965 May 30	New Zealand	5
1966 November 12	SW Central America	2
1967 November 2	South Atlantic. Axis of Moon's shadow missed the earth's surface	
1968 September 22	N of Siberia	$\frac{2}{3}$
1970 March 7	Central Pacific	3
1972 July 10	Japan	3
1973 June 30	Guiana	7
1974 June 20	Indian Ocean	?*
1976 October 23	Tanzania	5
1977 October 12	N Pacific	3
1979 February 26	Off W coast of N America	3
1980 February 16	Central Atlantic	4
1981 July 31	Black Sea	1
1983 June 11	Indian Ocean	5
1984 November 22	New Guinea	2
1985 November 12	South Pacific	?
1986 October 3	W of Iceland	?
1988 March 18	Indian Ocean	3
1990 July 22	Baltic	3
1991 July 11	W of Hawaii	6
1992 June 30	Near Montevideo	?
1994 November 3	W of South America	4
1995 October 24	Iran	3
1997 March 9	Central Asia	3
1998 February 26	Central Pacific	4
1999 August 11	E of New York	2†

* Duration is uncertain.
† Visible in W Cornwall.

NOTES

THE MOON

GENERAL

(See Table of Satellite Data page 52.)

The Moon's orbit is usually described as being around the Earth. In point of fact, the Moon's orbit is actually always concave towards the Sun, and because of the comparatively small distance of the Moon from Earth compared with that from the Sun, the path of the Moon from last quarter through new moon towards first quarter, although envisaged as convex towards the Sun, is actually not so. The Earth and Moon form a binary system whose barycentre travels round the Sun in an elliptical orbit.

There are numerous perturbations of the orbit of the Moon, which for ease of calculation is regarded as being round the Earth. This apparent orbit is regarded as lying in a plane through the Earth's centre, inclined at an angle of 5° 8′ and forms an ellipse with eccentricity about 1:18, which is variable. The nodes of this orbit have a retrograde motion of about 19° per annum. There is also a progression of the major axis in a direct sense completing a revolution in about nine years. The inclination of this orbit to the ecliptic is not quite constant, but is subject to periodic variations. The eccentricity also varies together with the rates of motion of the nodes and the sidereal period.

The Moon rotates on its axis in the same period as it takes to travel round the Earth: once per lunar month. The axis of rotation is inclined some 6·5° to the perpendicular, with the result that the North and South poles of the Moon are alternatively slightly presented to the Earth. This is called 'libration in latitude'.

Owing to the elliptical shape of the lunar orbit, the angular velocity of the Moon is not constant, while the rate of rotation is practically uniform. Thus, at apogee we see a little round the eastern side, and at perigee a little round the western side, in the classical sense. This is called 'libration in longitude'.

There is also a further libration caused by the rotation of the Earth carrying the observer eastwards, and this causes us to see a little round the western side when the Moon is rising and round the eastern side when it is setting. This is called 'diurnal libration'. Librations allow a total of 59 per cent of the lunar surface to be seen from Earth.

Surface

The surface of the Moon has been studied for many years. A very cursory examination through a small telescope, or even binoculars, is sufficient to show that the surface is covered by dark comparatively smooth areas called maria and rougher lighter areas formed of mountain ranges and ring formations. There is, however, a difference between the proportions of these features as between the near and far sides of the Moon. The near side has more maria than the far side, which is almost entirely covered by mountainous types of formations. Compare the two maps between pages 100 and 101.

For want of better terms the darker rock, as seen in the maria, has been termed 'lunabase' and the lighter coloured mountainous type 'lunarite'. This darker type is of a basaltic nature.

The origin of the craters or ring mountains has long been debated. The theory of meteoritic impact has been pitted against that of vulcanistic activity. It now appears that both sets of forces have been employed in structuring the Moon's surface. It may easily be that while the basaltic rocks indicate a vulcanistic form of activity, this activity might have been originated by meteoritic bombardment. The Apollo experiments seem to show a layer of rock in some places about 15m (50ft) deep, of the texture of ash, but not necessarily composed of ash. Under this lies the basalt.

It is evident that many lunar craters follow a linear arrangement, often graded in order of size, and that they follow fracture lines along the surface. Inner rings in some craters suggest an origin other than meteoritic and it is suggested that the same forces that produced the ring mountains also produced the maria. The sequence would seem to be: maria, medium-sized craters, wrinkle ridges, domes, chains of craters and pits, small craters, rilles, valleys and faults, and the small pits.

Lunar rocks contain large amounts of rare earths; elements such as chromium, titanium, yttrium, zirconium are typical of the metal rich content. There is some ten times more chromium in lunar rocks than is found in terrestrial rock, and 12 per cent of titanium oxide as against only $4\frac{1}{2}$ per cent found in the richest lodes on Earth.

Natural glass spheres are also found measuring some half a millimetre in diameter, with felspar crystals and melted basalt. Rocks are mostly volcanic, with only some 2 per cent meteoric debris. Estimates of the age of these rocks vary between 3,300 and 4,600 million years. There is an overlay of meteoric dust to a varying depth of some few inches, on average.

Transient Lunar Phenomena

The lunar scene is not altogether inactive, since from time to time there appear emanations from the surface. These are seen as ruddy glows lasting for some minutes. They are more numerous during perigee, which suggests a gravitational couple that relieves the pressure on the lunar surface and enables gases to be released from below the lunar crust. Following the release, the rocks fall in to seal the opening, or the opening is sealed by the formation of ice, as the Moon moves away from perigee. These Transient Lunar Phenomena (TLPs for short) are more usual near the borders of the maria than elsewhere on the Moon. They have been notably observed in Aristarchus, Alphonsus, Gassendi, Plato, and less frequently in a number of other sites.

Mascons. The density of the underlying lunar rocks has been found to vary, the distribution of high-density areas called 'mascons' (mass concentrations), generally following the positions of the floors of the maria. It is suggested from this that the Moon was formed by cold accretion from material in interplanetary space and, in view of the marked difference between lunar and terrestrial rocks in their content of metallic and other elements, the Moon never formed part of the Earth. (See map below.)

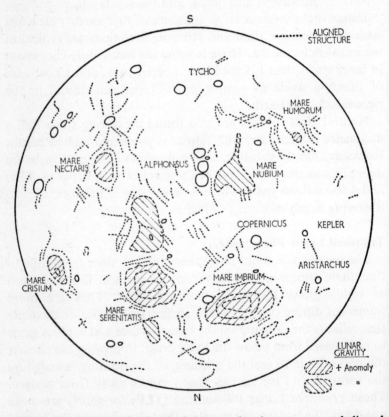

Fig 9   Map of the Moon after R. J. Livesey showing mascons and aligned features

Fig 10 Near Side of the Moon
(after Patrick Moore, drawn by Patricia A. Cullen)

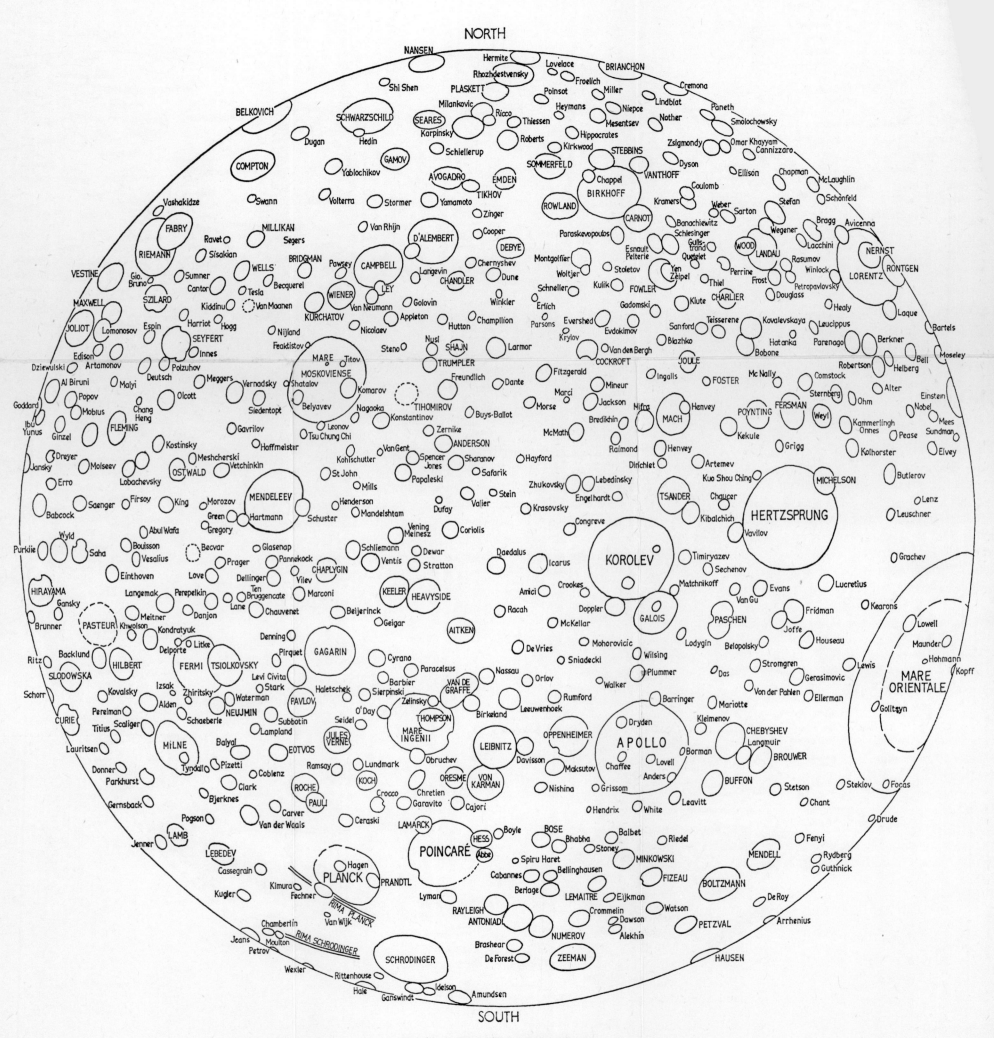

Fig 11   Far Side of the Moon

Magnetic Field. The Moon, as a body, has a very small magnetic field. There are also traces of magnetic fields in the lunar rocks probably fixed during the formation of the lunar surface.

Moonquakes. The lunar crust is not static, for the seismometers left behind by the Apollo crews have recorded some hundreds of moonquakes, averaging about one per terrestrial day. More severe quakes occur from time to time, originating from nine individual sites once per month during perigee.

Bombardment. Meteorites constantly bombard the surface. Most are very small with an occasional larger body about once per month, but not large enough to cause a large splash crater visible from Earth. The lingering reverberation from quakes and impacts indicates crust strength. The solar wind also constantly bombards the Moon.

Ionosphere. This has been suggested above the surface and is probably the residue of escaped gases like helium trapped from antiquity.

The Core is probably peridotite, a primitive rock type, not like the molten areas of the Earth's core. There appears to be no free water inside the Moon, and rocks seem to be welded together much more tightly than in the case of the Earth.

LIST OF FORMATIONS: NEAR SIDE

Name of formation	Diam (miles)	Height (feet)	Name of formation	Diam (miles)	Height (feet)
Abenezra	27	10,000	Berzelius	24	
Abulfeda	40	10,000	Bessarion	6	
Æstuum Sinus			Bessel	12	3,600
Agatharchides	30	5,000	Bianchini	25	
Agrippa	30	8,000	Biela	46	
Albategnius	80	14,000	Billy	32	4,000
Alfraganus	12		Biot	10	
Alhazen	20		Birmingham	66	
Almanon	30	6,000	Birt	11	
Aliacensis	52		Blancanus	57	12,000
Alpetragius	27	12,000	Blanchinus	33	
Alphonsus	70	7,000	Bode	11	
Alps		11,800	Boguslawsky	60	11,000
Altai Scarp		6,000	Bohnenberger	22	
Anaxagorus	32	10,000	Bond, WC	100	
Anaximander	54	9,000	Bonpland	36	
Anaximenes	50	8,000	Borda	26	
Ansgarius	50		Boscovich	27	
Apennines		18,500	Boussingault	70	
Apianus	39	9,000	Brayley	10	
Apollonius	30	5,000	Briggs	33	
Arago	18		Buch	30	
Archimedes	50	4,300	Bullialdus	39	8,000
Archytas	21	5,000	Burckhardt	35	13,000
Argelander	20		Burg	28	6,000
Ariadaeus	9		Busching	36	
Aristarchus	29	2,000	Byrgius	40	
Aristillus	35	11,000	Calippus	19	
Aristoteles	60	11,000	Campanus	30	
Arzachel	60	13,500	Capella	30	
Atlas	55	11,000	Capuanus	35	
Australe, Mare	400 × 200		Cardanus	32	4,000
			Carlini	5	
Autolycus	24	9,000	Carpathian		
Azophi	27	10,000	Mountains		7,000
Bailly	183	14,000	Casatus	65	
Beaumont	30		Cassini	36	
Beer	8		Catharina	55	
Behaim	35		Caucasus		
Bellot	12		Mountains		12,000
Bernouilli	25	13,000	Cauchy	8	

Name of formation	Diam	Height	Name of formation	Diam	Height
Cavalerius	40	10,000	Euclides	7	2,000
Cavendish	32	7,000	Eudoxus	40	11,000
Cayley	9		Euler	19	
Censorinus	3		Fabricus	55	
Cepheus	28		Faraday	40	
Charconac	30		Faye	22	
Challis	35		Firmicus	35	5,000
Cichus	20		Flammarion	45	
Clavius	145	12,000	Flamsteed	9	
Cleomedes	78	9,000	Foecunditatis,		
Cleostratus	40		Mare		
Colombo	50		Fontana	30	
Condamine	30		Fontenelle	23	
Copernicus	56	17,000	Fourier	36	
Crisium, Mare	280 ×		Fracastorius	60	
	350		Fra Mauro	50	
Crozier	15		Fraunhofer	30	5,000
Crüger	30		Frigoris, Mare		
Curtius	50		Furnerius	80	
Cuvier	50		Gärtner	63	
Cyrillus	60		Gassendi	55	9,000
Damoiseau	25		Gauricus	40	
Darwin	100		Gauss	100	
Davy	20		Gay-Lussac	15	
Dawes	14		Geber	25	
Delambre	32	15,000	Geminus	55	16,000
De la Rue	35		Gemma Frisius	80	
Delaunay	50?	(Irregular shape)	Gerard	50	
			Gioja	26	
De L'Isle	16		Goclenius	32	5,000
Democritus	23		Godin	27	
Demonax	75		Goldschmidt	68	
Deslandres	100	(Irregular shape)	Grimaldi	120	8,000
			Gruithuisen	10	
Dionysius	12		Guericke	36	
Diophantus	13		Gutenberg	45	
Doppelmayer	40	2,500	Haemus		
Drebbel	18		Mountains		8,000
Egede	23		Hagecius	50	
Encke	20		Hainzel	60	
Endymion	78	15,000	Halley	22	
Epidemiarum,			Hanno	40	
Palus			Hansteen	32	4,000
Eratosthenes	38	16,000			

Name of formation	Diam	Height	Name of formation	Diam	Height
Harbinger			Lagrange	100	
Mountains		8,000	La Hire, Mount		5,000
Harpalus	22		Lalande	15	
Hase	48		Lambert	18	
Heinsius	45		Landsberg	28	
Helicon	13		Langrenus	85	9,000
Hell	20		La Peyrouse	45	
Hercules	45	11,000	Legendre	46	
Herodotus	23	4,000	Le Monnier	34	
Herschel	28		Letronne	70	
Herschel,			Le Verrier	11	
Caroline	8		Licetus	46	
Herschel, John	90		Lichtenberg	12	
Hesiodus	28		Lilius	32	
Hevel	70	6,000	Linné	7	
Hind	16		Littrow	22	
Hippalus	38		Lohrmann	28	
Hipparchus	100	4,000	Longomontanus	90	
Hommel	75		Lubiniezky	24	
Horbiger	100		Macrobius	42	13,000
(Now			Mädler	20	
Deslandres)			Magelhaens	25	
Hörtensius	10		Maginus	110	
Humboldt, Wm	120	16,000	Mairan	25	15,000
Humboldtianum,			Manilius	25	
Mare			Manzinus	55	14,000
Humorum, Mare			Marginis, Mare		
Hyginus	4		Marinus	30	
Imbrium, Mare			Marius	22	
Inghirami	60	10,000	Maskelyne	19	
Iridum, Sinus			Mason	15	
Isidorus	30		Maurolycus	68	
Jacobi	41		Mayer, Tobias	22	
Janssen	121		Medii, Sinus		
Julius Caesar		(Irregular	Menelaus	20	8,000
		shape)	Mercator	28	5,000
Kant	20		Mercurius	33	
Kepler	22		Mersenius	45	8,000
Kies	25	2,500	Messala	80	
Kinau	26		Messier	9	
Kirch	7		Metius	50	
Klaproth	60		Meton	100	
Krafft	30		Milichius	8	
Kunowsky	12		Miller	30	

Name of formation	Diam	Height	Name of formation	Diam	Height
Moretus	75	9,000	Plutarch	40	
Mortis, Lacus			Polybius	20	
Mösting	16		Pons	20	
Murchison	35		Pontanus	28	
Mutus	50	14,000	Pontécoulant	60	
Nasireddin	30		Posidonius	62	
Neander	30		Prinz	(about	
Nearch	38			34)	
Nebularum, Palus			Procellarum, Oceanus		
Neper	70		Proclus	18	8,000
Newcomb	32		Ptolemaeus	90	9,000
Newton	143	24,000	Purbach	75	8,000
Nicolai	27	6,000	Putredinis, Palus		
Nicollet	10		Pyrénées		
Nubium, Mare			Mountains		12,000
Œnopides	42		Pythagoras	75	17,000
Oken	50	6,000	Pytheas	12	
Olbers	40		Rabbi Levi	50	
Orontius	52		Regiomontanus	80 × 65	7,000
Palitzsch	60 × 20		Reichenbach	30	
Pallas	30		Reiner	20	10,000
Parrot	40		Reinhold	30	9,000
Parry	26		Rhaeticus	28	
Peirce	12	7,000	Rheita	42	14,000
Pentland	45				
Percy Mountains (Gassendi)			Riccioli	100	
Petavius	100	11,000	Riccius	50	
Phillips	75		Riphaean		
Philolaus	46	12,000	Mountains		3,000
Phocylides	60		Ritter	19	
Piazzi	80	6,500	Rocca	60	
Piazzi Smyth	6	3,500	Rømer	35	11,000
Picard	21	8,000	Roris, Sinus		
Piccolomini	56	15,000	Rosenberger	50	
Pico (mtn.)		8,000	Ross	18	
Pitatus	50		Rosse	10	
Pitiscus	50	10,000	Sabine	18	
Piton (mtn.)		7,000	Sacrobosco	52	12,000
Plana	24		Santbech	44	15,000
Plato	60	7,000	Sasserides	60	
Playfair	28		Scheiner	70	15,000
Plinius	30		Schickard	134	8,000

Name of formation	Diam	Height	Name of formation	Diam	Height
Schiller	112 × 60		Teneriffe Mountains		8,000
Schneckenberg, Mount		700	Thales	24	
			Theaetetus	16	
Schömberger	40		Thebit	30	
Schröter	20		Theon Junior	10	
Scoresby	36		Theon Senior	11	
Seleucus	32	10,000	Theophilus	65	18,000
Serenitatis, Mare		125,000 sq miles	Timaeus	21	
			Timocharis	25	7,000
Sharp	22		Torricelli	12	
Silberschlag	8		Tralles	28	13,700
Sirsalis	20		Tranquilitatis, Mare		
Smythii, Mare					
Snellius	50		Triesnecker	14	
Sommering	17		Tycho	54	
Somnii, Palus			Ukert	14	
Somniorum, Lacus			Ulugh Beigh	30	
			Undarum, Mare		
Sosigenes	14		Vaporum, Mare		
South	60		Vasco da Gama	50	
Spitzbergen Mountains			Vendelinus	100	
			Vieta	50	15,000
Stadius	40		Vitello	30	4,000
Stag's-Horn Mountains (Straight Wall)			Vitruvius	20	
			Vlacq	56	10,000
			Walter	90	
Steinheil	45	11,000	Wargentin	55	(Plateau)
Stevinus	50		Webb	14	
Stiborius	23		Werner	45	15,000
Stöfler	90		Wichmann	8	
Strabo	32		Wilhelm, I	60	11,000
Straight Range		6,000	Wilkins	40	
Straight Wall		800	Wright	18	
Struve, Otto	100		Wurzelbauer	50	
Sulpicius Gallus	8	8,000	Xenophanes	67	
Sven Hedin	60		Zagut	50	
Tacitus	25	11,000	Zucchius	50	10,000
Taquet	6		Zupus	12	
Taruntius	35	3,500			
Taurus Mountains		10,000			

LIST OF FORMATIONS: FAR SIDE

(As approved by the International Astronomical Union in 1970, with room for additional notes such as heights and diameter between the columns.)

Abbe	Bose	Coriolis
Abul Wafa	Boyle	Coulomb
Aitken	Bragg	Crocco
Al-Biruni	Brashear	Crommelin
Alden	Bredikhin	Crookes
Alekhin	Bridgman	Curie
Alter	Brouwer	Cyrano
Amici	Brunner	
Anders	Buffon	Daedalus
Anderson	Buisson	D'Alembert
Antoniadi	Butlerov	Danjon
Apollo	Buys-Ballot	Dante
Appleton		Das
Arrhenius	Cabannes	Davisson
Artamonov	Cajori	Dawson
Artem'ev	Campbell	Debye
Avicenna	Cannizzaro	De Forest
Avogadro	Cantor	Dellinger
	Carnot	Delporte
Babcock	Carver	Denning
Backlund	Cassegrain	De Roy
Bladet	Ceraski	Deutsch
Banachiewicz	Chaffee	De Vries
Barbier	Chamberlin	Dewar
Barringer	Champollion	Dirichlet
Bartels	Chandler	Donner
Becquerel	Chang Heng	Doppler
Bečvar	Chant	Douglass
Beijerinck	Chaplygin	Dreyer
Bell	Chapman	Drude
Bellingshausen	Chappell	Dryden
Belopolsky	Charlier	Dufay
Belyayev	Chaucer	Dugan
Bergstrand	Chauvenet	Dunér
Berkner	Chebyshev	Dyson
Berlage	Chernyshev	Dziewulski
Bhabha	Chrétien	
Birkeland	Clark	Ehrlich
Birkhoff	Coblentz	Eijkman
Bjerknes	Cockcroft	Einthoven
Blazhko	Compton	Ellerman
Bobone	Comrie	Ellison
Boltzmann	Comstock	Elvey
Bolyai	Congreve	Emden
Borman	Cooper	Engelhardt

Eötvös	Harriot	Koch
Erro	Hartmann	Kohlschütter
Esnault-	Harvey	Kolhörster
Pelterie	Hatanaka	Komarov
Espin	Hayford	Kondratyuk
Evans	Healy	Konstantinov
Evdokimov	Heaviside	Kopff
Evershed	Hedin	Korolev
	Helberg	Kostinsky
Fabry	Henderson	Kovalevskaya
Fechner	Hendrix	Kovalsky
Fenyi	Henyey	Kramers
Feoktistov	Hertz	Krasovsky
Fermi	Hertzsprung	Krylov
Fersman	Hess	Kugler
Firsov	Heymans	Kulik
Fitzgerald	Hilbert	Kuo Shou
Fizeau	Hippocrates	Ching
Fleming	Hirayama	Kurchatov
Focas	Hoffmeister	
Foster	Hogg	Lacchini
Fowler	Hohmann	Lamarck
Freundlich	Holetschek	Lamb
Fridman	Houzeau	Lampland
Froelich	Hutton	Landau
Frost		Lane
	Ibn Yunus	Langemak
Gadomski	Icarus	Langevin
Gagarin	Idelson	Langmuir
Galois	Ingalls	Larmor
Gamow	Ingenii, Mare	Laue
Gansky	Innes	Lauritsen
Ganswindt	Izsak	Leavitt
Garavito		Lebedev
Gavrilov	Jackson	Lebedinsky
Geiger	Jenner	Leeuwenhoek
Gerasimovic	Joffe	Leibnitz
Gernsback	Joule	Lemaitre
Ginzel		Lenz
Glasenap	Kamerlingh	Leonov
Golitsyn	Onnes	Leucippus
Golovin	Karpinsky	Leuschner
Grachev	Kearons	Levi-Civita
Green	Keeler	Lewis
Gregory	Kékulé	Ley
Grigg	Khwolson	Lindblad
Grissom	Kibal'chich	Litke
Grotrian	Kidinnu	Lobachevsky
Gullstrand	Kimura	Lodygin
Guthnick	King	Lorentz
Guyot	Kirkwood	Love
	Kleimenov	Lovelace
Hagen	Klute	Lovell

Lowell
Lucretius
Lundmark
Lyman

Mach
Maksutov
Malyi
Mandel'shtam
Marci
Marconi
Mariotte
Maunder
McKeller
McLaughlin
McMath
McNally
Mees
Meggers
Meitner
Mendel
Mendeleev
Merrill
Mesentsev
Meshchersky
Metchnikov
Michelson
Milanković
Millikan
Mills
Milne
Mineur
Minkowski
Mitra
Möbius
Mohorovičić
Moiseev
Montgolfier
Moore
Morozov
Morse
Moulton

Nagaoka
Nassau
Nernst
Neujmín
Niépce
Nijland
Nikolaev
Nishina
Nobel
Nöther

Numerov
Nušl

Obruchev
O'Day
Ohm
Olcott
Omar
  Khayyam
Oppenheimer
Oresme
Orlov
Ostwald

Paneth
Pannekoek
Papaleksi
Paracelsus
Paraskevo-
  poulos
Parenago
Parkhurst
Parsons
Paschen
Pasteur
Pauli
Pavlov
Pawsey
Pease
Perelman
Perepelkin
Perkin
Perrine
Petrie
Petropav-
  lovsky
Petzval
Pirquet
Pizzetti
Planck
Planck
  (Rima)
Plaskett
Plummer
Pogson
Poincaré
Poinsot
Polzunov
Popov
Poynting
Prager
Prandtl
Priestly

Purkyně

Quételet

Racah
Raimond
Ramsay
Rasumov
Rayet
Rayleigh
Ricco
Riedel
Riemann
Rittenhouse
Ritz
Roberts
Robertson
Roche
Roshdest-
  vensky
Rowland
Rumford
Rydberg

Saenger
Šafařik
Saha
St John
Sanford
Sarton
Scaliger
Schaeberle
Schjellerup
Schlesinger
Schliemann
Schneller
Schönfeld
Schorr
Schrödinger
Schrödinger
  (Rima)
Schuster
Schwarzschild
Seares
Sechenov
Segers
Seidel
Seyfert
Shajn
Sharonov
Shatalov
Shi Shen
Shternberg

LIST OF IMPORTANT LUNAR PROBES

Date	Country of origin	Description
1959 January	USSR	Lunik I, first probe near Moon
1959 September	USSR	Lunik II, first crash-landing on Moon
1959 October	USSR	Lunik III, far side of Moon photographed
1961 August to 1965 March	USA	Nine Rangers launched, numbers 7, 8 and 9 successful, close-up photographs of lunar surface taken
1965	USSR	Zond 3, improved photographs of far side of the Moon
1966 February	USSR	Lunik 9, first soft landing on Moon. Also known as 'Luna 9'
1966 April	USSR	Luna 10, circum lunar probe
1966 June to 1968 May	USA	Surveyor vehicles, five out of seven successful soft landings. 1967 Surveyor III trenched lunar surface
1966 December	USSR	Luna 13, excellent photographs
1966 to 1967	USA	Orbiters I to V take excellent close-up photographs
1968	USSR	Zond 5, first moon probe recovered
1969 July	USA	Apollo 11, first landing on Moon by Armstrong and Aldrin, with Collins as third man. Surface specimens taken. Seismometer set up, etc
1969 November	USA	Apollo 12, landing within 200 yards of Surveyor 3 in Oceanus Procellarum by Conrad and Bean with Gordon as third man. Samples collected
1970 September	USSR	Luna 16 soft landing, automatic transport of samples to Earth

Date	Country of origin	Description
1970 November	USSR	Luna 17, with vehicle Lunokhod-1 landed on Moon and patrolling surface under command from Earth, and analysing surface specimens
1971 February	USA	Apollo 14 landing by Shepard and Mitchell, with Roosa as third man
1971 July/August	USA	Apollo 15 landing on Moon with Lunar Rover vehicle
1972 February	USSR	Luna 20
April	USA	Apollo 16

OBSERVATION

Observation of the Moon has been conducted for many years, but it is now sometimes said that all the work of drawing and photographing the Moon is today superseded by the Orbiter pictures etc. To some degree this is true, but there is at least one field of work still open to visual observers; this is the patrolling of the lunar surface in search of Transient Lunar Phenomena with suitable red and blue filters, which can be rapidly interchanged to give a 'blink' effect. For this work a telescope of 8in diameter in the case of a reflector, and 4–6in in the case of a refractor is required. Reflectors are much more trustworthy for this kind of observation because they are comparatively colour free. Colour aberration in a refractor can easily be misleading. A magnification of about two to three hundred diameters is recommended.

Occultations of stars by the Moon are used to check the predicted against the observed position of the Moon at the moment of a star's disappearance or reappearance at the limb. Similarly, when they occur, occultations of the planets are observed. Timing accurately to the nearest tenth of a second is required and a small refractor is quite adequate for this work. A stopwatch may be used to advantage. Accurate observations are helpful for the correction of the Moon's position and orbit.

Occultations of stars by the Moon are frequent, but the following are outstanding examples:

Occultations series of five bright stars by the Moon

We give here the beginning and the end of the series taking place between 1940 and 2020. These times are given in years and one decimal. For example, 1987·1 means the beginning of 1987, 2010·9 is the end of the year 2010, etc. These times may be 0·1 year in error. They are taken from a paper by Meeus in *Ciel et Terre*, March–April 1971 (vol 87).

For Regulus and Spica, the series marked with an * begin in

E

the Northern Hemisphere and end in the Southern one. The other series begin in the Southern Hemisphere and end in the Northern one.

The occultation series of Aldebaran and Antares begin *and* end in the Northern Hemisphere. For Alcyone (Eta Tauri, the brightest star of the Pleiades) the series begin and end in the Southern Hemisphere.

Regulus	Spica
1942·5–1943·9	1949·9–1951·5*
1951·3–1952·6*	1956·7–1958·2
1961·1–1962·5	1968·5–1970·0*
1969·8–1971·3*	1975·3–1976·8
1979·7–1981·1	1987·1–1988·6*
1988·4–1989·9*	1993·9–1995·4
1998·3–1999·7	2005·7–2007·2*
2007·0–2008·5*	2012·5–2014·0
2016·9–2018·3	

Aldebaran	Antares	Alcyone
1940·6–1944·2	1949·2–1954·2	1949·3–1955·1
1959·2–1962·8	1967·8–1972·8	1967·9–1973·7
1977·8–1981·4	1986·3–1991·4	1986·5–1992·3
1996·4–2000·0	2004·9–2010·0	2005·1–2010·9
2015·0–2018·6		

FORTHCOMING LUNAR ECLIPSES

Year	Month	Day	Magnitude*	Approximate time (UT) of mid-eclipse
1973	December	10	0·10	01h 48m
1974	June	4	0·80	22 14
	November	29	1·30	15 16
1975	May	25	1·50	05 46
	November	18	1·10	22 24
1976	May	13	0·10	19 50
1977	April	4	0·20	04 21
1978	March	24	1·50	16 25
	September	16	1·30	19 03
1979	March	13	0·90	21 10
	September	6	1·10	10 54
1981	July	17	0·60	04 48
1982	January	9	1·40	19 56
	July	6	1·70	07 30
	December	30	1·20	11 26
1983	June	25	0·30	08 25
1985	May	4	1·20	19 57
	October	28	1·10	17 43
1986	April	24	1·20	12 44
	October	17	1·30	19 19
1987	October	7	0·01	03 59

* Magnitude is the magnitude of the eclipse; 1 or greater being total, anything less than 1 is partial.

NOTES

MERCURY

GENERAL

Because its orbit has a mean radius of only some 58 million kilometers (36 million miles), as seen from Earth, Mercury is usually too close to the Sun to be observed other than with reasonably large telescopes, and this in full daylight.

Opportunities, however, do occur when Mercury is at elongation, either westerly before sunrise, or easterly just after sunset. On these occasions Mercury can be easily seen by the naked eye near the horizon as a bright, usually pinkish star-like object. The maximum possible angle of elongation from the Sun is 27° 45′ of arc, and the best times to view are when (in the Northern Hemisphere) elongation occurs either during spring evenings or autumn mornings. Every third elongation, east or west, is more favourable than the other two.

The maximum observable diameter of the planet is only 10″ of arc, that is 1/192 that of the Moon; the real diameter is one and a half times that of the Moon. So, to obtain a view of Mercury comparable to that of the Moon with the naked eye, we need to use a magnification of 200 diameters. To obtain the equivalent of a binocular view of the Moon, we need to use a magnification of 1,400 diameters. It is thus evident that to do useful work on Mercury a telescope in the 26cm (10in) range or larger is required.

At inferior conjunction, when Mercury is between the Sun

and Earth, the average apparent diameter is 1/180 that of the Sun.

When close to the Sun, an 'Ashen Light' similar to that of Venus has been detected edging the dark limb of Mercury.

The albedo of the surface of Mercury is 6 per cent and approximates the percentage of light reflected by terrestrial rocks. Radar measurements suggest Mercury is rougher than the Moon and there is also evidence for the truncation of the southern cusp at evening elongations of the planet (see Fig 12). These facts tie in with the recently discovered phase anomaly of Mercury, which has the effect of making the crescent illuminated appear thinner than it should do.

Surface spots are usually considered to be grey or pale maroon in colour. Colour filters give a reaction of minus red and minus violet, which support the grey hue. Mercury has been noted as featureless in blue light, which in contrast to the dark areas visible in red or amber light might be taken as suggesting the presence of some atmosphere. It has been suggested that Mercury has an escaping atmosphere constantly replenished by solar plasma and hence largely composed of hydrogen. The escape velocity is only 4·3km/s (2·6 miles/s).

Violet, red or amber filters improve visibility of surface detail. It is from the study of these details that the rotation period of Mercury was thought to be 87·969 days. Recently, radar methods have indicated a rotation period of 58·646 days. These two periods can be reconciled when one realises that 58·646 is two thirds of 87·969, while every third elongation is favourable for observation. Thus drawings will fit either the 87·969 day or the 58·646 day period while three times the synodic period almost equals six times the rotation period. At eastern elongations, the surface exhibits three oblique bands, while at western elongations there appears what is known as the 'figure 5 pattern'. Drawings of the planet should be made to the scale of 2in to the diameter of the planet. High powers cannot be employed in the telescope because observation has to be made either when Mercury is near the horizon, or when it is at a higher altitude with the Sun heating up the atmosphere.

Accurate drawings showing the phase and any markings on the disk of the planet can be of value, but photography is not easy because of the conditions mentioned.

While it has been emphasised that larger instruments are necessary to observe Mercury satisfactorily in full daylight, smaller instruments can be employed during the twilight periods with the planet near the horizon. Seeing conditions, being normally poor, are somewhat offset by the steadier image in a smaller instrument under these conditions. It must not, however, be forgotten that detail will be lost in the smaller instrument as compared with the larger one at good moments of seeing.

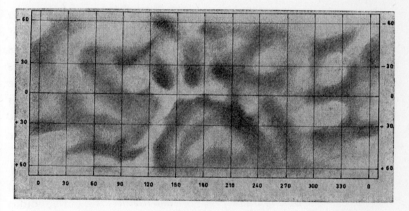

Fig 12 Albedo map of Mercury. Names have not yet been assigned to the features

TRANSITS AD 1631–1914

1631 November 7	1786 May 3
1644 November 8	1789 November 5
1651 November 2	1799 May 7
1661 May 3	1802 November 9
1664 November 4	1815 November 12
1677 November 7	1822 November 5
1690 November 10	1832 May 5
1697 November 3	1835 November 7
1707 May 6	1845 May 8
1710 November 6	1848 November 9
1723 November 9	1861 November 12
1736 November 11	1868 November 5
1740 May 2	1878 May 8
1743 November 5	1881 November 8
1753 May 6	1891 May 8
1756 November 7	1894 November 10
1769 November 9	1907 November 12
1776 November 2	1914 November 6
1782 November 12	

TRANSITS AD 1924–2078

Date of transit	Time (UT) of mid-transit	
	hours	mins
1924 May 8	1	42
1927 November 10	5	46
1937 May 11	9	00
1940 November 11	23	22
1953 November 14	16	54
1957 May 6	1	15
1960 November 7	16	54
1970 May 9	8	17
1973 November 10	10	33
1986 November 13	4	08
1993 November 6	3	58
1999 November 15	21	42
2003 May 7	7	54
2006 November 8	21	42
2016 May 9	14	59

Date of transit	Time (UT) of mid-transit	
	hours	mins
2019 November 11	15	21
2032 November 13	8	55
2039 November 7	8	48
2049 May 7	14	26
2052 November 9	2	32
2062 May 10	21	39
2065 November 11	20	09
2078 November 14	13	44

Other transits can be found by extrapolation, using the forty-six year period. For example, 1970 May 9 plus forty-six years equals 2016 May 9. This method is, however, not always accurate because adjustment has to be made for leap years.

ELONGATIONS AD 1956–2000

Date	Elonga-tion	Mag	Date	Elonga-tion	Mag
	°			°	
1956 Jan 11	19·0E	−0·3	Dec 29	22·4W	−0·1
Feb 21	26·5W	+0·3	1959 March 12	18·3E	0·0
May 2	20·9E	+0·5	April 26	27·2W	+0·7
June 20	22·8W	+0·6	July 8	26·2E	+0·7
Aug 31	27·2E	+0·5	Aug 23	18·4W	+0·1
Oct 12	18·0W	−0·3	Nov 3	23·6E	0·0
Dec 25	19·9E	−0·3	Dec 12	21·0W	−0·2
1957 Feb 2	25·3W	+0·2	1960 Feb 23	18·1E	−0·2
April 15	19·7E	+0·4	April 7	27·8W	+0·6
June 1	24·5W	+0·7	June 19	24·9E	+0·7
Aug 13	27·4E	+0·5	Aug 5	19·2W	+0·2
Sept 25	17·9W	−0·2	Oct 15	24·9E	+0·1
Dec 8	21·0E	−0·2	Nov 24	19·8W	−0·3
1958 Jan 16	23·8W	+0·1	1961 Feb 6	18·2E	−0·3
March 29	18·8E	+0·2	March 20	27·7W	+0·5
May 14	26·1W	+0·7	June 1	23·3E	+0·7
July 26	27·1E	+0·6	July 19	20·4W	+0·4
Sept 9	18·0W	0·0	Sept 28	26·0E	+0·3
Nov 20	22·2E	−0·1	Nov 7	18·9W	−0·2

Date	Elongation °	Mag	Date	Elongation °	Mag
1962 Jan 20	18·7E	−0·3	Oct 31	18·6W	+0·1
March 3	27·1W	+0·4	1969 Jan 13	18·9E	−0·3
May 13	21·7E	+0·6	Feb 23	26·7W	+0·3
July 1	21·8W	+0·6	May 5	21·1E	+0·5
Sept 10	26·9E	+0·4	June 23	22·6W	+0·7
Oct 22	18·3W	−0·2	Sept 3	27·1E	+0·5
1963 Jan 4	19·4E	−0·3	Oct 14	18·1W	−0·3
Feb 13	26·0W	+0·2	Dec 27	19·8E	−0·3
April 26	20·4E	+0·4	1970 Feb 5	25·5W	+0·2
June 13	23·5W	+0·7	April 18	19·9E	+0·3
Aug 24	27·4E	+0·5	June 5	24·3W	+0·7
Oct 5	17·9W	−0·2	Aug 16	27·4E	+0·5
Dec 18	20·3E	−0·3	Sept 28	17·9W	−0·1
1964 Jan 26	24·7W	+0·1	Dec 10	20·8E	−0·2
April 7	19·3E	+0·1	1971 Jan 19	24·1W	+0·1
May 24	25·2W	+0·7	April 1	19·0E	+0·2
Aug 5	27·3E	+0·6	May 17	25·8W	+0·7
Sept 18	17·9W	−0·1	July 29	27·2E	+0·7
Nov 30	21·5E	−0·2	Sept 12	17·9W	0·0
1965 Jan 8	23·2W	0·0	Nov 23	22·0E	−0·1
March 21	18·6E	0·0	1972 Jan 1	22·6W	−0·1
May 6	26·6W	+0·7	March 14	18·4E	0·0
July 18	26·8E	+0·7	April 28	27·1W	+0·7
Sept 2	18·1W	+0·1	July 10	26·4E	+0·7
Nov 13	22·8E	−0·1	Aug 25	18·3W	+0·1
Dec 21	21·8W	−0·2	Nov 5	23·4E	0·0
1966 March 5	18·2E	−0·1	Dec 14	21·2W	−0·2
April 18	27·5W	+0·6	1973 Feb 25	18·1E	−0·2
June 30	25·7E	+0·7	April 10	27·7W	+0·6
Aug 16	18·7W	+0·3	June 22	25·1E	+0·7
Oct 26	24·1E	0·0	Aug 8	19·1W	+0·2
Dec 4	20·5W	−0·2	Oct 18	24·7E	+0·1
1967 Feb 16	18·1E	−0·2	Nov 27	20·0W	−0·3
March 31	27·8W	+0·5	1974 Feb 9	18·2E	−0·3
June 12	24·2E	+0·7	March 23	27·8W	+0·5
July 30	19·7W	+0·4	June 4	23·5E	+0·7
Oct 9	25·4E	+0·2	July 22	20·2W	+0·5
Nov 17	19·4W	−0·3	Oct 1	25·9E	+0·3
1968 Jan 31	18·4E	−0·3	Nov 10	19·1W	−0·2
March 13	27·5W	+0·4	1975 Jan 23	18·6E	−0·3
May 24	22·6E	+0·6	March 6	27·2W	+0·3
July 11	21·0W	+0·7	May 16	22·0E	+0·6
Sept 20	26·4E	+0·3	July 4	21·6W	+0·7

	Date	Elongation °	Mag		Date	Elongation °	Mag
	Sept 13	26·8E	+0·4		June 26	22·3W	+0·7
	Oct 25	18·4W	−0·3		Sept 6	27·1E	+0·5
1976	Jan 7	19·2E	−0·3		Oct 17	18·2W	−0·3
	Feb 16	26·2W	+0·2		Dec 30	19·6E	−0·3
	April 28	20·4E	+0·3	1983	Feb 8	25·7W	+0·2
	June 15	23·3W	+0·7		April 21	20·0E	0·0
	Aug 26	27·2E	+0·5		June 8	24·0W	+0·7
	Oct 7	17·9W	−0·3		Aug 19	27·4E	+0·6
	Dec 20	20·1E	−0·3		Oct 1	17·9W	−0·2
1977	Jan 28	24·9W	+0·1		Dec 13	20·6E	−0·3
	April 10	19·5E	+0·3	1984	Jan 22	24·3W	+0·1
	May 27	25·0W	+0·7		April 3	19·1E	+0·2
	Aug 8	27·4E	+0·6		May 19	25·6W	+0·7
	Sept 21	17·9W	−0·2		July 31	27·2E	+0·6
	Dec 3	21·3E	−0·2		Sept 14	17·9W	−0·1
1978	Jan 11	23·4W	0·0		Nov 25	21·8E	−0·1
	March 24	18·7E	0·0	1985	Jan 3	22·8W	0·0
	May 9	26·4W	+0·7		March 17	18·4E	0·0
	July 22	26·9E	+0·7		May 1	26·9W	+0·7
	Sept 4	18·1W	−0·2		July 14	26·5E	+0·7
	Nov 16	22·6E	0·0		Aug 28	18·3W	+0·1
	Dec 24	22·0W	−0·1		Nov 8	23·2E	0·0
1979	March 8	18·2E	−0·1		Dec 17	21·4W	−0·2
	April 21	27·4W	+0·6	1986	Feb 28	18·2E	−0·1
	July 3	25·9E	+0·7		April 13	27·7W	+0·6
	Aug 19	18·6W	+0·1		June 25	25·3E	+0·7
	Oct 29	23·9E	+0·1		Aug 11	18·9W	+0·2
	Dec 7	20·7W	−0·2		Oct 21	24·5E	+0·2
1980	Feb 19	18·1E	−0·2		Nov 30	20·2W	−0·3
	April 2	27·8W	+0·6	1987	Feb 12	18·2E	−0·3
	June 14	24·5E	+0·7		March 26	27·8W	+0·5
	Aug 1	19·5W	+0·4		June 7	23·8E	+0·7
	Oct 11	25·2E	+0·2		July 25	20·0W	+0·5
	Nov 19	19·6	−0·2		Oct 4	25·7E	+0·2
1981	Feb 2	18·3E	−0·3		Nov 13	19·2W	−0·3
	March 16	27·6W	+0·4	1988	Jan 26	18·5E	−0·3
	May 27	22·8E	+0·7		March 8	27·3W	+0·4
	July 14	20·8W	+0·6		May 19	22·2E	+0·6
	Sept 23	26·3E	+0·3		July 6	21·4W	+0·6
	Nov 3	18·7W	−0·3		Sept 15	26·7E	+0·4
1982	Jan 16	18·8E	−0·3		Oct 26	18·4W	−0·2
	Feb 26	26·8W	+0·3	1989	Jan 9	19·1E	−0·3
	May 8	21·3E	+0·6		Feb 18	26·4W	+0·2

Date	Elonga-tion	Mag	Date	Elonga-tion	Mag
	°			°	
May 1	20·7E	+0·5	March 1	27·0W	+0·3
June 18	23·0W	+0·7	May 12	21·5E	+0·6
Aug 29	27·3E	+0·5	June 29	22·1W	+0·7
Oct 10	18·0W	−0·2	Sept 9	27·0E	+0·4
Dec 23	20·0E	−0·2	Oct 20	18·2W	−0·3
1990 Feb 1	25·1W	+0·1	1996 Jan 2	19·5E	−0·3
April 13	19·6E	+0·3	Feb 11	25·9W	+0·2
May 31	24·7W	+0·7	April 23	20·2E	+0·4
Aug 11	27·4E	+0·6	June 10	23·8W	+0·7
Sept 24	17·9W	−0·1	1966 Aug 21	27·4E	+0·6
Dec 6	21·1E	−0·2	Oct 3	17·9W	−0·2
1991 Jan 14	23·7W	0·0	Dec 15	20·5E	−0·3
March 27	18·8E	+0·1	1997 Jan 24	24·5W	0·0
May 12	26·2W	+0·7	April 6	19·2E	+0·2
July 25	27·0E	+0·7	May 22	25·4W	+0·7
Sept 7	18·0W	0·0	Aug 4	27·3E	+0·6
Nov 19	22·4E	−0·1	Sept 16	17·9W	−0·1
Dec 27	22·2W	−0·1	Nov 28	21·7E	−0·1
1992 March 9	18·3E	0·0	1998 Jan 6	23·0W	0·0
April 23	27·3W	+0·6	March 20	18·5E	0·0
July 6	26·0E	+0·7	May 4	26·7W	+0·7
Aug 21	18·5W	+0·1	July 17	26·7E	+0·7
Oct 31	23·7E	+0·1	Aug 31	18·2W	+0·1
Dec 9	20·9W	−0·2	Nov 11	23·0E	0·0
1993 Feb 21	18·1E	−0·3	Dec 20	21·6W	−0·2
April 5	27·8W	+0·5	1999 March 3	18·2E	−0·2
June 17	24·7E	+0·7	April 16	27·6W	+0·6
Aug 4	19·4W	+0·3	June 28	25·5E	+0·7
Oct 14	25·0E	+0·2	Aug 14	18·8W	+0·2
Nov 22	19·7W	−0·3	Oct 24	24·3E	+0·1
1994 Feb 4	18·3E	−0·3	Dec 2	20·3W	−0·3
March 19	27·7W	+0·5	2000 Feb 15	18·2E	−0·2
May 30	23·1E	+0·7	March 28	27·8W	+0·5
July 17	20·6W	+0·5	June 9	24·0E	+0·7
Sept 26	26·1E	+0·3	July 27	19·8W	+0·5
Nov 6	18·8W	−0·3	Oct 6	25·5E	+0·3
1995 Jan 19	18·7E	−0·3	Nov 15	19·3W	−0·3

NOTES

VENUS

GENERAL

Venus has been known for many centuries. To the Babylonians of 1600 BC it was Nin-dar-Anna—'Mistress of the Heavens'; to the Chinese, Tai-pe—'The Beautiful White One'; to the Greeks, Hesperus—the Evening Star, and Phosphorus—the Morning Star.

The Babylonians knew Nin-dar-Anna as one body long before the Greeks previous to AD 180 regarded it as two. In Nineveh it was realised around 173 BC that eight Earth years equals thirteen Venus years. In AD 1640 it was known that the orbit of Venus is wholly within that of the Earth.

At inferior conjunction its apparent diameter can reach 63″ of arc; at superior conjunction this is reduced to about 10″, a decrease in apparent area ratio of some forty to one, which on occasions can reach forty-seven to one.

The mean distance from Earth varies between these two extremes and is relative to the respective positions of the two planets in their orbits. The nearest Venus approaches Earth is about 42 million kilometres (26 million miles) and the furthest from Earth about 256 million kilometres (160 million miles).

The apparent brilliance of Venus depends not only on its distance from Earth, but also on the phase illuminated. Maximum brilliance occurs between 34 and 37 days either side of inferior conjunction. Its proximity to Earth, with its increase of apparent size of the planet, offsets the smaller angle of illuminated phase.

The maximum elongation of Venus, east or west of the Sun, is about 47°, and in this position its apparent magnitude reaches —4·1, while the maximum brilliance reached is —4·4 mag.

Apparent features occur near the tops of clouds in the cloud cover of Venus:

Terminator shading: usually visible, but in varying intensity and extent.

Terminator irregularities: probably caused by solar illumination of high-altitude clouds on Venus with spaces between them.

Dichotomy: when the disk is visually cut in half. There is usually a phase anomaly of some days by which amount the phase is smaller than that predicted by calculation. This is variable.

Light areas: contrasting with the dark shadings or otherwise perhaps high-altitude illuminated clouds.

Dark shadings: not easy to see at first but less difficult than the light areas without filters. They are probably shadows of one cloud upon another, or interstices through which we see deeper into the darker levels of the atmosphere.

Cusp caps: light areas near the points (cusps) of the crescent. These are illuminated clouds and there is some evidence that they indicate the positions of the poles of the planet. There is a tendency towards periodicity in their appearance, and they appear bright in green light.

Four-day cycle: in the cloud patterns this suggests a regular weather behaviour.

Ashen light: this must not be confused with the purely subjective appearance of a dark disk completing the figure of the crescent phase planet. The true Ashen Light is brighter than the twilight sky background, and an occulting bar to cut off the bright crescent of Venus must be used if it is to be seen properly. It is sometimes noted to be of a coppery hue and may be searched for with a Wratten 35 (purple) filter with main transmission around 4,400Å and 7,000Å in the telescope, with the bright crescent hidden by the occulting bar. It seems to occur most often at about 10° either side of inferior conjunction.

Collars: these are noted quite regularly and take the shape of sloping streaks from points near the equatorial sides of cusp caps near the terminator. They are not permanent features as is sometimes stated, but they are a usual feature, and probably indicate areas comparatively free from cloud above the surface of the planet. They have been attributed to contrast and this may enhance their appearance.

Extension of cusps: horns of the crescent sometimes noted when the crescent is thin near inferior conjunction. Thought to be an effect of refraction of solar light within the atmosphere, it is more clearly seen at long wavelengths, such as yellow and red.

Inferior conjunction ring: when the planet is between Earth and Sun, but North or South of the ecliptic, Venus can often be seen as a shape approaching a ring. The black body of the planet is surrounded by the luminescence of its thick atmosphere.

Date	Country and name	Remarks	Indicated temperature (°C)	Atmospheric Pressure (Earth: 1)	Chemical composition of atmosphere	Notes on atmosphere
1961	USSR Venera 1	Radio contact lost	—	—		
1962	USA Mariner 1	Failure	—	—		
1962	USA Mariner 2	Passed within 21,600 miles of Venus	130 to 480			
1964	USSR Zond 1	Failure	—	—		
1965	USSR Venera 2	Passed within 15,000 miles of Venus	No signals			
1966	USSR Venera 3	Possibly crash-landed on Venus	—	—		
1967	USSR Venera 4	Soft landing on dark side near equator. Temperature extrapolated to surface 271°C at 179*	40 to 280 Temp varies with wavelengths	15 to 20	80–98% CO_2 1·5% H-O and oxygen. No nitrogen	Weak hydrogen corona above atmosphere of Venus
1967	USA Mariner 5		475 Cloud temp 367	92	72–87% CO_2 No oxygen or H_2O	Hydrogen corona at 2,800km above Venus inert and escaping
1969	USSR Venera 5		400	60	93–7% CO_2	Differences attributed to unevenness of surface
1969	USSR Venera 6	Temperature extrapolated to surface 530°C at 140*			2–5%N and inert gases	
1970	USSR Venera 7	Soft landing and first observations from surface	475	90		

Further US probes are envisaged for 1975, 1976 and 1978.

* Microwave temperature, effective brightness temperature of black body, not realised on a planet.

ELONGATIONS AD 1970–1999

Eastern	Degrees	Western	Degrees
1970 September 1	46·2	1971 January 20	47·0
1972 April 8	45·8	1972 August 27	45·9
1973 November 13	47·2	1974 April 4	46·4
1975 June 18	45·4	1975 November 7	46·6
1977 January 24	47·0	1977 June 15	45·8
1978 August 29	46·2	1979 January 18	47·0
1980 April 5	45·9	1980 August 24	45·9
1981 November 10	47·2	1982 April 1	46·5
1983 June 16	45·3	1983 November 4	46·6
1985 January 22	47·1	1985 June 12	45·8
1986 August 27	46·1	1987 January 15	47·0
1988 April 3	45·9	1988 August 22	45·8
1989 November 8	47·2	1990 March 30	46·5
1991 June 13	45·3	1991 November 2	46·6
1993 January 19	47·1	1993 June 10	45·8
1994 August 25	46·1	1995 January 13	47·0
1996 April 1	45·9	1996 August 19	45·8
1997 November 6	47·1	1998 March 27	46·5
1999 June 11	45·3	1999 October 31	46·6

The stellar magnitude for these elongations remains almost constant at −4·0 to −4·1.

INFERIOR CONJUNCTIONS AD 1961–2023

1961	April 10	N	1993	April 1	N
1962	November 12	S	1994	November 2	S
1964	June 19	S	1996	June 10	S
1966	January 26	N	1998	January 16	N
1967	August 29	S	1999	August 20	S
1969	April 8	N	2001	March 30	N
1970	November 10	S	2002	October 31	S
1972	June 17	S	2004	June 8	S
1974	January 23	N	2006	January 13	N
1975	August 27	S	2007	August 18	S
1977	April 6	N	2009	March 27	N
1978	November 7	S	2010	October 29	S
1980	June 15	S	2012	June 6	N
1982	January 21	N	2014	January 11	N
1983	August 25	S	2015	August 15	S
1985	April 3	N	2017	March 25	N
1986	November 5	S	2018	October 26	S
1988	June 12	S	2020	June 3	N
1990	January 18	N	2022	January 9	N
1991	August 22	S	2023	August 13	S

After eight years, the same geocentric phenomena of Venus occur again, but two and a half days earlier. This follows the rule previously mentioned as known in Nineveh about 173 BC. The letters N and S indicate whether Venus is North or South of the ecliptic.

TRANSITS AD 1631–2368

Transits of Venus occur in pairs with an eight-year interval between each pair. The pairs occur with intervals of alternately 113 years and 130 years between each pair's commencing date:

1631	1639
1761	1769
1874	1882
2004	2012
2117	2125
2247	2255
2360	2368

PHASE ANOMALY AD 1956–1971

(Difference between observed and calculated dichotomy.)

Year	Morning or evening elonga- tion	DICHOTOMY		Difference (0–C)
		Observed	Calculated	
1956	PM	April 8/9	April 12	− 4
1956	AM	Undetermined		?
1957	PM	November 12/13	About November 17	Say − 4
1958	AM	April 11/14	April 11	Say + 2
1959	PM	June 15	June 21	− 6
1959	AM	November 14	November 11	+ 3
1961	PM	January 23	January 31	− 8
1961	AM	June 24	June 20	+ 4
1962	PM	August 18/19	September 1	− 12
1963	AM	January 27	January 23	+ 4
1964	PM	April 4·7	April 12	− 7·5
1964	AM	About September 3	August 29	+ 5
1965	PM	November 8·5	November 16·7	− 8·2
1966	AM	April 14·75	April 7·6	+ 7·1
1967	PM	June 13·5	June 20	− 6·5
1967	AM	November 21	November 8·6	+ 12·4
1969	PM	January 23·2	January 29	− 5·8
1969	AM	June 25	June 19·5	+ 5·5
1970	PM	August 18·5	August 29·6	− 11·1
1971	AM	January 25·0	January 20·7	+ 4·3

It will be noted that dichotomy is observed late during morning elongations and early during evening elongations.

OBSERVATION

Venus may be observed satisfactorily with telescopes of 15cm (6in) or larger diameter, although a refractor of 7·5cm (3in) diameter can be useful. The great necessity is clarity of vision without over-illumination and at the same time not too dull an image. The best magnification will be found to be in the region of some twenty to thirty diameters per inch of aperture.

Observation should normally be made in daylight, either after sunset or before sunrise, unless with circles Venus can be found in full daylight. This is because of the inherent brilliance of the planet, which after dark makes satisfactory work almost impossible.

Much useful work can be undertaken using colour filters, not only to enhance the delicate shadings but also to enable cloud patterns at various wavelengths of light to be seen and recorded. For phase determinations, the Wratten 15 (yellow) filter is recommended to limit the colour perception of the observer, which has a detrimental effect on accuracy of phase seen in the telescope. Other filters used are Wratten No 25 or 29 (red), 47 or 47B (blue) with green on occasions when cusp caps appear. These are enhanced in green light.

Unless micrometer measurements of phase are made, it is advisable to draw the planet to a scale of 5cm (2in) diameter and then measure the phase observed from the drawing. Simple estimates of phase are notoriously inaccurate.

The observer will discover for himself the best magnification to use with due regard to the size of his instrument and the prevailing local conditions of steadiness and transparency of the atmosphere.

Photography with adequate equipment may be undertaken and provide valuable records, both of phase and cloud patterns.

NOTES

MARS

GENERAL

Mars revolves around the Sun at a mean distance of 1·52 astronomical units, or 227·94 million kilometres (141,640,000 miles). Its sidereal period of revolution is 686·98 days and this being longer than the Earth's year gives rise to a synodic period of 779·94 days with the result that Mars reaches opposition approximately once every 2 years 50 days. It is thus visible at opposition during alternate years, with a lag of 50 days between oppositions.

The axial rotation takes 24h 37m 23s. To see the same portion of his globe, one must therefore look some 37m later each night. There is some oblateness of the globe.

The equatorial diameter is 6,800km (4,225 miles) and the polar diameter 6,748km (4,193 miles).

A small telescope is adequate near opposition to show the polar caps, which undergo seasonal changes. The mean diameter of Mars is 6,790km (4,219 miles) and at mean opposition it subtends an equatorial diameter of about 18″ of arc. In other parts of its orbit, when it is further from Earth, this angle is proportionately smaller. The maximum and minimum apparent diameters are 25″ and 3·5″ of arc. Thus, observation of the surface features is best carried out near opposition.

The dark areas appear greyish but some colour is detectable with seasonal changes, when intensities are compared in light of various wavelengths, suggestive of primitive vegetation. The light areas, or 'deserts', are of a pink or red colour.

Irregular markings tend to appear connected when at the limit of vision, and once gave rise to the suggestion of 'canals' on the surface of the planet. This is now known to be illusory, and the surface is known to be covered with craters similar to those found on the Moon.

SURFACE

Spacecraft have been used to study the surface of Mars. Mariner 4 in 1965 travelled within 9,788km (6,118 miles) of Mars and sent back twenty-one pictures of the surface showing the craters on a craggy barren surface, while the atmosphere was found to be much thinner than was expected, with carbon dioxide the main constituent. Mariners 6 and 7 in 1969 flew within 3,200km (2,000 miles) of Mars, and measured a high intensity of radiation at the surface, together with the absence of water in sufficient quantity to permit growth of any known terrestrial form of life. It must, however, be remembered that this series of observations was only conducted over a part of the Martian globe. Further probes were launched towards Mars by both USA and USSR in 1971. Soft landings are envisaged for the future as well as more photographic surveys, but from photographs already obtained it is clear that the surface is jumbled and collapsed land, with chaotic areas and regions of comparative flatness. Undiminished sunlight breaks down aggregates of molecules and makes life improbable.

Martian craters are more worn down than lunar ones. It is interesting that the area known as Hellas has no craters as large as 300m (358yd) in diameter, while the polar regions have a temperature as low as $-100°C$. The dark areas are no longer regarded as depressions; some of them are elevated above the surrounding terrain, and they are rougher than the desert regions.

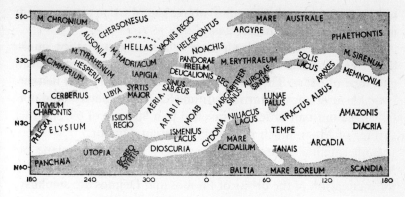

Fig 13   Map of the surface of Mars

ATMOSPHERE

The atmosphere, now regarded as 98 per cent carbon dioxide, appears as a haze 8–16km (5–10 miles) thick. The noon ground temperature is about 10°–20°C in the bright tropical regions, and 20°–30°C in the dark parts. The night temperature drops to −60° or −80°C, and the atmosphere is probably some 30°C lower than the ground temperature.

SATELLITES

There are two satellites of Mars. The nearer one, Phobos, has a sidereal period of only 7h 39m and accordingly is seen to transit the Martian meridian by an observer on Mars once every 7h 39m 26·6s. As this period is much shorter than the rotational period of Mars itself, the satellite is seen to rise in the West and set in the East. Phobos thus overtakes the rotation of Mars; it travels only 5,920km (3,700 miles) above the Martian surface, and is gradually getting closer. Mariner observations indicate a diameter for Phobos of about 16km (10 miles). Deimos revolves around Mars once in 30h 18m and thus transits the Martian meridian once every 1d 6h 21m 16s. It therefore rises in the East and sets in the Martian West in a normal manner. It travels 20,000km (12,500 miles) above the Martian surface, and is gradually getting further away.

The characteristics of both these orbits suggest that the satellites were formed by accretion of material in the primaeval envelope of Mars. They are so close to the primary that neither is visible at or above Martian latitude 82° and Phobos would not be visible until an observer travelled to a latitude of 69°, on the surface of Mars, much nearer the Martian equator.

Both satellite orbits are inclined very little to the plane of Mars' equator, but since Mars itself has an inclination of 23° 59′, the inclination of the orbits of Phobos and Deimos are similarly inclined to the ecliptic. Observation of these satellites is not easy because they are situated close to the planet, but they can be seen with adequate telescopic size, 30cm (12in) or thereabouts, and an occulting device to hide the bright planet.

OBSERVATION

Observation of Mars requires an instrument 20–25cm (8–10in) in diameter for serious work, but at opposition an objective as small as 7·6cm (3in) diameter shows the main features, such as the poles, Mare Acidalium and the Syrtis Major. Some authorities maintain that in certain parts of the world the atmospheric disturbances will not usually permit the use of a large telescope on Mars, and the best results will probably be obtained with a diameter of 12–30cm (5–12in). The magnification used is largely a matter of experiment, but an average of some forty times per inch of diameter will be found acceptable.

Coloured filters can be used to assist seeing difficult features. Orange or red will bring out the ground detail, while blue will accentuate the atmospheric and cloud appearances.

Changes in Martian Longitude can be calculated from the following table:

Time elapsed	Change in Martian longitude (degrees)
1m	0·24
3m	0·73
5m	1·22
10m	2·44
15m	3·66
20m	4·87
30m	7·31
45m	10·97
50m	12·18
1h	14·62
3h	43·86
5h	73·10
6h	87·72

Other values can be found by interpolation or multiplication.

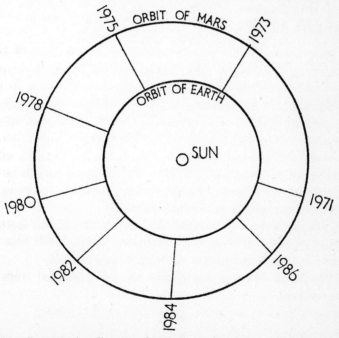

Fig 14 Comparative distances for various oppositions of Mars. Favourable oppositions as regards nearness to the Earth occur in August and September when Mars is south of the Equator, thus making observing conditions poor for Northern Hemisphere observers. The diagram is not to scale

OPPOSITIONS AD 1971–1999

Date of opposition			Apparent diameter (*seconds*)	Declination (*degrees*)
1971	August 10	7hr	24·9	−22
1973	October 25	3hr	21·5	+10
1975	December 15	4hr	16·6	+26
1978	January 22	0hr	14·3	+24
1980	February 25	6hr	13·8	+14
1982	March 31	10hr	14·7	− 1
1984	May 11	9hr	17·6	−18
1986	July 10	5hr	23·2	−28
1988	September 28	3hr	23·8	− 2
1990	November 27	20hr	18·1	+23
1993	January 7	23hr	14·9	+27
1995	February 12	2hr	13·9	+18
1997	March 17	8hr	14·2	+ 5
1999	April 24	18hr	16·2	−11

NOTES

THE ASTEROIDS

GENERAL

These small bodies, the largest 686km (429 miles) in diameter, travel in orbits mainly situated between those of Mars and Jupiter. Orbital inclinations vary, reaching a maximum of some 43° in the case of Hidalgo; eccentricities also vary, one asteroid even coming within the orbit of Mercury, and another travelling out beyond the orbit of Jupiter.

At distances where an asteroid would have a revolution period of a simple fraction of the period of Jupiter, the cumulative perturbations by Jupiter cause the asteroid to follow a different path. The gaps left are known as 'Kirkwood gaps'. On the other hand, some asteroids move in the same orbit as Jupiter 60° away, and these are known as the Trojan Group. Other groups are known as the Hilda Group, the Minerva Group, the Hestia Group and the Flora Group, but the Trojan Group is the most notable and has seven asteroids 60° in front of Jupiter and five behind; all these groups have a similar motion to Jupiter. Perturbations by Saturn also occur in certain cases.

NOTES

Eros, with an irregular shape 28km (18 miles) longest diameter, passed Earth at 24 million kilometres (15 million miles) in 1931 and will do so again in 1975. Rotation period 5h 17m by change in mag.

LIST OF INTERESTING ASTEROIDS

Number	Name	Year of discovery	Diameter (miles)	Sidereal period (years)
1	Ceres	1801	429	4·60
2	Pallas	1802	281	4·61
3	Juno	1804	150	4·36
4	Vesta	1807	370	3·63
5	Astraea	1845	112	4·14
6	Hebe	1847	106	3·78
7	Iris	1847	94	3·68
8	Flora	1847	77	3·27
9	Metis	1848	133	3·69
10	Hygiea	1849	222	5·60
11	Parthenope	1850	75	3·84
12	Victoria	1850	94	3·56
13	Egeria	1850	123	4·14
14	Irene	1851	98	4·16
15	Eunomia	1851	146	4·30
16	Psyche	1852	201	4·99
18	Melpomene	1852	82	3·48
19	Fortuna	1852	100	3·82
20	Massalia	1852	112	3·74
22	Kalliope (Calliope)	1852	156	4·96
27	Euterpe	1853	94	3·60
29	Amphitrite	1854	114	4·08
30	Urania	1854	56	3·64
39	Lactitia	1856	160	4·60
40	Harmonia	1856	56	3·41
44	Nysa	1857	62	3·77
51	Nemausa	1858	94	3·64
63	Ausonia	1861	92	3·70
192	Nausicaa	1879	120	3·72
324	Bamberga	1892	122	4·40
349	Dembrovska	1892	160	5·00
511	Davida	1903	217	5·72
532	Herculina	1904	138	4·61
	Eros	1898	11	1·76
	Hidalgo	1920	27	3·96
(See	Amor	1932	2	2·67
notes)	Apollo	1932	2	1·81
	Adonis	1936	1	2·76
	Hermes	1937	1	1·47
	Icarus	1949	1	1·12

Hidalgo travels beyond the orbit of Jupiter with an inclined eccentric orbit.

Hermes passed within 780,000km (485,000 miles) of Earth in 1937.

Icarus passed Earth at 6·4 million kilometres (4 million miles) distance in 1969 and reached a magnitude of 13, being visible in a moderately large telescope. Radar echoes were obtained at this time. Icarus is the only asteroid known to pass within the orbit of Mercury.

OBSERVATION

Observation and search is carried on mainly by photography, but the brighter asteroids can be observed visually with binoculars or telescopes. They can be detected by repeated comparisons with star maps, when their individual motions will show up. On photographs the stars show as spots of light, but the motion of an asteroid causes its image to be drawn out as a line.

NOTES

JUPITER

GENERAL

The largest planet in the Solar System, with the greatest number of satellites. According to one theory Jupiter has a ferrous core with rocky silicates, and an outer core of liquid or solid hydrogen, over which is laid the atmosphere.

Chemical composition. This outer gas envelope is largely hydrogen, but has an admixture of hydrogen compounds, such as ammonia and methane, with some helium and small quantities of other elements. It is also suggested that the atmosphere has some water vapour at depth, together with some ammonia droplets and ammonia vapour as well as ammonia crystals at higher levels.

Temperature at the base of the atmosphere is probably high, but at higher levels it drops to about −146°C.

Rotation varies with latitude, being most rapid at the Jovian equator where each rotation takes 9h 50m 30s. Nearer the poles this falls off to a much slower rate. The rapid rotation produces bulging near the equator with the result that the equatorial diameter is 142,800km (88,700 miles) while the polar diameter is 133,500km (82,800 miles). This is quite noticeable in a telescope.

Turbulence in the Jovian atmosphere, much of it caused by differential rotation, is considerable. Rapid and violent change is therefore continual, but despite this, a regular overall pattern is maintained, which is expressed in terms of belts and zones. Belts are dark while zones are light areas, shown in Fig 15.

The great red spot is a prominent feature which changes in appearance from time to time. Sometimes it is prominently brick red and at others it is pale almost to the point of disappearance, when only the hollow in which it lies between the South Equatorial and the South Temperate Belts is noticeable. Sometimes the Red Spot is more intense one end from the other. It does not always keep its position in longitude fixed, moving slightly, and this suggests it is not a ground-based phenomena but perhaps a floating raft in the Jovian atmosphere, changing its depth from time to time. It has also been suggested it is the top of a column of stagnant gas.

Magnetosphere of Jupiter is thought to be about one hundred times as strong as that of the Earth, and to have areas similar to our Van Allen Belts. It has been noted that radio emissions seem to be associated with the position of the satellite Io, the innermost of the four great satellites, and that the belt areas are extensive.

SATELLITES

(For details see the table of satellite data on page 52.)

It should be noted that of the twelve satellites of Jupiter, the four outer ones, Nos XII, XI, VIII and IX, have retrograde motions. The four major ones are listed below with notes on their appearances etc:

Io (No I) has an albedo of 0·656 and is yellow. In transit over the disk of Jupiter it appears dusky.

Europa (No II) with an albedo of 0·715 is white, and retains its whiteness in transit over the Jovian disk.

F

Ganymede (No III) with an overall albedo of 0·405 is half bright and half dark, and yellow. It is sometimes lost in transit on the disk of Jupiter.

Callisto (No IV) with an albedo of 0·266 is fainter than the other three major satellites and appears to have a polar cap, which is not, as is sometimes supposed, composed entirely of snow. It appears comparatively dark in transit on the Jovian disk.

Observation of the four major satellites is possible with small instruments. Binoculars will often show them, and it has been claimed that they are visible under good conditions by the naked eye on rare occasions. With adequate instrumentation there is opportunity to observe the shape and the markings on the small bodies as seen from Earth, their transits, eclipses and occultations, and when the Earth passes through the planes of their orbits, their mutual eclipses and occultations. In the case of transits it will be noted that the shadow of the satellite precedes the satellite before Jupiter's opposition, and follows it after opposition.

It sometimes happens that the four major satellites are at first glance invisible, being either in eclipse, occultation or transit on the disk, simultaneously. This will happen on 1980 Apl 9 when I will be in transit, II and III occulted, with IV in eclipse. Subsequently I will still be in transit, II occulted and eclipsed, with III and IV both eclipsed.

Again on 1990 Jun 15, I will be eclipsed and occulted, II in transit, III occulted and IV eclipsed.

On 1991 Jan 2, I will be in transit, II occulted and eclipsed, III occulted and IV eclipsed.

On 1997 Aug 27, I will be occulted, II in transit, III occulted and eclipsed with IV eclipsed.

OBSERVATION

Jupiter can be observed with a telescope of 15cm (6in) in diameter, although quite a small instrument will show the belts and zones. High magnification is not necessary. It is usual to time the passage of visible features across the meridian, as indicated by an imaginary line bisecting vertically the disk of the planet. These times of meridian passage are then plotted on a graph of longitude against date. The resultant slope indicates the actual movement over a period of days. Drawings of the entire disk or any special feature are also useful, but the time taken to draw the whole disk must not be more than about twenty minutes because of the rapid rotation. The disk for drawings should be oblate: 4·95 by 5·3cm (1·96 by 2·10in). Good photographs are also useful for recording appearances. The main point to bear in mind is to record accurately the meridian passage of features and the accurate drawing of the disk or other features.

Since the equatorial region of Jupiter rotates more rapidly than the rest of the planet, and this rotation rate decreases as one goes nearer the poles, each region has its own individual rotation period.

It is obviously out of the question to apply a suitable system of longitude to each belt or zone, and so we must compromise. It is normal practice to use System I for the Equatorial Zone and the North and South Equatorial Belts. The rest of the disk is assumed to rotate more slowly in an even manner and is designated as System II. The changes in longitude under these two systems are tabulated below:

CHANGE OF LONGITUDE IN INTERVALS OF MEAN TIME

System I: Period 9h 50m 30s

h	°	h	°	m	°	m	°	m	°
1	36·6	6	219·5	10	6·1	1	0·6	6	3·7
2	73·2	7	256·1	20	12·2	2	1·2	7	4·3
3	109·7	8	292·7	30	18·3	3	1·8	8	4·9
4	146·3	9	329·2	40	24·4	4	2·4	9	5·5
5	182·9	10	5·8	50	30·5	5	3·0	10	6·1

System I applies to all objects situated on or between the north component of the south equatorial belt and the south component of the north equatorial belt.

CHANGE OF LONGITUDE IN INTERVALS OF MEAN TIME

System II: Period 9h 55m 40·65s

h	°	h	°	m	°	m	°	m	°
1	36·3	6	217·6	10	6·0	1	0·6	6	3·6
2	72·5	7	253·8	20	12·1	2	1·2	7	4·2
3	108·8	8	290·1	30	18·1	3	1·8	8	4·8
4	145·1	9	326·4	40	24·2	4	2·4	9	5·4
5	181·3	10	2·6	50	30·2	5	3·0	10	6·0

System II applies to all objects situated north of the south component of the north equatorial belt or south of the north component of the south equatorial belt.

OPPOSITIONS

1971	May 23	in constellation of Scorpio
1972	June 24	in constellation of Sagittarius
1973	July 30	in constellation of Capricornus
1974	September 5	in constellation of Aquarius
1975	October 13	in constellation of Pisces
1976	November 18	in constellation of Taurus
1977	December 23	in constellation of Gemini
1979	January 24	in constellation of Cancer
1980	February 24	in constellation of Leo

Note the synodic period is 398·88 days

THE BELTS AND ZONES

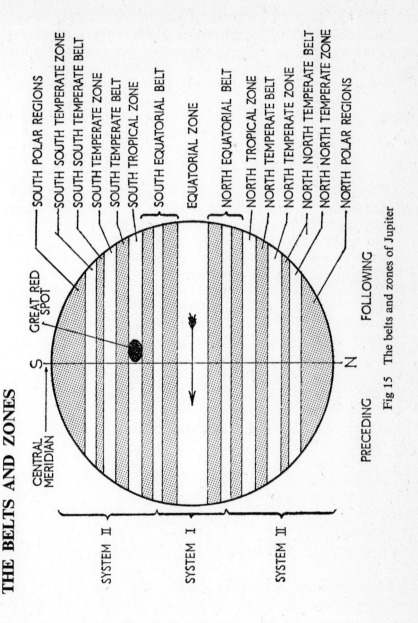

CENTRAL MERIDIAN

GREAT RED SPOT

S

N

SOUTH POLAR REGIONS
SOUTH SOUTH TEMPERATE ZONE
SOUTH SOUTH TEMPERATE BELT
SOUTH TEMPERATE ZONE
SOUTH TEMPERATE BELT
SOUTH TROPICAL ZONE
SOUTH EQUATORIAL BELT
EQUATORIAL ZONE
NORTH EQUATORIAL BELT
NORTH TROPICAL ZONE
NORTH TEMPERATE BELT
NORTH TEMPERATE ZONE
NORTH NORTH TEMPERATE BELT
NORTH NORTH TEMPERATE ZONE
NORTH POLAR REGIONS

SYSTEM II
SYSTEM I
SYSTEM II

PRECEDING   FOLLOWING

Fig 15   The belts and zones of Jupiter

NOTES

SATURN

RINGS

Saturn, with its rings, is the most beautiful of all the inanimate bodies in the Solar System. The rings are not solid, but are composed of millions of individual bodies, probably ammonia ice crystals, each one in its particular orbit round Saturn. Gaps occur in and between the rings through harmonic perturbations of the planet's and the satellites' gravitational pulls. The ring system is composed as follows:

The outer Crêpe Ring or Dusky Ring of indefinite extension, and whose reality is doubted.

Ring A with outer diameter 272,300km (169,000 miles) and inner diameter 239,600km (149,000 miles) having the Encke Division in it.

Cassini's Division 4,000km (2,500 miles) wide and cleared by the effects of the harmonic perturbations of the inner satellites, particularly by Mimas.

Ring B, 234,200km (145,000 miles) outer diameter, appears brighter than Ring A, probably because the component bodies are more closely packed than in Ring A.

Ring C or Crêpe Ring, or Dusky Ring, with outer diameter of about 181,000km (112,500 miles) and extending inwards to within 14,500km (9,000 miles) of the surface of Saturn, but somewhat transparent and seen against the ball of Saturn as a dark band.

Ring D: the Inner Crêpe Ring discovered photographically at the Pic du Midi in 1970.

The Rings are seen edge on once every fifteen years as the Earth passes through the plane of the system (see table, p 152).

PASSAGES OF THE RINGS' PLANE

| THROUGH THE EARTH | | THROUGH THE SUN | |
Date	Direction	Date	Direction
1848 April	N to S		
1848 September	S to N	1848 August	N to S
1849 January	N to S		
1861 November	S to N		
1862 January	N to S	1862 May	S to N
1862 August	S to N		
1878 March	N to S	1878 February	N to S
1891 September	S to N	1891 October	S to N
1907 April	N to S		
1907 October	S to N	1907 July	N to S
1908 January	N to S		
1920 November	S to N		
1921 February	N to S	1921 April	S to N
1921 August	S to N		
1936 June	N (Odeg)		
		1936 December	N to S
1937 February	N to S		
1950 September	S to N	1950 September	S to N
1966 April	N to S		
1966 October	S to N	1966 June	N to S
1966 December	N to S		
1979 October	S to N		
1980 March	N to S	1980 March	S to N
1980 July	S to N		
1995 May	N to S		
1995 August	S to N	1995 November	N to S
1996 February	N to S		

When the plane of Saturn's rings passes through the Earth, the rings are edge on and are almost invisible except in large telescopes. When the plane passes through the Sun, the rings appear dark through mutual eclipses of the particles forming the rings.

DATA ON THE RINGS

DIAMETERS OF SATURN'S RINGS

		At unit distance	At mean opposition distance	Miles	km
		"	"		
Ring A	outer	375·4	43·96	169,200	272,300
	inner	330·4	38·69	148,900	239,600
Ring B	outer	322·8	37·80	145,500	234,200
	inner	249·7	29·24	112,500	181,000
Ring C	inner	206·0	24·12	92,800	149,300

Thickness of the rings is misleading in the telescope because the eye registers the brightness as an extension of the width against the dark background. The thickness can hardly be more than 16km (10 miles) and may be even less.

Appearances of the rings differ from time to time. They are most open when Saturn is in the constellation Sagittarius and again in Leo and Gemini. They are edgewise to the Sun in the constellations of Pisces and Leo. On occasion stars have been seen through the rings. When edge on to Earth the rings are often quite invisible and Saturn has been suspected of being eccentrically placed with regard to the rings.

THE GLOBE

The Globe of Saturn is similar in appearance to that of Jupiter, with considerable flattening polewise. The diameters are equatorial 119,000km (74,000 miles) and polar 107,000km

(67,000 miles). It has a gaseous surface, but large spots and disturbances are much more rare than in the case of Jupiter. Saturn is considered to be 60 per cent hydrogen by mass, and with a lower temperature than Jupiter (−180°C); activity is not marked on Saturn. The Equatorial Zone carries white oval clouds similar to those on Jupiter, but the belts are less prominent, with more methane and less ammonia than on Jupiter.

SATELLITES

(For details see the table of satellite data on page 52.)

Titan, the largest satellite travelling round Saturn, has a diameter of 4,800km (3,000 miles) and is the only satellite in the solar system to possess an atmosphere, possibly methane. Titan can be well seen in a small telescope as a star-like point accompanying Saturn, and its movement may be traced from night to night as it circles Saturn.

Mimas, Enceladus, and Tethys have densities similar to water and have been thought to be huge balls of snow.

Iapetus, with an orbit outside that of Titan, appears brighter when west of Saturn than when east, probably through having an irregular shape and possibly dark areas on the surface. It seems as if Iapetus keeps the same face towards Saturn.

Phoebe, the outermost satellite, has a highly inclined orbit of 150°, and thus has retrograde motion around Saturn. It has been suggested Phoebe is a captured asteroid.

Janus, the nearest to Saturn, was discovered in December 1966.

Observation of the satellites is of value photometrically because neither the magnitudes nor their variations are well established. Small instruments may be used for the brighter satellites and Titan can be seen with 5cm (2in) aperture, while Tethys with 10cm (4in) must be searched for when farthest from Saturn. Mimas is difficult because of nearness to the planet; Enceladus is also difficult for the same reason. For the fainter members of Saturn's family, it is necessary to use instruments capable of grasping magnitudes as faint as 14, and in the case of Phoebe,

16·5. But Saturn should be hidden to make the best of the conditions.

Observation of Saturn can be undertaken with a telescope of quite moderate dimensions. Saturn will bear magnification better than Jupiter, so high powers are recommended when possible.

Rotation: knowledge of the rotation periods at various latitudes is still inadequate, largely because definite markings are rare. It is therefore necessary to record any such objects as they cross the meridian, as in the case of the observation of Jupiter. The following tables make calculations easier.

No of rotations		Period			To observe the same part of the Equatorial Zone of Saturn:				
1			10h	14m	after	1 day	observe 3h	32m	earlier
2			20	28	after	2 days	3	10	later
3		1d	6h	42m	after	3	—	22	earlier
4		1	16	56	after	4	there will be no repeat		
5		2	3	10			appearance		
10		4	6	20	after	5	2	38	later
15		6	9	30	after	6	—	44	earlier
20		8	12	40	after	7	4	16	earlier
25		10	15	50	after	8	2	26	later
30		12	19	—	after	9	1	6	earlier
35		14	22	10	after	10	4	38	earlier
40		17	1	20	after	20	—	58	later
45		19	4	30					
50		21	7	40					

Adopting a rotation period of 10h 14m the change of longitude will be
as follows:

Number of days lapsed	Change in longitude	Number of days lapsed	Change in longitude
50	95·0deg	4	137·2deg
40	292·0	3	12·9
30	129·0	2	248·6
20	326·0	1	124·3
15	64·5	*Time lapsed*	
10	163·0	12h	62·2
9	38·7	6	211·1
8	274·4	3	105·5
7	150·1	2	70·4
6	25·8	1	35·2
5	261·5	½	17·6

For smaller time intervals divide
accordingly

In addition to watching for and recording the times of transit
of any markings on the globe, it should be also noted what
intensities of illumination are shown by the various zones and
belts on a scale of zero to ten, the latter representing darkness
while zero is the intensity of the brightest part of Ring B. Notes on
colour should also be made as well as variations in the brightness
of the satellites if the telescope used is large enough for these to
be accurately observed.

Occultations of stars by Saturn, while rare, are important for
indicating the variations in the density of the rings as indicated
by the change in brightness of a star as Saturn passes in front
of it.

The shadows of the globe on the rings and the rings on the
globe should also be noted.

Drawings of the planet should be made, when conditions are
good enough, to a size of 4 inches by 2 inches.

OPPOSITIONS AD 1971–1980

1971 November 25 in constellation Taurus
1972 December 8 in constellation Taurus
1973 December 22 in constellation Gemini with rings wide open
1975 January 6   in constellation Gemini

1976	January 20	in constellation Cancer
1977	February 2	in constellation Cancer
1978	February 16	in constellation Leo
1979	March 1	in constellation Leo (with rings edge on three times during 1979–80)
1980	March 14	in constellation Leo

Note synodic period is 378·09 days

NOTES

URANUS, NEPTUNE AND PLUTO

URANUS

Uranus, with its five satellites (see page 52), is unique in the Solar System in so far as its inclination of 98° is past the vertical, and so causes the rotation of both planet and satellites to be retrograde. With a revolution period of 84 years, its seasons are quite unlike those of any other planet. It is accordingly seen sometimes in the normal way with its equator presented towards Earth (as in 1965), and at others it is seen pole on (as in 1946). Its poles suffer a night period of 21 years with a corresponding period of day. The surface temperature is −190°C.

The five satellites are all comparatively faint and when Uranus presents its pole towards Earth, their orbits appear circular.

Observation of the apparently small disk requires large apertures to detect the belts and zones. Some variation in the brightness of Uranus has been detected. Binoculars show Uranus as a star-like point, but larger instruments are required to show the disk.

NEPTUNE

Neptune is similar to Uranus in appearance, but slightly bluish in colour. The surface temperature is −220°C, and disk details are difficult to see.

There are two satellites: Triton has an almost circular orbit and retrograde motion, while Nereid is very small with an orbit similar to that of a comet with direct motion (see page 52).

PLUTO

Pluto, normally the outermost planet, has an eccentric orbit that carries it within the orbit of Neptune as shown in the diagram below; perihelion will be in 1989. Its orbit with an inclination of 17° does not permit collision with Neptune. It may once have been a satellite of Neptune. With a diameter of about 5,900km (3,700 miles) it seems doubtful if it could disturb the orbits of Uranus and Neptune as much as seems to be the case; it could be larger, more dense or perhaps not the real cause of the perturbations. Surface temperature is −211°C to −229°C. It is probably a terrestrial-type planet with a rock body overlaid with ice.

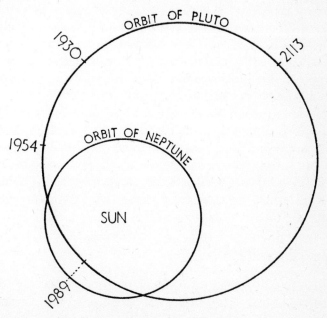

Fig 16   Pluto comes within the orbit of Neptune to reach perihelion in 1989. The diagram is not to scale

Observation requires large instruments, and it was not until the 508cm (200in) Mount Palomar telescope was available that the diameter of the disk could be measured. Its magnitude is below 14, which means that a telescope of considerable aperture is required to show it.

NOTES

THE ZODIACAL LIGHT AND
GEGENSCHEIN OR COUNTERGLOW

THE ZODIACAL LIGHT

A faint glow seen in the sky near the ecliptic, especially during late evenings in March and early mornings in September. Although the light is predominantly white, a pink or warm glow has been reported.

The glow is thought to be due to light reflected from thinly spread matter extending out from the Sun beyond the orbit of Earth; the outer part of the solar corona. It has also been suggested that it is due to a tail of dust, similar to a comet's tail, following the Earth.

THE GEGENSCHEIN

This is a hazy patch of light seen opposite the Sun's position, best seen in September as a patch about forty times the diameter of the Moon. It is extremely hard to see and the slightest artificial light is enough to make it invisible.

It is probably due to light reflected from interplanetary material, or an enhancement of illumination of such material by refraction of sunlight through the atmosphere of Earth.

COMETS

GENERAL

These objects can be divided into two classes: 1. Periodic Comets, which approach the Sun at regular forecastable intervals (see p 166). 2. Comets that appear without warning and are not seen again after one visit to the Sun (that is, after travelling around and near to the Sun). There is no evidence of comets coming from anywhere outside the Solar System and it is assumed that these are really comets with very long periods travelling in very large orbits. They appear near the Sun and are not seen again for many years or even centuries; this also means that when such a comet is seen, its previous appearance may well have been long before records were kept, or even perhaps before man existed.

Cometary orbits are normally nearly parabolic ellipses, but perturbations by the larger planets, notably Jupiter, can produce orbits of lesser or greater eccentricity. Hyperbolic orbits have also been indicated by the motion of a comet. It is possible that both these latter are really parts of large ellipses disturbed by planetary perturbations.

Structure. The structure of a comet is understandable in terms of gravity and the radiation pressure on bodies of different sizes. Smaller bodies have larger surface areas in proportion to their mass than larger ones, and are thus proportionately more

162

susceptible to radiation pressure. Thus, when a comet approaches the Sun near perihelion passage, the smaller bodies and gas molecules in the cloud of material forming the comet are repelled, while the larger stones or rocks obey the laws of gravity without being displaced by the Sun's radiation pressure. Hence a comet always keeps its tail pointing away from the Sun, except when it approaches the Sun from a very long distance away in space.

The *nucleus*, the central portion of a comet's head, is usually of stellar appearance and fainter than the surrounding coma. It is probably composed of meteorites or small rocks. The *coma*, surrounding the nucleus, is of gaseous appearance and normally bright. The *tail*, appearing as a continuation of the coma, generally becomes broader as it streams away from the head of the comet. It is supposed that magnetic fields provide a coupling mechanism between the solar wind and cometary particles, together with the weak interplanetary field. Ionised gases thus follow the radius vector of the solar wind, while dust tails lag behind, and are thus curved in appearance. Gas tails are comparatively straight. The gases show emission spectra while dust tails reflect sunlight.

Brightness varies inversely with the distance from the Sun and the Earth according to certain rules, but no comet behaves accurately in this way. We accordingly adopt a general expression in terms of stellar magnitude scale for each of the main classes of comets.

For parabolic comets:

$$M = m + 10 \log r + 5 \log D$$

For short period comets:

$$M = m + 15 \log r + 5 \log D$$

where M is the observed magnitude of the comet, m is the magnitude when the distances from both Sun and Earth are unity, r is the actual distance from the Sun and D is the actual distance from Earth.

The different values of m observed for different comets are attributed to their different physical and chemical compositions.

Fluctuations also occur when a comet is a long way from the Sun and the temperature is too low to expel gaseous matter from the nucleus. A third formula is often used to give a magnitude derived from the proportionate distances of a comet from Earth and Sun:

Mag $= 5 \cdot 0 + 5 \log D + 10 \log r$

There is only one comet that can be observed every year, which is Schwassmann-Wachmann I. This comet was discovered in 1925, and is notable because its orbit is nearly circular. The orbit lies between those of Jupiter and Saturn. The comet shows sudden changes of brightness, which are thought to be due to bombardment by corpuscles emitted by the Sun. Its normal magnitude is about 18 and it is therefore beyond the capabilities of smaller telescopes. Its period of revolution round the Sun is $16 \cdot 1$ years.

Tidal action of the Sun. This is observed in most cases, the heads changing shape when the comet is near the Sun. Biela's Comet with a period of $6 \cdot 75$ years is a notable case. In 1846 it became pear-shaped and then separated into two parts.

The origin of comets is supposed to lie in a spherical shell some 150,000 astronomical units away from the Sun, forming part of the Solar System. Cometary orbits are probably distributed spherically around the Solar System but each orbit is a near parabola. Comets observed are those that happen to be making a perihelion passage in any particular period of time. Asteroid fragments impacting on comet nuclei can change their orbits.

Chemical Constitution. Chemically, comets can be analysed by their spectra. These show, in addition to reflected sunlight, bright bands indicating the presence of:

C_2, CH, CH_2, NH, NH_2, OH, CO, N_2^+, and OH^+.

These bands are not permanent, since the molecules combine with others to form various carbon gases which are driven off into the tail. When near the Sun the spectrum also shows the presence of bright lines of sodium, iron and nickel.

Naming of comets. A comet is usually named after its discoverer, or in some rare cases, after the computer of its orbit. Comets are also designated by the year of discovery plus the letter assigned in order of appearance during that year, thus: 1970a, 1971a, 1971b, etc, or by the order of their perihelion passage each year, eg 1963 VIII.

LIST OF PERIODIC COMETS

Name of comet	Period (years)	Last perihelion passage	Remarks
Encke	3·30	1971 Jan	Separately discovered by Méchain in 1786, by Caroline Herschel and Pons in 1805. Due again 1972 March
Grigg-Skjellerup	5·12	1967 Jan	
Honda-Mrkos-Pajdusakova	5·22	1969 Sept	Great increase in brightness near perihelion, comet diffuse
Tempel II	5·26	1967 Aug	
Neujmin II	5·47	1971 Jan	Last seen 1927
Tuttle-Giacobini-Kresak	5·50	1967 Nov	Favourable return 1973
Kojima	6·21	1970 Oct	
D'Arrest	6·23	1970 May	
De Vico-Swift	6·31	1965 Aug	First recovery since 1894
Toit-Neujmin-Delporte	6·31	1970 Oct	1970 July first recovery since 1941
Pons-Winnecke	6·34	1970 July	
Giacobini-Zinner	6·40	1966 March	
Tempel-Swift	6·41	1970 Jan	Last seen 1908
Kopff	6·41	1970 Oct	
Forbes	6·42	1967 Dec	Last seen 1961
Schwassmann-Wachmann II	6·52	1968 March	
Churyumov-Gerasimenko	6·55	1969 Sept	
Wolf-Harrington	6·55	1971 Sept	
Tsuchinshan I	6·62	1965 Jan	
Wirtanen	6·65	1967 Dec	
Harrington-Wilson	6·69	1964 Oct	Last seen 1951

Name of comet	Period (years)	Last perihelion passage	Remarks
Brooks II	6·72	1967 March	Not seen 1967
Perrine-Mrkos	6·72	1968 Nov	
Reinmuth II	6·74	1967 Aug	
Johnson	6·77	1970 March	
Tsuchinshan II	6·79	1965 Feb	
Gunn	6·80	1969 April	
Harrington II	6·82	1967 April	
Arend-Rigaux	6·83	1971 April	
Finlay	6·91	1967 July	
Borrelly	6·99	1967 June	
Holmes	7·04		Lost, and recovered 1964, due again 1972 Jan
Daniel	7·09	1964 April	Predicted 1971 June: Period 7·12
Harrington-Abell	7·19	1969 May	
Shajn-Schaldach	7·27	1971 Oct	Not seen since discovery in 1949
Faye	7·40	1969 Oct	
Ashbrook-Jackson	7·42	1971 March	
Whipple	7·47	1970 Oct	
Reinmuth I	7·59	1965 Aug	
Arend	7·76	1967 June	
Schaumasse	8·19	1968 April	Last seen 1960
Jackson-Neujmin	8·39	1970 Aug	First recovered 1970 after 1936
Wolf I	8·43	1967 Aug	
Comas-Solá	8·55	1969 Oct	
Kearns-Kwee	8·95	1963 Dec	
Neujmin, III	10·57	1961 Dec	Not recovered
Gale	10·90	1970 Nov	Last seen 1938
Klemola	10·91	1965 Aug	
Väisälä	11·28	1971 Sept	Recovered 1970 Dec
Slaughter-Burnham	11·62	1970 April	
Van Biesbroeck	12·4	1966 July	
Wild	13·19	1960 March	
Tuttle	13·61	1967 March	
Schwassmann-Wachmann I	16·10	See notes	
Neujmin I	17·93	1966 Dec	
Crommelin	27·87	1956 Oct	
Stephan-Oterma	38·96	1942	
Westphal	61·73	1913	

Name of comet	Period (years)	Last perihelion passage	Remarks
Brorsen-Metcalf	69·06	1919	
Olbers	69·57	1956 June	
Pons-Brooks	70·88	1954 May	
Halley	76·03	1910	
Herschel-Rigollet	156·00	1939	
Grigg-Mellish	164·30	1907	

SOME GREAT COMETS AD 1066–1970

Year	Comet
1066	Halley's Comet
1106	Comet with 63° tail
1145	Comet first seen in China, possibly Halley's comet
1264	Possibly two comets. Tail over 100° long
1301	Halley's Comet
1378	Halley's Comet
1402	Comet visible in daylight
1456	Halley's Comet
1531	Halley's Comet
1578	Star as large as the Sun, Brahe's comet of 1577
1607	Halley's Comet
1618	Comet with 70° tail
1680	Period calculated as 8,814 years
1682	Halley's Comet
1744	Cheseaux, multiple tail. Klinkenberg, 90° tail
1758–9	Halley's Comet. First predicted return
1811	Flaugergues, half across the sky, lasted seventeen months. 70° tail
1835	Halley's Comet
1843	Comet with 40° tail, visible in daylight
1858	Donati's Comet with curved tail 40° long
1861	Tebbutt, Earth passed through tail 119° long
1882	Head disrupted, period calculated as 400,000 years. Probably the brightest comet observed
1910	Great Comet visible in daylight
1910	Halley's Comet
1956	Arend Roland
1957	Comet Mrkos
1962	Comet Seki-Lines
1965	Comet Ikeya-Seki
1970	Comet Bennett

RECORDED APPEARANCES OF HALLEY'S COMET

AD 66	989	1607
141	1066	1682
218	1145	1759
295	1301	1835
451	1378	1910
760	1456	due 1986
	1531	

OBSERVATION

Observation of comets is usually carried out photographically and positions relative to the background stars accurately measured on the photographic plates. Most comets are discovered on sky photographs, although wide-angle telescopes and binoculars are often employed in comet searching. This requires an accurate knowledge of the sky and for this reason is often undertaken by teams of observers who are allotted their own special areas of sky in which to search.

NOTES

METEORS

GENERAL

Meteors are small bodies travelling around the Sun as minute planets and are usually of the dimensions of a grain of sand. They become visible on collision with the Earth's atmosphere and are sometimes termed 'shooting stars'. The relative speeds of the Earth and a meteor may be as high as 72km/s (45 miles/s). Resistance in the atmosphere of the Earth causes the body to vaporise and usually to be consumed at heights of from 80–112km (50–70 miles) above the Earth's surface. Occasionally, however, a particularly large body of a size approximating to that of a walnut, or perhaps on occasion larger, survives the catastrophe and lands on the ground as a meteorite, but there seems to be a fundamental difference between these classes.

Some twenty million of these minute bodies collide with the Earth each day.

There is a third class, known as micrometeorites, that are extremely small indeed, measuring only some 0·1mm (1/250ths of an inch) in diameter, which because of their small mass do not become visible by vaporisation. They are studied from space vehicles.

Meteors can be classed as *shower* types and *sporadic* types. The shower type travels round the Sun in swarms and is associated with comets. As the Earth passes through the swarm, a shower occurs and these showers occur at regular times each year. The main showers are listed in the following tables.

LIST OF MAIN SHOWERS

Shower	Epoch		ZHR at max	Radiant		Notes
	maximum	normal limits		RA	Dec	
Quadrantids	January 4	January 1–5	100	15h 28m	N 50 deg	Blue coloured meteors with silver trains. Rich in faint meteors
April Lyrids	April 22	April 19–24	14	18 08	N 32	Bright meteors
Eta Aquarids	May 5	May 1–8	18	22 24	O	Persistent trains
June Lyrids	June 16	June 10–21	10	18 32	N 35	Blue coloured meteors with persistent trains
Ophiuchids	June 20	June 17–26	15	17 20	S 20	
Capricornids	July 25	July 10 to August 5	15	21 00	S 15	
Delta Aquarids	July 29	July 15 to August 15	36	22 36 / 22 36	S 17 / O	Double radiant
Pisces-Australids	July 30	July 15 to August 20	14	22 40	S 30	
Alpha-Capricornids	August 1	July 15 to August 25	10	20 36	S 10	Yellow coloured fireballs
Iota-Aquarids	August 5	July 15 to August 25	13	22 32 / 22 04	S 15 / S 6	Double radiant

Perseids	August 12	July 25 to August 18	70	03 04	N 58	Bright meteors with persistent trains
Kappa Cygnids	August 20	August 18–22	10	19 20	N 55	Bright exploding fireballs
Orionids	October 21	October 16–27	35	06 24	N 15	Persistent trains
Taurids	November 1	October 10 December 5	16	03 28 03 36	N 14 N 21	Double radiant. Brilliant meteors
Leonids	November 17	November 14–20	*	10 08	N 22	Many bright meteors with persistent trains
Phoenicids	December 5	December 5	25?	01 00	S 55	
Geminids	December 13	December 7–15	55	07 28	N 32	Many bright meteors
Ursids	December 22	December 17–24	18	14 28	N 78	

* The number seen varies considerably from year to year. Every 33 years rates as high as many thousands per hour have been recorded, the last of these occasions being 1967. A reasonable rate is recorded most years.

NB: The dates given in the table should be treated only as a guide. There are small variations due to the calendar and for any one year reference should be made to the corresponding yearbook or handbook.

The values for the ZHR (Zenith Hourly Rate) are approximate as the actual value varies from year to year. They are given solely as a guide.

The Perseids are a rich consistent shower following the orbit of Comet Tuttle III and are known as the Tears of St Lawrence.

Sporadic meteors can appear at any time and come from all parts of the sky. There is, however, a preponderance from the leading side of the Earth as it travels in its orbit. Meteors overtaking the Earth naturally meet it more slowly than those encountered at the Earth's leading side. There is also evidence suggesting the Earth encounters more meteors during the day than at night, particularly during the afternoon.

It has been suggested that some meteorites carry evidence of extra-terrestrial life, but this claim is not proven.

Elements. No unfamiliar elements have been found in them and the iron type (siderites) are usually 90 per cent iron with some nickel and cobalt. The stony type (aerolites) are partly stone and partly nickel-iron, but the distinction is not sharp between the types. Of the many meteorites found on the Earth's surface, the largest is that at Hoba West, in South West Africa, which weighs over 60 tons.

Large craters caused by meteoritic impact have been found in many parts of the globe; those at Barringer in Arizona, the Wolf Creek Crater in Australia, that of 1908 in Siberia, are especially well known, while many more very bright objects have been seen to land, and continue to be observed from time to time, without making a crater in the ground. These bright objects are called fireballs, and can leave material suspended in the air for days.

The danger of being struck by one of these falling objects is quite negligible.

OBSERVATION

When observing meteors, the following points should be recorded:

1   Date and time of the occurrence.
2   Magnitude by comparison with stars.
3   Right ascension and declination of first appearance.
4   Right ascension and declination of disappearance.
5   Length of the track.
6   Duration of visibility.
7   Apparent colour, and presence of streak or train.
8   Radiant point if the meteor is part of a shower; this point is apparent as a result of perspective.

Items 3 and 4 can be obtained by reference to a star atlas.

A number of observations as above can be compared and the true path of a meteor deduced. Observers should therefore work as a team and be well spread out so as to provide bearings at various angles on a long base line.

The main aims of meteor observing are to determine:
1   The radiant points of new showers and strong minor streams.
2   Hourly rates and times of maxima of showers.
3   Diurnal and annular variations in hourly rates.
4   Magnitude distributions of shower or sporadic meteors.
5   Details of meteor spectra when possible, but this is a difficult matter.

Cameras may be used, for long exposure times will record meteors as streaks across the picture, and will thus show the radiant points by back producing the traces. In this case the camera must be driven to compensate for the Earth's diurnal rotation.

Wide-field telescopes and binoculars can also be used to detect telescopic meteors, ie those too faint to be seen with the naked eye.

NOTES

STARS

ALPHABETICAL LIST OF CONSTELLATIONS

Name	English equivalent	Abbreviation		Area (sq deg)
Andromeda	Daughter of Cepheus	And or	Andr	722
Antlia	The Air Pump	Ant	Antl	239
Apus	Bird of Paradise	Aps	Apus	206
Aquarius	Water Bearer	Aqr	Aqar	980
Aquila	The Eagle	Aql	Aqil	652
Ara	The Altar	Ara	Arae	237
Aries	The Ram	Ari	Arie	441
Auriga	The Charioteer	Aur	Auri	657
Bootes	The Bear Driver	Boo	Boot	907
Caelum	The Sculptor's chisel	Cae	Cael	125
Camelopardus	The Giraffe	Cam	Caml	757
Cancer	The Crab	Cnc	Canc	506
Canes Venatici	The Hunting Dogs	CVn	C. Ven	465
Canis Major	The Greater Dog	CMa	C. Maj	380
Canis Minor	The Lesser Dog	CMi	C. Min	183
Capricornus	The Goat	Cap	Capr	414
Carina	The Keel (of Argo Navis)	Car	Cari	494
Cassiopeia	Mother of Andromeda	Cas	Cass	598
Centaurus	The Centaur	Cen	Cent	1,060
Cepheus	King of Ethiopia	Cep	Ceph	588
Cetus	Sea Monster (The Whale)	Cet	Ceti	1,231
Chamaeleon	The Chameleon	Cha	Cham	132
Circinus	The Compasses	Cir	Circ	93
Columba	The Dove	Col	Colm	270

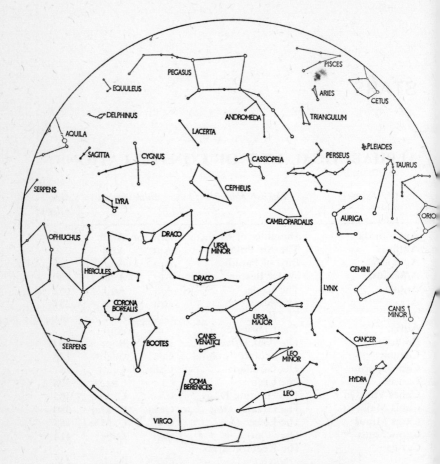

Fig 17   Constellations of the Northern Hemisphere

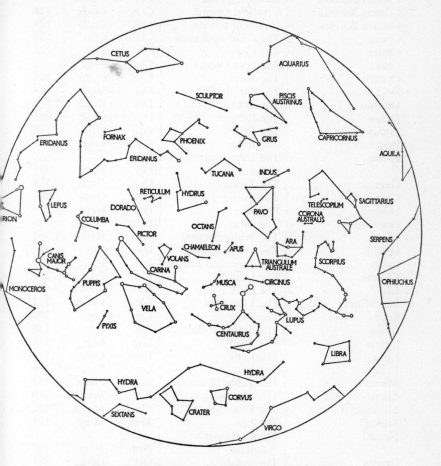

Fig 18   Constellations of the Southern Hemisphere

Name	*English equivalent*	*Abbreviation*	*Area (sq deg)*
Coma Berenices	Berenice's Hair	Com or Coma	386
Corona Australis	Southern Crown	CrA CorA	128
Corona Borealis	Northern Crown	CrB CorB	179
Corvus	The Crow or Raven	Crv Corv	184
Crater	The Cup	Crt Crat	282
Crux	Southern Cross	Cru Cruc	68
Cygnus	The Swan	Cyg Cygn	804
Delphinus	The Dolphin	Del Dlph	189
Dorado	The Swordfish	Dor Dora	179
Draco	The Dragon	Dra Drac	1,083
Equuleus	The Foal	Equ Equl	72
Eridanus	The River	Eri Erid	1,138
Fornax	The Laboratory Furnace	For Forn	398
Gemini	The Twins	Gem Gemi	514
Grus	The Crane	Gru Grus	366
Hercules	Hercules	Her Herc	1,225
Horologium	The Clock	Hor Horo	249
Hydra	The Water Serpent	Hya Hyda	1,303
Hydrus	The Water Snake	Hyi Hydi	243
Indus	The American Indian	Ind Indi	294
Lacerta	The Lizard	Lac Lacr	201
Leo	The Lion	Leo Leon	947
Leo Minor	The Lion Cub	LMi LMin	232
Lepus	The Hare	Lep Leps	290
Libra	The Scales or Balance	Lib Libr	538
Lupus	The Wolf	Lup Lupi	334
Lynx	The Lynx	Lyn Lync	545
Lyra	The Lyre	Lyr Lyra	286
Mensa	The Table Mountain	Men Mens	153
Microscopium	The Microscope	Mic Micr	210
Monoceros	The Unicorn	Mon Mono	482
Musca	The Fly	Mus Musc	138
Norma	The Carpenter's Square	Nor Norm	165
Octans	The Octant	Oct Octn	291
Ophiuchus	The Serpent Holder	Oph Ophi	948
Orion	The Great Hunter	Ori Orio	594
Pavo	The Peacock	Pav Pavo	378
Pegasus	The Winged Horse	Peg Pegs	1,121
Perseus	The Hero, Son of Zeus	Per Pers	615
Phoenix	The Phoenix	Phe Phoe	469
Pictor	The Painter's Easel	Pic Pict	247
Pisces	The Fishes	Psc Pisc	889

Name	English equivalent	Abbreviation		Area (sq deg)
Piscis Austrinus	The Southern Fish	PsA or PscA		245
Puppis	The Stern (of Argo Navis)	Pup	Pupp	673
Pyxis	The Compass Box	Pyx	Pyxi	221
Reticulum	The Net	Ret	Reti	114
Sagitta	The Arrow	Sge	Sgte	80
Sagittarius	The Archer	Sgr	Sgtr	867
Scorpius	The Scorpion	Sco	Scor	497
Sculptor	The Sculptor's Workshop	Scl	Scul	475
Serpentarius	See Ophiuchus			
Scutum	The Shield	Sct	Scut	109
Serpens	The Serpent	Ser	Serp	637
Sextans	The Sextant	Sex	Sext	314
Taurus	The Bull	Tau	Taur	797
Telescopium	The Telescope	Tel	Tele	252
Triangulum	The Triangle	Tri	Tria	132
Triangulum Australe	The Southern Triangle	TrA	TrAu	110
Tucana	The Toucan	Tuc	Tucn	295
Ursa Major	The Greater Bear	UMa	UMaj	1,280
Ursa Minor	The Lesser Bear	UMi	UMin	256
Vela	The Sail (of Argo Navis)	Vel	Velr	500
Virgo	The Virgin or Maiden	Vir	Virg	1,294
Volans	The Flying Fish	Vol	Voln	141
Vulpecula	The Fox	Vul	Vulp	268

PROPER NAMES

These have largely fallen into disuse, but a list of the better-known ones may be useful:

Constellation	Greek letter	Name	Constellation	Greek letter	Name
Andromeda	Alpha	Alpheratz		Mu	Alkalurops
	Beta	Mirach			
	Gamma	Almaak	Cancer	Alpha	Acubens
Aquarius	Alpha	Sadalmelik		Gamma	Asellus Borealis
	Beta	Sadalsuud		Delta	Asellus Australis
	Gamma	Sadachiba		Zeta	Tegmine
	Delta	Scheat			
	Epsilon	Albali			
			Canes Venatici	Alpha	Cor Caroli
Aquila	Alpha	Altair			
	Beta	Alshain	Canis Major	Alpha	Sirius
	Gamma	Tarazed		Beta	Mirzam
	Zeta	Dheneb		Gamma	Muliphen
	Lambda	Althalimain		Delta	Wezea
Ara	Alpha	Choo		Epsilon	Adara
				Zeta	Phurad
Argo Navis	Alpha	Canopus		Eta	Aludra
	Beta	Miaplacidus			
	Delta	Koo She	Canis Minor	Alpha	Procyon
	Epsilon	Avior		Beta	Gomeisa
	Zeta	Suhail Radar			
	Iota	Tureis	Capricornus	Alpha	Al Giedi
	Kappa	Markeb		Beta	Dabih
	Lambda	Al Suhail Al Wazn		Delta	Deneb Al Giedi
	Rho	Turais			
			Cassiopeia	Alpha	Shedir
Aries	Alpha	Hamal		Beta	Chaph
	Beta	Sheratan		Gamma	Tsih
	Gamma	Mesartim		Delta	Ruchbah
Auriga	Alpha	Capella	Centaurus	Alpha	Al Rijil (or Rigel Kent)
	Beta	Menkarlina			
	Zeta	Sadatoni		Beta	Agena
Bootes	Alpha	Arcturus		Gamma	Menkent
	Beta	Nekkar			
	Gamma	Seginus	Cepheus	Alpha	Alderamin
	Epsilon	Izar		Beta	Alphirk
	Eta	Saak		Gamma	Alrai

Constellation	Greek letter	Name	Constellation	Greek letter	Name
Cetus	Alpha	Menkar		Theta	Acamar
	Beta	Diphda			
	Gamma	Alkaffaljid-hina		Omicron[1]	Beid
	Zeta	Baiten Kaitos		Omicron[2]	Keid
	Iota	Deneb Kaitos-Shemali	Gemini	Alpha	Castor
				Beta	Pollux
	Omicron	Mira		Gamma	Alhena
				Delta	Wasat
Columba	Alpha	Phakt		Epsilon	Mebsuta
	Beta	Wezn		Zeta	Mekbuda
				Eta	Propus
Corona Borealis	Alpha	Alphekka		Mu	Tejat
	Beta	Nusakan	Grus	Alpha	Alnair
Corvus	Alpha	Alkhiba		Beta	Al Dhanab
	Gamma	Minkar			
	Delta	Algorel	Hercules	Alpha	Rasalgethi
				Beta	Kornephoros
Crater	Alpha	Alkes		Zeta	Rutilicus
				Kappa	Marsik
Crux Australis	Alpha	Acrux		Lambda	Masym
	Beta	Mimosa (not generally used)	Hydra	Alpha	Alphard
Cygnus	Alpha	Deneb	Leo	Alpha	Regulus
	Beta	Albireo		Beta	Denebola
	Gamma	Sadr		Gamma	Algieba
	Epsilon	Gienah		Delta	Zosma
	Pi	Azelfafage		Epsilon	Asad Australis
Delphinus	Alpha	Svalocin		Zeta	Adhafera
	Beta	Rotanev		Theta	Chort
Draco	Alpha	Thuban		Lambda	Alterf
	Beta	Alwaid		Mu	Rassalas
	Gamma	Etamin	Lepus	Alpha	Arneb
	Delta	Tais		Beta	Nihal
	Eta	Aldhibain	Libra	Alpha	Zubenel-genubi
	Iota	Edasich		Beta	Zubenel-chemali
	Xi	Juza		Gamma	Zubenelhak-rabi
Eridanus	Alpha	Achernar		Sigma	Zubenalgubi
	Beta	Kursa			
	Gamma	Zaurak	Lupus	Alpha	Men
	Delta	Theemini			
	Eta	Azha			

Constellation	Greek letter	Name	Constellation	Greek letter	Name
	Beta	Ke Kouan		Pi	Albaldah
Lyra	Alpha	Vega		Sigma	Nunki
	Beta	Sheliak			
	Gamma	Sulaphat	Scorpio	Alpha	Antares
				Beta	Graffias
Ophiuchus	Alpha	Rasalhague		Gamma	(see Sigma
	Beta	Cheleb			Librae)
	Delta	Yed Prior		Delta	Dschubba
	Epsilon	Yed Post		Epsilon	Wei
	Zeta	Han		Theta	Sargas
	Eta	Sabik		Kappa	Girtab
				Lambda	Shaula
Orion	Alpha	Betelgeux		Nu	Jabbah
	Beta	Rigel		Sigma	Alniyat
	Gamma	Bellatrix		Upsilon	Lesath
	Delta	Mintaka			
	Epsilon	Alnilam	Serpens	Alpha	Unukalhai
	Zeta	Alnitak		Theta	Alya
	Eta	Algjebbah			
	Kappa	Saiph	Taurus	Alpha	Aldebaran
	Lambda	Heka		Beta	Alnath
				Gamma	Hyadum
Pegasus	Alpha	Markab			Primus
	Beta	Scheat		Epsilon	Ain
	Gamma	Algenib		Eta	Alcyone
	Epsilon	Enif		17	Electra
	Zeta	Homan		19	Taygete
	Eta	Matar		20	Maia
				21	Asterope
Perseus	Alpha	Mirphak		23	Merope
	Beta	Algol		27	Atlas
				28	Pleione
Phoenix	Alpha	Ankaa			
			Triangulum	Alpha	Rasalmo-
Pisces	Alpha	Kaitain			thallah
Piscis			Triangulum		
Australis	Alpha	Fomalhaut	Australe	Alpha	Atria
Sagittarius	Alpha	Rukbat	Ursa Major	Alpha	Dubhe
	Beta	Arkab		Beta	Merak
	Gamma	Alnasr		Gamma	Phad
	Delta	Kaus		Delta	Megrez
		Meridionalis		Epsilon	Alioth
	Epsilon	Kaus		Zeta	Mizar
		Australis		Eta	Alkaid or
	Zeta	Ascella			Benetnasch
	Lambda	Kaus Borealis		Iota	Talita

Constellation	Greek letter	Name	Constellation	Greek letter	Name
	Mu	Tania Australis		Zeta	Alifa
	Pi	Ta Tsun		Eta	Alasco
	80	Alcor	Virgo	Alpha	Spica
				Beta	Zawijah
Ursa Minor	Alpha	Polaris		Gamma	Postvarta
	Beta	Kocab		Epsilon	Vindemiatrix
	Gamma	Pherkad Major		Eta	Zaniah
	Delta	Yildun		Iota	Syrma

STELLAR MAGNITUDES

The magnitude of a star is related to its brightness, either apparent or absolute. The relative brightness of different stars is indicated by a number. The higher the number, the fainter the star. Thus a star of magnitude 1 will be bright to the naked eye, whereas to see a star of magnitude 10 will require optical aid.

Hipparchus in 130 BC compiled a star catalogue. He called the twenty brightest stars he could see stars of the first magnitude. All stars just visible to the naked eye he called sixth magnitude stars, placing the remainder in intermediate classes. Ptolemy (AD 140) introduced subdivisions of magnitudes, using the words 'greater' or 'less' in conjunction with the magnitudes. Argelander, with Schönfeld and Krüger (AD 1852–63), compiled the *Bonn Dürchmusterung Catalogue*, using decimal divisions of the stellar magnitudes: 8·3, 4·6, etc. At about this time, Sir John Herschel noted that a decrease of light in geometrical progression corresponded to an increase of magnitude in arithmetical progression, in accordance with the law called Fechner's Law (AD 1859), which states that if stimulus is increased in geometrical progression, its resulting sensation increases in an arithmetic progression.

It was also established that a star of the first magnitude is one hundred times as bright as a star of the sixth magnitude.

N. Pogson (AD 1850) proposed that a fixed scale be adopted as the uniform ratio between magnitudes. For ease in calculation he suggested the ratio should be 2·512, a figure of which the logarithm to the base 10 is 0·4. This approximates very closely to the average figure among a number of observers.

Magnitude steps thus become longer as we descend the scale, by a factor of 2·512. Thus a star of magnitude 1 is:

2·512 times as bright as a star of magnitude 2;

2·512 squared times as bright as a star of magnitude 3 (6·30 times);

2·512 cubed times as bright as a star of magnitude 4 (15·84 times), and so on.

Each step of one magnitude represents a dimming, from magnitude one, equal to multiplying each consecutive step by 2·512 progressively all down the scale.

Bright stars above magnitude 1 are classed as magnitude 0. Brighter than this we move into negative figures, for example, Sirius is magnitude −1·42.

Magnitude can be in terms of Apparent, Absolute, Bolometric or Photographic (see Glossary for definitions of these terms).

Differences between the magnitudes of stars expressed in the various terms arise from the variations of brightness in different parts of the stars' spectra. A red star may be bright to the eye and be recorded so in the visual sense, but a star strong in blue light will be recorded brighter than a red one on a blue sensitive plate or film, even if they appear of equal brilliance to the naked eye. Furthermore, a star faint in visible light may be strong in emission at longer wavelengths, and so be quoted as bright on the Bolometric scale.

MAGNITUDES AND BRIGHTNESS RATIOS

Magnitude difference	Brightness ratio
0·1	1·096
0·2	1·202
0·3	1·318
0·4	1·445
0·5	1·585
0·6	1·738
0·7	1·905
0·8	2·089
0·9	2·291
1·0	2·512
2·0	6·310
3·0	15·849
4·0	39·811
5·0	100·000

Thus a star of one magnitude fainter than another has a brightness ratio of 2·512, while a star five magnitudes below another is one hundred times fainter.

Though the nomenclature is rather loose, it is customary to say that stars of above magnitude 1·3 are of the 'first magnitude'; stars between magnitudes 1·3 and 2·5 are of the 'second magnitude'; between 2·5 and 3·5 'third magnitude', and so on. However, it is clearly more satisfactory to give the precise values.

STANDARD STARS FOR EACH MAGNITUDE

Approximate magnitude	Name of star	Exact magnitude
1½	Alpha Geminorum	1·58
	Lambda Scorpii	1·60
	Gamma Orionis	1·64
2	Beta Ursae Minoris	2·04
	Kappa Orionis	2·06
	Alpha Andromedae	2·06
2½	Gamma Ursae Majoris	2·44
	Epsilon Cygni	2·46
	Alpha Pegasi	2·50
	Delta Leonis	2·57
3	Zeta Aquilae	2·99
	Gamma Bootis	3·05
	Delta Draconis	3·06
	Zeta Tauri	3·07
3½	Alpha Trianguli	3·45
	Zeta Leonis	3·46
	Beta Bootis	3·48
	Epsilon Tauri	3·54
4	Beta Aquilae	3·90
	Gamma Coronae Borealis	3·93
	Delta Ceti	4·04
	Delta Cancri	4·17
4½	Nu Andromedae	4·42
	Delta Ursae Minoris	4·44
	Nu Cephei	4·46
	Psi Ursae Majoris	4·54
5	Rho Ursae Majoris	4·99
	Eta Ursae Minoris	5·04
	Delta Trianguli	5·07
	Zeta Canis Minoris	5·11
5½	Theta Ursae Minoris	5·33
	Rho Coronae Borealis	5·43
	Epsilon Trianguli	5·44

LIST OF THE BRIGHTEST STARS

The 286 stars brighter than apparent magnitude 3·55.

Star. If the star is a visual double the letter *A* indicates that the data are for the brighter component. The brightness and separation of the second component *B* are given in the last column. Sometimes the double is too close to be conveniently resolved and the data refer to the combined light, *AB*; in interpreting such data the magnitudes of the two components must be considered.

Visual Magnitude (*V*). These magnitudes are based on *photoelectric observations*, with a few exceptions, which have been adjusted to match the yellow colour-sensitivity of the eye. The photometric system is that of Johnson and Morgan in *Ap J*, vol 117, p 313, 1953. It is as likely as not that the true magnitude is within 0·03 mag of the quoted figure, on the average. Variable stars are indicated with a 'v'. The type of variability, range, *R*, in magnitudes, and period in days are given.

Colour index (*B–V*). The blue magnitude, *B*, is the brightness of a star as observed photoelectrically through a blue filter. The difference *B–V* is therefore a measure of the colour of a star. The table reveals a close relation between *B–V* and spectral type. Some of the stars are slightly reddened by interstellar dust. The probable error of a value of *B–V* is only 0·01 or 0·02 mag.

Type. The customary spectral (temperature) classification is given first. The Roman numerals are indicators of *luminosity class*. They are to be interpreted as follows: Ia—most luminous supergiants; Ib—less luminous supergiants; II—bright giants; III—normal giants; IV—subgiants; V—main sequence stars. Intermediate classes are sometimes used, eg Iab. Approximate absolute magnitudes can be assigned to the various spectral and luminosity class combinations. Other symbols used in this column are: p—a peculiarity; e—emission lines; v—the spectrum is variable; m—lines due to metallic elements are abnormally strong; f—the O-type spectrum has several broad emission lines; n or nn—unusually wide or diffuse lines. A composite spectrum, eg M1 Ib+B, shows up when a star is composed of two nearly equal but unresolved components. In the far southern sky, spectral types in italics were provided through the kindness of Prof R. v. d. R. Woolley, Australian Commonwealth Observatory. Types in parentheses are less accurately defined (g— giant, d—dwarf, c—exceptionally high luminosity). All other types were very kindly provided especially for this table by Dr W. W. Morgan, Yerkes Observatory.

Parallax (P). From 'General Catalogue of Trigonometric Stellar Parallaxes' by Louise F. Jenkins, Yale Univ Obs, 1952.

Absolute visual magnitude (M_v), and *distance in light-years* (D). If π is greater than 0·030″ the distance corresponds to this trigonometric parallax and the absolute magnitude was computed from the formula $M_v = V + 5 + 5 \log \pi$. Otherwise a generally more accurate absolute magnitude was obtained from the luminosity class. In this case the formula was used to *compute* π and the distance corresponds to this 'spectroscopic' parallax. The formula is an expression of the inverse square law for decrease in light intensity with increasing distance. The effect of absorption of light by interstellar dust was neglected, except for three stars, ζ Per, σ Sco and ζ Oph, which are significantly reddened and would therefore be about a magnitude brighter if they were in the clear.

Annual proper motion (PM), and *radial velocity* (R). From 'General Catalogue of Stellar Radial Velocities' by R. E. Wilson, Carnegie Inst Pub 601, 1953. Italics indicate an average value of a variable radial velocity.

The star names are given for all the officially designated navigation stars and a few others. Throughout the table, a *colon* (:) indicates an uncertainty.

Star	RA 1970 (h m)	Declination (° ′)	Visual Magnitude V	Colour Index B–V	Spectral (letter)	Type	Parallax P (″)	Absolute Magnitude Mᵥ	Distance D (ly)	Proper Motion PM (″)	Radial Velocity R (km/sec)	Notes
SUN			−26·73	+0·63	G2	V		+4·84				Sun
α And	00 06·8	+28 55	2·06	−0·08	B9p	IV	0·024	−0·1	90	0·209	−11·7	Alpheratz. Manganese star
β Cas	07·6	+58 59	2·26	+0·34	F2	IV	0·072	+1·6	45	0·555	+11·8	Caph
γ Peg	11·7	+15 01	2·84v	−0·23	B2	IV	−004	−3·4	570	0·010	+04·1	β CMa type, R in V2·83–2·85, 0·15d. γ Peg = Algenib
β Hyi	24·2	−77 25	2·78	+0·62	G1	IV	0·153	+3·7	21	2·255	+22·8	
α Phe	24·8	−42 28	2·39	+1·08	K0	III	0·035	+0·1	93	0·442	+74·6	Ankaa
δ And A	37·7	+30 42	3·25:	+1·26	K3	III	0·024	−0·2	160	0·161	−07·3	B 12m 28″
α Cas	38·8	+56 22	2·16	+1·18	K0	II–III	0·009	−1·1	150	0·058	−03·8	Schedar. Var?
β Cet	42·1	−18 09	2·02	+1·03	K1	III	0·057	+0·8	57	0·234	+13·1	Diphda
η Cas A	47·3	+57 39	3·47	+0·56	G0	V	0·182	+4·8	18	1·221	+09·4	B7–26m 9″
γ Cas A	54·9	+60 33	2·13v	−0·16v	B0	IV:pe	0·034	−0·3:	96:	0·026	−06·8	Var B8–18m 2″
β Phe AB	01 04·7	−46 53	3·30	+0·88	G8	III	0·017	+0·3	190	0·035	−01·1	A4·1m B4·1m 2″
η Cet	07·1	−10 20	3·47	+1·16	K3	III	0·032	+1·0	102	0·250	+11·5	
β And	08·0	+35 20	2·02	+1·57	M0	III	0·043	+0·2	76	0·211	+00·3	Mirach
δ Cas	23·8	+60 05	2·67	+0·13	A5	V	0·029	+2·1	43	0·301	+06·7	
γ Phe	27·1	−43 28	3·44	+1·56	K5	Ib	−003	−4·6	1300	0·209	+25·7	
α Eri	36·6	−57 23	0·51	−0·16	B5	IV:	0·023	−2·3	118	0·098	+19·0	Achernar. Ecl? R0–08:m 759d
τ Cet	42·7	−16 06	3·50	+0·72	G8	Vp	0·275	+5·7	12	1·921	−16·2	

Star	RA 1970 h m	Dec ° '	V	B–V	Type	P "	M_v	D ly	PM "	R km/sec	
α Tri	01 51·4	+29 26	3·45	+0·46	F6 IV	0·050	+2·0	65	0·230	−12·6	
ε Cas	52·2	+63 31	3·33	−0·15	B3 IV:p	0·007	−2·7	520	0·038	−08·1	
β Ari	53·0	+20 40	2·68	+0·14	A5 V	0·063	+1·7	52	0·147	−01·9	
α Hyi	57·8	−61 43	2·84	+0·28	F0 V		+2·9	31	0·265	+07·0	
γ And A	02 02·1	+42 11	2·14:	+1·16:	K3 II	0·005	−2·4	260	0·068	−11·7	B 5·4m C 6·2m A–BC 10" B–C 0·7" γ And = Almach
α UMi A	02·5	+89 08	1·99v	+0·60v	F8 Ib	0·003	−4·6	680	0·046	−17·4	Cep, R0·11m 4·0d, B 8·9m 18" Polaris
α Ari	05·5	+23 19	2·00	+1·15	K2 III	0·043	+0·2	76	0·241	−14·3	Hamal
β Tri	07·8	+34 51	3·00	+0·13	A5 III	0·012	−0·1	140	0·156	+09·9	
o Cet A	17·8	−03 07	2·00v		A2 V (gM6e)	0·013	−0·5	103	0·232	+63·8	LP, R 2·0–10·1, 332d, B 10m 1" Mira
γ Cet AB	41·7	+03 07	3·48	+0·11	A2 V	0·048	+2·0	68	0·203	−05·1	A 3·57m B 6·23m 3"
θ Eri AB	57·1	−40 25	2·92	+0·13	A3 V	0·028	+1·7	65	0·061	+11·9	Acamar
α Cet	03 00·7	+03 58	2·54	+1·63	M2 III	0·003	−0·5	130	0·075	−25·9	Menkar
γ Per	02·6	+53 23	2·91:	+0·72:	G8 III:+A3:	0·011	+0·3	113	0·004	+02·5	
ρ Per	03·1	+38 43	3·50v		M4 II–III	0·008	−1·0	260	0·172	+28·2	Irr R 3·2–3·8
β Per	06·0	+40 50	2·06v	−0·07	B8 V	0·031	−0·5	105	0·006	+04·0	Ecl R 2·06–3·28, 2·87d Algol
α Per	22·2	+49 45	1·80	+0·48	F5 Ib	0·029	−4·4	570	0·035	−02·4	Mirfak
δ Per	40·8	+47 42	3·03	−0·14	B5 III	0·007	−3·3	590	0·046	−09·0	
η Tau	45·7	+24 20	2·86	−0·09	B7 III	0·005	−3·2	541	0·050	+10·1	in Pleiades Alcyone
γ Hyi	47·7	−74 20	3·30	+1·61	M2 II–III	·001	−1·5	300	0·125	+16·0	B 9·36m 13"
ζ Per A	52·1	+31 48	2·83	+0·13	B1 Ib	0·007	−6·1	1000	0·015	+20·6	
ε Per A	55·8	+39 55	2·88	−0·17	B0–5 V	·001	−3·7	680	0·036	−01	B7·99m 9"
γ Eri	56·6	−13 36	3·01	+1·58	M0 III	0·003	−0·5	160	0·126	+61·7	
α Ret A	04 14·0	−62 33	3·33	+0·91	G6 II	0·008	−2·1	390	0·064	+35·6	B 12m 49"
ε Tau	26·9	+19 07	3·54	+1·02	K0 III	0·018	+0·1	160	0·118	+38·6	
θ²Tau	26·9	+15 48	3·42	+0·17	A7 III	0·025	+0·2	140	0·108	+39·5	
α Dor	33·3	−55 06	3·28	−0·08	A0 IIIp	0·011	−1·2	260	0·051	+25·6	Silicon star
α Tau A	34·2	+16 27	0·86v	+1·52	K5 III	0·048	−0·7	68	0·202	+54·1	Irr? R 0·78–0·93, B13m 31" Aldebaran
π³Ori	48·2	+06 55	3·17	+0·45	F6 V	0·125	+3·65	26	0·468	+24·3	
ι Aur	55·0	+33 07	2·64:	+1·49	K3 II	0·015	−2·4	330	0·021	+17·5	

Star	RA 1970 h m	Dec ° '	V	B-V	Type	P "	M_v	D ly	PM "	R km/sec	Notes
ε Aur	04 59·8	+43 47	3·00v	+0·50:	F0 Iap	0·004	−7·1	3400	0·008	−02·5	Ecl R 0·81m 9886d
ε Lep	05 04·2	−22 25	3·21	+1·46	K5 III	0·006	−0·4	170	0·077	+01·0	
η Aur	04·4	+41 12	3·17	−0·18	B3 V	0·013	−2·1	370	0·077	+07·4	
β Eri	06·4	−05 07	2·79	+0·13	A3 III	0·042	+0·9	78	0·122	−08·0	
μ Lep	11·6	−16 14	3·29	−0·09	B9 IIIp	0·018	−2·1	390	0·049	+27·7	Manganese star
β Ori A	13·1	−08 14	0·14v	−0·04	B8 Ia	−·003	−7·1	900	0·001	+20·7	Rigel — Irr? R 0·08-0·20, B 6·65m 9"
α Aur	14·5	+45 58	0·05	+0·80	G8 III:+F	0·073	−0·6	45	0·435	+30·2	Capella
η Ori AB	23·0	−02 25	3·32v	−0·18	B0·5 V	0·004	−3·7	940	0·008	+19·8	Ecl R 3·32-3·50, 8·0d, A 3·59m B 4·98m 1"
γ Ori	23·5	+06 19	1·64	−0·23	B2 III	0·026	−4·2	470	0·015	+18·2	Bellatrix
β Tau	24·4	+28 35	1·65	−0·13	B7 III	0·018	−3·2	300	0·178	+08·0	Elnath
β Lep A	27·0	−20 47	2·81	+0·82	G5 III	0·014	+0·1	113	0·090	−13·5	B 9·4m 3"
δ Ori A	30·5	−00 19	2·20v	−0·20	O9·5 II	0·004	−6·1	1500	0·002	+16·0	Ecl R 2·20-2·35, 5·7d, B 6·74m 53"
α Lep	31·4	−17 51	2·58	+0·22	F0 Ib	0·002	−4·6	900	0·006	+24·7	
λ Ori AB	33·5	+09 55	3·40	−0·18	O8 III	0·006	−5·1	1800	0·006	+33·5	A 3·56m B 5·54m 4" C 10·92m 29"
ι Ori AB	34·0	−05 56	2·76	−0·24	O9 III	0·021	−6·1	2000	0·005	+21·5	A 2·78m B 7·31m 11"
ε Ori	34·7	−01 13	1·70	−0·19	B0 Ia	−·007	−6·8	1600	0·000	+26·1	Alnilam
ζ Tau	35·9	+21 08	3·07:	−0·13:	B2 III:p	−·002	−4·2	940	0·023	+24·3	Shell star
α Col A	38·6	−34 05	2·64	−0·11	B8 Ve	−·005	−0·6	140	0·026	+35·0	B 12m 12"
ζ Ori AB	39·2	−01 57	1·79	−0·22	O9·5 Ib	0·022	−6·6	1600	0·004	+18·1	A 1·91m B 4·05m 3"
κ Ori	46·3	−09 41	2·06	−0·17	B0·5 Ia	0·009	−6·9	2100	0·004	+20·6	
β Col	49·9	−35 47	3·12	+1·16	(gK1)	0·023	+0·0	140	0·402	+89·4	
α Ori	53·5	+07 24	0·41v	+1·87:	M2 Iab	0·005	−5·6	520	0·028	+21·0	Betelgeuse — Irr? R 0·06:-0·75:m
β Aur	57·3	+44 57	1·86	+0·06	A2 V	0·037	−0·3	88	0·051	−18·2	
θ Aur AB	57·7	+37 13	2·65	−0·07	B9-5pv	0·018	+0·1	108	0·097	+29·3	Silicon star A 2·67m B 7·14m 3"
η Gem A	06 13·1	+22 31	3·33v	+1·58	M3 III	0·013	−0·6	200	0·066	+19·0	R 0·27m, B 6·70m 1"
ζ CMa	19·2	−30 03	3·04	−0·18	B2·5 V	−·003	−2·4	390	0·004	+32·2	
μ Gem	21·1	+22 32	2·92v	+1·63	M3 III	0·021	−0·6	160	0·129	+54·8	R 0·14m
β CMa	21·4	−17 56	1·96v	−0·24	B1 II-III	0·014	−4·8	750	0·004	+33·7	β CMa type variable
α Car	23·3	−52 41	−0·72	+0·16	F0 Ib-II	0·018	−3·1	98	0·025	+20·5	Canopus
γ Gem	36·0	+16 26	1·93	0·00	A0 IV	0·031	−0·6	105	0·066	−12·5	

Star	RA 1970 h m	Dec ° '	V	B-V	Type	P "	M_v	D ly	PM "	R km/sec	
ν Pup	06 36.8	−43 10	3.19	−0.10	B7 *III*		−3.2	620	0.010	+28.2	
ε Gem	42.1	+25 10	3.00	+1.39	G8 *Ib*		−4.6	1080	0.016	+09.9	
ξ Gem	43.6	+12 56	3.38	+0.43	F5 *IV*		+1.9	64	0.224	+25.3	
α CMa *A*	43.8	−16 41	−1.42	+0.01	A1 *V*	0.375	+1.45	8.7	1.324	−07.6	B 8.66m 1960: 9", θ = 90° **Sirius**
α Pic	48.1	−61 54	3.27	+0.21	A5 *V*		+2.1	57	0.272	+20.6	
τ Pup	49.2	−50 35	2.97	+1.17	K0 *III*		+0.1	124	0.079	+36.4	
ε CMa *A*	57.4	−28 56	1.48:	−0.18:	B2 *II*		−5.1	680	0.004	+27.4	B 7.5m 8" **Adhara**
σ² CMa	07 01.8	−23 47	3.02	−0.09	B3 Ia		−7.1	3400	0.000	+48.4	
δ CMa	07.2	−26 21	1.85	+0.65	F8 Ia		−7.1	2100	0.005	+34.3	
L₂ Pup	12.6	−44 36			(gM5e)	−.018	−3.1	650	0.342	+53.0	LP, R 3.4–6.2, 141ᵈ
π Pup	16.1	−37 03	2.81	+1.56:	(gK4)	0.016	−0.3	140	0.008	+15.8	
η CMa	22.9	−29 14	2.46	−0.08	B5 Ia	0.023	−7.1	2700	0.008	+41.1	
β CMi	25.7	+08 21	2.91	−0.09	B7 *V*		−1.1	210	0.065	+22.0	
σ Pup *A*	28.3	−43 14	3.28	+1.49	(gK5)	0.020	−0.4	180	0.195	+88.1	B 9.4m 22"
α Gem *A*	32.7	+31 57	1.97	+0.00:	A1 *V*	0.013	+1.3	45	0.199	+06.0	5", B−V +0.02, C 9.08vm 73" *Castor*
α Gem *B*	32.7	+31 57	2.95	+0.07:	A5m	0.072	+2.3	45	0.199	−01.2	
α CMi *A*	37.7	+05 18	0.37	+0.41	F5 *IV–V*	0.288	+2.7	11.3	1.250	−03.2	B 10.7m 5" **Procyon**
β Gem	43.5	+28 06	1.16	+1.02	K0 III	0.093	+1.0	35	0.625	+03.3	**Pollux**
ξ Pup	48.0	−24 48	3.34	+1.23	G3 Ib	−.003	−4.6	1240	0.005	+02.7	
χ Car	56.0	−52 54	3.48	−0.18	(B3)		−2.1	430	0.039	+19.1	
ζ Pup	08 02.5	−39 55	2.23	−0.26	O5f		−7.1	2400	0.033	−24.0	
ρ Pup	06.3	−24 13	2.80v	+0.42	F6 IIp	0.031	+0.3:	105:	0.098	+46.6	Var R 2.72–2.87
γ Vel *A*	08.6	−47 16	1.88	−0.26	WC7		−4.1	520	0.011	+35.0	B 4.31m 41"
ε Car	21.9	−59 24	1.97	+1.14:	(K0+B)		−3.1:	340	0.030	+11.5	*Avior*
ο UMa *A*	27.8	+60 49	3.37	+0.83	G5 III	0.004	+0.1	150	0.171	+19.8	B 15m 7"
δ Vel *AB*	43.9	−54 36	1.95	+0.05	A0 *V*	0.043	+0.2	76	0.086	+02.2	A 2.0m B 5.1m 3" CD 10m 69"
ε Hya *ABC*	45.2	+06 32	3.39	+0.68	G0 comp	0.010	+0.6	140	0.198	+36.4	A 3.7m B 5.2m 0.2" 15", C 6.8m 3" D 12m 20"
ζ Hya	53.8	+06 04	3.11	+1.00	K0 II–III	0.029	−1.1	220	0.101	+22.8	
ι UMa *A*	57.2	+48 09	3.12	+0.19	A7 *V*	0.066	+2.2	49	0.505	+12.2	BC 10.8m 7"

Star	RA 1970 (h m)	Dec (° ')	V	B–V	Type	P (")	M_v (")	D (ly)	PM (")	R (km/sec)	Notes	Name
λ Vel	09 06·9	−43 19	2·24	+1·64:	K5 Ib	0·015	−4·6	750	0·026	+18·4		*Suhail*
a Car	10·2	−58 50	3·43	−0·17	B3 IV		−2·9	590	0·028	+23·3		
β Car	12·9	−69 36	1·67	+0·01	A0 III	0·038	−0·4	86	0·183	−05·0		*Miaplacidus*
ι Car	16·3	−59 08	2·25	+0·17	F0 Ib	0·021	−4·6	750	0·019	+13·3		
α Lyn	19·3	+34 32	3·17	+1·54	M0 III	0·007	−0·5	180	0·217	+37·6		
κ Vel	21·2	−54 53	2·45	−0·15	B2 IV	0·017	−3·4	470	0·012	+21·9		
α Hya	26·1	−08 32	1·98	+1·44	K4 III	0·015	−0·3	94	0·034	−04·3		*Alphard*
N Vel	30·3	−56 54	3·19	+1·56	(gK5)		−0·4	170	0·036	−13·9		
θ UMa A	30·8	+51 49	3·19	+0·46	F6 IV	0·052	+1·8	63	1·094	+15·4	B 14m 5"	
ε Leo	44·1	+23 54	2·99	+0·81	G0 II	0·002	−2·1	340	0·048	+05·0		
1 Car	44·4	−62 23	4·10v		(cG0) II	0·019	−5·5	2700	0·016	+04·0	Cep max 3·4m min 4·8m, 35·2^d	
ν Car AB	46·4	−64 56	2·95	+0·26	A7 II	0·020	−2·1	340	0·012	+13·6	A 3·02m B 6·03m 5"	
α Leo A	10 06·8	+12 07	1·36	−0·11	B7 V	0·039	−0·7	84	0·248	+03·5	B 8·1m 177"	*Regulus*
ω Car	13·0	−69 53	3·33	−0·08	B8·5 IV		−1·5	300	0·029	+04·0		
ζ Leo	15·1	+23 34	3·46	+0·30	F0 III	0·009	+0·5	130	0·023	−15·0		
λ UMa	15·3	+43 04	3·45	+0·03	A2 IV	−010	+0·1	150	0·170	+18·3		
q Car	16·1	−61 11	3·41v	+1·55	K5 Ib	0·018	−4·6	1300	0·023	+08·6	Var R 3·38–3·44	
γ Leo AB	18·3	+20 00	1·99	+1·13	K0 IIIp	0·019	+0·1	90	0·350	−36·6	A 2·29m B 3·54m 4"	
μ UMa	20·5	+41 39	3·05	+1·55	M0 III	0·031	+0·5	105	0·086	−20·5		
ρ Car	31·0	−61 32	3·30v	−0·11	B5 IVpe		−2·3	430	0·021	+26·0	Var R 3·22–3·39	
θ Car	41·9	−64 14	2·74	−0·22	B0 Vp		−4·0	710	0·018	+24·0	A 2·7m B 7·2m 2"	
μ Vel AB	45·5	−49 16	2·67	+0·89	G5 III		+0·1	108	0·085	+06·9		
ν Hya	48·1	−16 02	3·12	+1·25	K3 III	0·022	−0·2	150	0·221	−01·0		
β UMa	11 00·0	+56 33	2·37	−0·03	A1 V	0·042	+0·5	78	0·087	−12·0		*Merak*
α UMa AB	01·9	+61 55	1·81	+1·06	K0 III	0·031	−0·7	105	0·138	−08·9	A 1·88m B 4·82m 1"	*Dubhe*
ψ UMa	08·0	+44 39	3·00	+1·14	K1 III		+0·0	130	0·072	−03·8		
δ Leo	12·5	+20 41	2·57	+0·13	A4 V	0·040	+0·6	82	0·201	−20·6		
θ Leo	12·7	+15 36	3·34	0·00	A2 V	0·019	+1·1	90	0·104	+07·8		
λ Cen	34·4	−62 51	3·15	−0·05	B9 III		−2·1	370	0·039	+07·9		
β Leo	47·5	+14 44	2·14	+0·09	A3 V	0·076	+1·5	43	0·511	−00·1		*Denebola*

Star	RA 1970	Dec	V	B-V	Type		P	M_v	D	PM	R	
	h m	° '				V	″		ly	′	km/sec	
γ UMa	11 52·2	+53 52	2·44	0·00	A0		0·020	+0·2	90	0·094	*−12·9*	*Phecda*
δ Cen	12 06·8	−50 33	2·59v	−0·15:	B2	Ve		−2·7	370	0·042	+09·0	Var R 2·56–2·62
ε Crv	08·6	−22 27	3·04	+1·33	K3	III		−0·2	140	0·069	+04·9	
δ Cru	13·5	−58 35	2·81v	−0·23	B2	IV		−3·4	570	0·041	+26·4	Var R 2·78–2·84
δ UMa	13·9	+57 12	3·30	+0·07	A3	V	0·052	+1·9	63	0·106	−12·9	*Megrez*
γ Crv	14·3	−17 22	2·59	−0·10	B8	III		−3·1	450	0·163	−04·2	*Gienah*
α Cru A	24·9	−62 56	1·39	−0·25	B1	IV		−3·9	370	0·042	*−11·2*	**Acrux** 5″, C 4·90m 89″
α Cru B	24·9	−62 56	1·86	−0·25	(B3)		0·018	−3·4	370	0·042	*−00·6*	
δ Crv A	28·3	−16 21	2·97	−0·04	B9·5	V:n		+0·1	124	0·255	+09·0	B 8·26m 24″
γ Cru	29·5	−56 57	1·69	+1·55	M3	II		−2·5	220	0·274	+21·3	**Gacrux**
β Crv	32·8	−23 14	2·66	+0·89	G5	III	0·027	+0·1	108	0·059	−07·7	
α Mus	35·4	−68 58	2·70v	−0·20	B3	IV	0·006	−2·9	430	0·037	+18·0	Var R 2·66–2·73
γ Cen AB	39·9	−48 48	2·17	+0·00	A0	IV:		−0·5	160	0·197	−07·5	A 2·9m B 2·9m 1″
γ Vir AB	40·1	−01 17	2·76	+0·34	F0	V	0·101	+3·5	32	0·567	−19·7	A 3·50m B 3·52m 4″
β Mus AB	44·4	−67 57	3·06	−0·17	B3	V		−2·1	470	0·041	+42·0	A 3·7m B 4·0m 1″
β Cru	46·0	−59 32	1·28	−0·25	B0	III	0·008	−4·6	490	0·049	+20·0	**Beta Crucis**
ε UMa	52·7	+56 07	1·79	−0·03	A0pv	V:n	0·023	+0·2	68	0·113	−09·3	Chromium-europium star **Alioth**
α CVn A	54·6	+38 29	2·90	−0·10	B9·5pv			+0·1	118	0·238	*−03·3*	Silicon-europium star. B 5·61m 20″
ε Vir	13 00·7	+11 08	2·86	+0·93	G9	II–III	0·036	+0·6	90	0·274	−14·0	
γ Hya	17·3	−23 01	2·98	+0·92	G8	III	0·021	+0·3	113	0·086	−05·4	
ι Cen	18·9	−36 33	2·76	+0·05	A2	V	0·046	+1·1	71	0·351	+00·1	
ζ UMa A	22·7	+55 05	2·26	+0·02	A2	V	0·037	+0·1	88	0·127	*−09·0*	*Mizar* B 3·94m 14″ (Alcor, 224″)
α Vir	23·6	−11 00	0·91v	−0·24	B1	V	0·021	−3·3	220	0·054	*+01·0*	**Spica** Ecl R 0·91–1·01, 4·0d
ζ Vir	33·2	−00 27	3·40	+0·10	A3	Vn	0·035	+1·1	93	0·287	−13·2	
ε Cen	38·0	−53 19	2·33	−0·23	B1	IV		−3·9	570	0·033	+05·6	
η UMa	46·4	+49 28	1·87	−0·20	B3	V	0·004	−2·1	210	0·123	−10·9	*Alkaid*
ν Cen	47·7	−41 32	3·42	−0·22	B2	IV		−3·4	750	0·037	+09·0	
μ Cen	47·8	−42 20	3·12v	−0·13:	B2	V:pne		−2·7	470	0·032	+12·6	Var R 3·08–3·17
η Boo	53·3	+18 33	2·69	+0·59	G0	IV	0·102	+2·7	32	0·370	*−00·1*	
ζ Cen	53·7	−47 09	2·56	−0·23:	B2	IV		−3·4	520	0·076	+06·5	

Star	RA 1970	Dec	V	B-V	Type	P	M_v	D	PM	R	
	h m	° ′				″		ly	″	km/sec	
β Cen *AB*	14 01·7	−60 13	0·63	−0·23:	B1 II:	0·016	−5·2	490	0·035	−12·0	A 0·7m B 3·9m 1″ **Hadar**
π Hya	04·7	−26 32	3·25	+1·13	K2 III	0·039	+1·2	84	0·156	+27·2	*Menkent*
θ Cen	04·9	−36 14	2·04	+1·03	K0 III-IV	0·059	+0·9	55	0·738	+01·3	
α Boo	14·3	+19 20	−0·06	+1·23	K2 IIIp	0·090	−0·3	36	2·284	−05·2	**Arcturus**
γ Boo	30·9	+38 27	3·05	+0·19	A7 III	0·016	+0·2	118	0·186	−35·5	
η Cen	33·6	−42 01	2·39v	−0·21	B1·5 V:ne		−3·0	390	0·049	−00·2	Var, R 2·33−2·45
α Cen *A*	37·6	−60 43	0·01	+0·68	G2 V	⎱·751	+4·39	4·3	3·676	−24·6	⎱ 18″ **Rigil Kentaurus**
α Cen *B*	37·6	−60 43	1·40:	+0·73:	(dK1)	⎰	+5·8	4·3		−20·7	⎰
α Lup	40·0	−47 16	2·32	−0·22	B1 V		−3·3	430	0·033	+07·3	
α Cir *AB*	40·1	−64 50	3·18	+0·25	F0 Vp	0·049	+1·6	66	0·308	+07·4	Strontium star. A 3·19m B 5·04m 3″
ε Boo *AB*	43·7	+27 12	2·37	+0·96	K1: III:+A	0·013	+0·0	103	0·051	−16·5	A 2·47m B 5·04m 3″
α Lib *A*	49·2	−15 52	2·76	+0·15	A3m	0·049	+1·2	66	0·130	−10·0	*Zubenelgenubi*
β UMi	50·8	+74 16	2·04	+1·47	K4 III	0·031	−0·5	105	0·033	+16·9	B 5·15m 231″ *Kochab*
β Lup	56·6	−43 01	2·69	−0·23	B2 IV		−3·4	540	0·066	−00·3	
κ Cen	57·1	−41 59	3·15	−0·21	B2 V		−2·7	470	0·033	+09·1	
β Boo	15 00·8	+40 30	3·48	+0·95	G8 III	0·022	+0·3	140	0·059	−19·9	
σ Lib	02·3	−25 10	3·31	+1·65	M4 III	0·056	+2·0:	58:	0·089	−04·3	
ζ Lup *A*	10·1	−51 59	3·42	+0·90:	K0 III	0·036	+1·2	90	0·135	−09·7	B 7·8m 71″
δ Boo *A*	14·3	+33 26	3·47	+0·95	G8 III	0·028	+0·3	140	0·148	−12·2	B 7·84m 105″
β Lib	15·4	−09 16	2·61	−0·11	B8 V	−0·012	−0·6	140	0·101	−35·2	
γ TrA	16·1	−68 34	2·94	−0·01	A0 IV	0·005	+0·2	113	0·067	00·0	
δ Lup	19·4	−40 32	3·24	−0·23	B2 Vp		−3·4	680	0·032	+02·0	Europium star
γ UMi	20·8	+71 56	3·08	+0·06	A3 II-III	−0·005	−1·5	270	0·026	−03·9	
ι Dra	24·3	+59 04	3·28	+1·18	K2 III	0·032	+0·8	102	0·012	−11·0	
γ Lup *AB*	33·1	−41 04	2·80	−0·22	B2 Vn		−2·7	570	0·037	+06·0	A 3·5m B 3·7m 1″
α CrB	33·4	+26 49	2·23v	−0·02	A0 V	0·043	+0·4	76	0·154	+01·7	Ecl R 0·11m, 17·4d *Alphecca*
α Ser	42·8	+06 31	2·65	+1·17	K2 III	0·046	+1·0	71	0·139	+02·9	
β TrA	52·5	−63 20	2·87	+0·28:	F2 V	0·078	+2·3	42	0·448	−00·3	
π Sco	57·0	−26 02	2·92	−0·19	B1 V	0·005	−3·3	570	0·034	−03·0	
η Lup *AB*	58·1	−38 19	3·45	−0·23	B2 V		−2·7	570	0·042	+07·0	A 3·47m B 7·70m 15″
δ Sco	58·6	−22 32	2·34	−0·13	B0 V		−4·0	590	0·032	−14·0	

Star	RA 1970	Dec	V	B–V	Type	P	M_v	D	PM	R	
	h m	° ′				″		ly	″	km/sec	
β Sco AB	16 03·7	−19 43	2·65	−0·09	B0·5	V	0·004	−3·7	650	0·027	−06·6	A 2·78m B 504m 1″, C 4·93m 14″
δ Oph	12·8	−03 36	2·72	+1·59	M1	III	0·029	−0·5	140	0·156	−19·9	
ε Oph	16·7	−04 38	3·22	+0·97	G9	III	0·036	+1·0	90	0·089	−10·3	
σ Sco A	19·4	−25 31	2·86v	+0·14	B1	III		−4·4	570	0·030	−00·4	βCMa R 2·82−2·90, 0·25d, B8·49m 20″
η Dra A	23·6	+61 34	2·71	+0·92	G8	III	0·043	+0·9	76	0·062	−14·3	B 8·7m 6″
α Sco A	27·6	−26 22	0·92v	+1·84	M1	Ib+B	0·019	−5·1	520	0·029	−03·2	A 0·86m−1·02m B 5·07m 3″ Antares
β Her	28·9	+21 33	2·78	+0·92	G8	III	0·017	+0·3	103	0·105	−25·5	
τ Sco	34·0	−28 09	2·85	−0·25	B0	V		+4·0	750	0·030	−00·7	
ζ Oph	35·5	−10 30	2·57	+0·00	O9·5	V	−·007	−4·3	520	0·022	−19·0	
ζ Her AB	40·2	+31 39	2·81	+0·64	G0	IV	0·110	+3·1	30	0·608	−69·9	A 2·91m B 5·46m 1″
η Her	41·9	+38 59	3·46	+0·92	G7	III-IV	0·053	+2·1	62	0·097	+08·3	
α TrA	45·5	−68 59	1·93	+1·43	K2	III	0·024	−0·1	82	0·044	−03·6	Atria
ε Sco	48·2	−34 15	2·28	+1·16	K2	III-IV	0·049	+0·7	66	0·664	−02·5	
μ¹ Sco	49·8	−38 00	2·99v	−0·20	B1·5	V		−3·0	520	0·033	−25·0	Ecl R 2·99−3·09, 1·4d
ζ Ara	56·1	−55 56	3·16	+1·61	(gK5)		0·036	+0·9	90	0·042	−06·0	
κ Oph	56·3	+09 26	3·18	+1·15	K2	III	0·026	−0·1	150	0·293	−55·6	
ζ Dra	17 08·7	+65 45	3·20	−0·12	B6	III	0·017	−3·2	620	0·026	−14·1	
η Oph AB	08·7	−15 41	2·46	+0·06	A2·5	V	0·047	+1·4	69	0·097	−00·9	Sabik
η Sco	10·0	−43 12	3·33	+0·38	F2	III	0·063	+2·3	52	0·293	−28·4	
α Her AB	13·3	+14 25	3·10v	+1·41	M5	II	−·007	−2·3	410	0·032	−33·1	A 3·2m ± 0·3 B 5·4m 5″ Ras-Algethi
δ Her	13·8	+24 52	3·13	+0·09	A3	IV	0·034	+0·8	96	0·164	−41·0	
π Her	14·0	+36 50	3·13	+1·43	K3	II	0·020	−2·4	410	0·029	−25·7	
θ Oph	20·2	−24 58	3·29	−0·22	B2	IV		−3·4	710	0·025	−03·6	
β Ara	22·8	−55 30	2·90	+1·45:	K3	Ib		−4·6	1030	0·035	−00·4	
γ Ara A	22·9	−56 21	3·32	−0·16	B1	V	0·026	−3·3	680	0·017	−04·0	B 10m 18″
υ Sco	28·7	−37 16	2·71	−0·22	B2	IV		−3·4	540	0·039	+18·0	
α Ara	29·5	−49 52	2·95	−0·18:	B2·5	V		−2·4	390	0·083	−02·0	
β Dra A	29·7	+52 20	2·77	+0·96	G2	II	0·009	−2·1	310	0·019	−20·0	B 11·49m 4″
λ Sco	31·6	−37 05	1·60	−0·24	B1	V		−3·3	310	0·031	00·0	Shaula
α Oph	33·5	+12 35	2·09	+0·16	A5	III	0·056	+0·8	58	0·260	+12·7	Rasalhague
θ Sco	35·2	−42 59	1·86	+0·39	F0	Ib	0·020	−4·6	650	0·012	+01·4	

Star	RA 1970 h m	Dec ° '	V	B–V	Type		P	M_v	D ly	PM "	R km/sec	
κ Sco	17 40·4	−39 01	2·39	−0·21	B2	IV		−3·4	470	0·031	−10·0	
β Oph	42·0	+04 35	2·77	+1·16	K2	III	0·023	−0·1	124	0·160	−12·0	
μ Her A	45·3	+27 45	3·42	+0·75	G5	IV	0·108	+3·6	30	0·811	−15·6	BC 9·78m 33"
ι¹ Sco	45·5	−40 06	2·99	+0·49	F2	Ia	0·032	−7·1	3400	0·004	−27·6	
G Sco	47·7	−37 02	3·21	+1·18	(gK1)		0·013	+0·7	102	0·064	+24·7	
γ Dra	55·9	+51 29	2·21	+1·52	K5	III	0·017	−0·4	108	0·026	−27·6	*Eltamin*
ν Oph	57·4	−09 47	3·32	+1·00	G9	III	0·015	+0·2	140	0·118	+12·4	
γ Sgr	18 03·9	−30 26	2·97	+1·00	K0	III	0·018	+0·1	124	0·200	+22·1	
η Sgr A	15·6	−36 47	3·17	+1·55	M3	II	0·038	+1·1:	86:	0·218	+00·5	B 10m 4"
δ Sgr	19·1	−29 50	2·71	+1·39	K2	III	0·039	+0·7	84	0·050	−20·0	
η Ser	19·7	−02 54	3·23	+0·94	K0	III–IV	0·054	+1·9	60	0·894	+08·9	
ε Sgr	22·2	−34 24	1·81	−0·02	B9	IV	0·015	−1·1	124	0·135	−11·0	*Kaus Australis*
λ Sgr	26·1	−25 27	2·80	+1·05	K2	III	0·046	+1·1	71	0·194	−43·3	
α Lyr	35·9	+38 45	0·04	0·00	A0	V	0·123	+0·5	26·5	0·345	−13·9	*Vega*
φ Lyr	43·8	−27 02	3·20	−0·11	B8	III		−3·1	590	0·052	+21·5	
β Lyr A	49·0	+33 20	3·38v	−0·05:	Bpe		−·011	−4·6	1300	0·007	*19·2*	Ecl R 3·38–4·36, 12·94, B 7·8m 46"
σ Sgr	53·4	−26 20	2·12	−0·21	B2	V		−2·7	300	0·059	−11·0	*Nunki*
ζ²Sgr	55·9	−21 08	3·51	+1·18:	(gK1)		0·006	+0·0	160	0·035	−19·9	
γ Lyr	57·8	+32 39	3·25	−0·05	B9	III	0·011	−2·1	370	0·007	−21·5	
ζ Sgr AB	19 00·7	−29 55	2·61	+0·08	A2	IV	0·020	+0·1	140	0·020	+22·0	A 3·3m B 3·5m 1"
ζ Aql A	04·0	+13 49	2·99	+0·01	A0	V:nn	0·036	+0·8	90	0·101	−26·3	B 12m 5"
λ Aql	04·7	−04 56	3·44	−0·07	B9:	V:n	0·025	−0·1	160	0·092	−14·0	
τ Sgr	05·1	−27 43	3·30	+1·18	F2		0·038	+1·2	86	0·261	+45·4	
π Sgr ABC	08·0	−21 04	2·89	+0·35	F2	II–III	0·016	−0·7	250	0·040	−09·8	A 3·7m B 3·8m C 6·0m <1"
δ Dra	12·5	+67 37	3·06	+1·00	G9	IV	0·028	+0·2	124	0·130	+24·8	
δ Aql	24·0	+03 03	3·38	+0·31	F0	IV	0·062	+2·3	53	0·267	−29·9	
β Cyg A	29·5	+27 54	3·07	+1·12	K3	II:+B:	0·004	−2·4	410	0·009	−24·0	*Albireo*
δ Cyg AB	44·0	+45 04	2·87	−0·03	B9·5	III	0·021	−1·7	270	0·060	−21·0	B 5·11m 35"
γ Aql	44·8	+10 32	2·67	+1·48	K3	II	0·006	−2·4	340	0·012	−02·1	A 2·91m B 6·44m 2"
α Aql	49·3	+08 47	0·77	+0·22	A7	IV, V	0·198	+2·2	16·5	0·658	−26·3	**Altair**

Star	RA 1970 h m	Dec ° '	V	B-V	Type	P "	M_v	D ly	PM "	R km/sec	
θ Aql	20 09·8	−00 54	3·31	−0·07	B9·5 III	0·008	−1·7	330	0·034	−27·3	Type gK0: + late B; B 5·97m 205"
β Cap A	19·3	−14 53	3·06	+0·76	comp	0·005	+0·1	130	0·039	−18·9	
γ Cyg	21·1	+40 09	2·22	+0·66	F8 Ib	−006	−4·6	750	0·001	−07·5	
α Pav	23·3	−56 50	1·95	−0·20	B3 IV	0·039	−2·9	310	0·087	+02·0	
α Ind	35·5	−47 23	3·11	+1·00	K0 III	−013	+1·1	84	0·082	−01·1	
α Cyg	40·4	+45 10	1·26	+0·09	A2 Ia		−7·1	1600	0·003	−04·6	**Deneb**
β Pav	42·3	−66 19	3·45	+0·16	A5 III	−026	−0·1	160	0·046	+09·8	
η Cep	44·7	+61 43	3·41	+0·92	K0 IV	0·071	+2·7	46	0·825	−87·3	
ε Cyg	45·0	+33 51	2·46	+1·03	K0 III	0·044	+0·7	74	0·481	−10·3	
ζ Cyg	21 11·7	+30 06	3·25:	+0·99	G8 II	0·021	−2·2	390	0·056	+17·4	
α Cep	17·9	+62 28	2·44	+0·24	A7 IV,V	0·063	+1·4	52	0·156	−10·0	*Alderamin*
β Cep	28·3	+70 25	3·15v	−0·22v	B2 III	0·005	−4·2	980	0·014	−08·2	β CMa R 3·14-3·16, 0·19d
β Aqr	30·0	−05 43	2·86	+0·82	G0 Ib	0·000	−4·6	1030	0·017	+06·5	
ε Peg A	42·7	+09 45	2·31	+1·55	K2 Ib	−005	−4·6	780	0·025	+04·7	*Enif* B 11m 82"
δ Cap	45·4	−16 16	2·92v	+0·29	A6m III:	0·065	+2·0	50	0·392	−06·3	Var R 2·88-2·95
γ Gru	52·1	−37 30	3·03	−0·10	B8 III:	0·008	−3·1	540	0·102	−02·1	
α Aqr	22 04·2	−00 28	2·96	+0·96	G2 Ib	0·003	−4·6	1080	0·016	+07·5	
α Gru	06·3	−47 07	1·76	−0·14	B5 V	0·051	+0·3:	64:	0·194	+11·8	*Al Na'ir*
ζ Cep	09·8	+58 03	3·31	+1·55	K1 Ib	0·019	−4·6	1240	0·015	−18·4	
α Tuc	16·4	−60 24	2·87	+1·40	K3 III-IV	0·019	+1·5	62	0·079	+42·2	
δ Cep A	28·1	+58 16	3·96v	+0·66v	F5-G2 Ib	0·005	−4·0	1300	0·012	−16·8	Cep R 3·51-4·42, 5·4d, B 6·19m 41"
ζ Peg	40·0	+10 41	3·40:	−0·08:	B8 V	−004	−0·6	210	0·077	+07·0	
β Gru	40·9	−47 02	2·17v	+1·59	M3 II	0·003	−2·5	280	0·134	+01·6	Var R 2·11-2·23
η Peg	41·6	+30 04	2·95	+0·85	G8 II:+F?	−002	−2·2	360	0·027	+04·3	
δ Aqr	53·1	−15 59	3·28	+0·08	A3 V	0·039	+1·2	84	0·047	+18·0	
α PsA	56·0	−29 47	1·19	+0·10	A3 V	0·144	+2·0	22·6	0·367	+06·5	**Fomalhaut**
β Peg	23 02·3	+27 55	2·50v	+1·67	M2 II-III	0·015	−1·5	210	0·234	+08·7	Var R 2·4-2·7 *Scheat*
α Peg	03·3	+15 02	2·50	−0·03	B9·5 III	0·030	−0·1	109	0·071	−03·5	*Markab*
γ Cep	38·1	+77 27	3·20	+1·02	K1 IV	0·064	+2·2	51	0·168	−4·24	

STELLAR MASSES, DENSITIES, VOLUMES AND DISTANCES

The masses of stars can be found using Kepler's Third Law as applied to visual binaries. From this we derive the following formula:

$$\frac{M1 + M2}{M\odot} = \frac{(a/A)^3}{P^2}$$

where M1 and M2 refer to the masses of the two stars forming a binary system, M⊙ the mass of the Sun, A the distance from the Sun to Earth, a the distance between the binary components, and P the period of the binary system.

Measurement of the distance of each star from the centre of gravity of the binary system enables us to obtain the masses of the two components on the assumption that

$$\frac{M}{m} = \frac{D}{d},$$

where M is the mass of the primary, D its distance from the centre, m is the mass of the secondary star, and d its distance from the gravity centre of the binary system. To establish the distance of the binary system from Earth, the following formula is applicable:

$$M1 + M2 = \frac{a''^3}{p''^3 P^2}$$

where a'' is the angular separation of the two components in seconds of arc, P the period, and p'' the parallax in seconds of arc.

Knowing its period, we can now find the masses in terms of the Sun equals one. For example, in the case of Alpha Centauri, the parallax is $0''{\cdot}760$, the separation $17''{\cdot}60$ and the period $80{\cdot}1$ years.

$$\text{Hence } M1 + M2 = \left(\frac{17{\cdot}60}{0{\cdot}760}\right)^3 \frac{1}{(80{\cdot}1)^2},$$

which equals $1{\cdot}95$ the mass of the Sun. We discover that the more massive a star is, the more luminous it actually is, by comparing numbers of specimen binary systems with each other. In other words we arrive at the Mass/Luminosity Relationship in terms of Mass and Absolute Magnitude.

Absolute Magnitude is the magnitude a star would have if it were placed at a standard distance from us of ten parsecs; this is expressed in terms of Bolometric Magnitude, which includes radiation at all wavelengths. Some examples are given below:

Star	Absolute bolometric magnitudes		Masses, Sun: 1	
	Star 1	Star 2	Star 1	Star 2
Eta Cassiopeiae	4·54	7·51	0·94	0·58
Sirius (Alpha Conis Majoris)	0·80	11·22	2·28	0·98
Procyon (Alpha Conis Minoris)	2·59	12·62	1·76	0·65

The Mass/Luminosity relationship is expressed by the following formula:

$$\log \left(\frac{L}{L\odot} \right) = 3.5 \log \left(\frac{M}{M\odot} \right)$$

where L is the luminosity of the star, L⊙ that of the Sun, M the mass of the star and M⊙ that of the Sun.

Densities of stars can be determined from their masses and radii. These latter vary tremendously whereas the masses are more constant. In the Main Sequence the densities do not differ markedly from that of the Sun, but when we move to the Giant Stars we find they are very much less dense. These two types are detectable by differences in their spectra, giant stars having finer absorption lines, and these are enhanced by the presence of more ionised atoms. It is thus possible to differentiate between Main Sequence and Giant Type stars, and to evaluate the densities from their Spectra.

Volumes of stars can be determined from their masses and densities, since volume equals mass divided by density. Deviation from the Mass/Luminosity rule indicates a difference in a star's internal structure, but each spectral type is indicative of a star's mass or luminosity as shown on the Hertzsprung-Russell diagram which follows:

THE HERTZSPRUNG-RUSSELL DIAGRAM

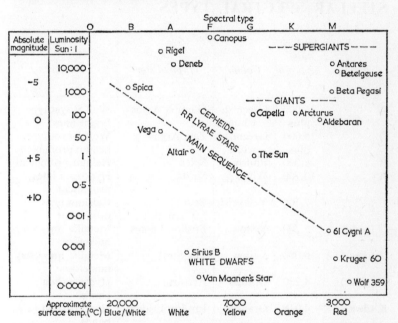

Fig 19 The Hertzsprung-Russell diagram showing the relationship between spectra and luminosity of stars

Super Giants are the largest stars but with very tenuous atmospheres.

Giants are similar but smaller than Super Giants.

Cepheid Variable Stars are pulsating examples of unstable stars.

RR Lyrae Stars are smaller, but similar to Cepheid pulsating types.

Main Sequence Stars may be regarded as normal types. They are most numerous.

White Dwarf Stars are very dense small stars of degenerate matter, the remains of more normal stars that have lost their outer envelopes; the end of the life sequence of stars.

A few of the brighter stars are shown individually on the diagram herewith in demonstration of the relationship between spectral type and luminosity.

STELLAR SPECTRAL TYPES

Type	Surface temperature (°C)	Colour	Typical star	Remarks
W	36,000 plus	Greenish-white	Gamma Argus	Wolf Rayet type, bright lines
O	36,000 plus	Greenish-white	Zeta Argus	Wolf Rayet type, helium prominent
B	28,000	Bluish	Spica	Helium prominent
A	10,700	White	Sirius	Hydrogen lines prominent
F	7,500	Yellowish	Beta Cassiopeiae	Calcium lines prominent
G (giant)	5,200	Yellow	Epsilon Leonis	Metallic lines very numerous
G (dwarf)	6,000	Yellow	The Sun	Metallic lines very numerous
K (giant)	4,230	Orange	Arcturus	Hydrocarbon bands
K (dwarf)	4,910	Orange	Epsilon Eridani	Hydrocarbon bands
M (giant)	3,400	Orange-red	Betelgeux	⎫ Broad titanium
M (dwarf)	3,400	Orange red	Wolf 359	⎬ oxide and calcium bands or flutings
R	2,300	Orange-red	U Cygni	⎭ Carbon bands
N	2,600	Red	S Cephei	Carbon bands reddest stars
S	2,600	Red	R Andromedae	Some zirconium oxide bands, mostly long-period variables

Q a special class reserved for Novae

SPECTROSCOPIC PARALLAX

It will be noted that the main factor in establishing a star's luminosity is its mass. This in turn determines its place on the Hertzsprung-Russell diagram and its consequent spectral type. The difference between its luminosity or its absolute magnitude (being its true brightness if placed ten parsecs from the observer) and its apparent magnitude is a function of its distance, which can be found by spectroscopic parallax.

Spectroscopic Parallax is limited in accuracy to the precision with which each individual star conforms to the Hertzsprung-Russell diagram pattern, but when taken in numbers the average figure gives a close approximation, and it can be used with some degree of accuracy. We are thus able to measure the distances of stars much further off than those for which pure trigonometrical methods can apply.

In practice it is found that certain lines in the spectra of stars vary with the star's luminosity, and by calibration of such relationships for stars whose parallax and absolute magnitudes have been directly obtained, it is possible to determine a definite relationship between absolute magnitude and intensity of the lines. Spectroscopic parallax is obtained by assuming the absolute magnitude to be equal to the mean for the spectral type. But it must be remembered that it is usually not possible to say whether a star is a giant or a dwarf without careful examination of the spectrum.

PROPER MOTIONS

Because of the vast scale of the Galaxy, the individual motions of the stars are not noticeable to the naked eye. They do, however, show up on large-scale photographs when their motions are at right angles to the line of sight. Today some 40,000 proper motions are known, the largest being that of Barnard's Star, with a displacement of 10·3 seconds of arc per annum. This is equivalent to the diameter of the Moon every 180 years.

The majority of stars with large proper motions are invisible to the naked eye. The brighter stars do show proper motion over very long periods of time.

This proper motion does not represent the true path of a star because it also incorporates movement in the line of sight; this is obtained by observing the displacement of the lines in the spectra in conjunction with the proper motion. We thus establish the true path by combining the two motions.

URSA MAJOR

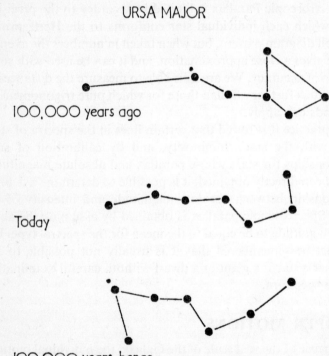

100,000 years ago

Today

100,000 years hence

Fig 20   Proper motions of the stars in the constellation of
Ursa Major over a period of 200,000 years

STELLAR ENERGY

It was at one time considered that the radiative energy of a star resulted from gravitational contraction, but this would not provide sufficient energy over the many millions of years of a star's lifetime. Mutual annihilation of protons and electrons was also suggested, but it is now known that atoms are too complicated for this to occur.

It is today considered that the required energy is produced by transformation of hydrogen atoms into atoms of helium. Four hydrogen nuclei make one nucleus of helium, while in the process a little mass is lost and energy is released. It is this energy that keeps the stars shining by radiation.

Taking the Sun as a typical Main Sequence star, we know it is composed of 93 per cent hydrogen, 5 per cent helium, and the remainder of various other elements including iron etc.

THE LIFE OF A STAR

The Hertzsprung-Russell diagram must not be regarded as a representation of the stages a star goes through in its lifetime. It is rather a diagram showing the various types of star developing from hydrogen clouds of various masses.

It is usual to envisage the beginning of a star as the condensation of hydrogen on a core with sufficient mass to effect the condensation by gravity. Nuclear reaction in the core raises the temperature to some 15 million °C and the star becomes a member of the Main Sequence, but where it joins the line depends on its mass; if very massive it will be near the top of the diagram as in the cases of Rigel or Spica. If small, the star will join near the bottom and spend a long time in the Main Sequence; large stars squander their energy rapidly and have shorter lives than the average. Hydrogen in the core becomes exhausted and the shell continuing to burn hydrogen gradually becomes exhausted. The star now shrinks by gravitational attraction of the core as radiation pressure is reduced. This raises the temperature of the helium core and new reactions take place. The helium begins to build up more complex elements and a higher temperature is reached in the core far beyond the 15 million °C previously mentioned; this leads to synthesis of heavier elements, and the star expands as radiation pressure acts on the more opaque envelope. The star is now a red giant with a helium burning shell.

Sometimes the outer shell is thrown off and a planetary nebula is produced, or perhaps a nova, but in most cases the core is left as a small dense body—a white dwarf, or possibly a pulsar. The track of the life history on the Hertzsprung-Russell diagram is thus: from the main sequence at some point, towards the top right-hand corner, then downwards towards the left bottom corner to the white dwarf type. (Not down the Main Sequence as was at one time believed.)

STAR POPULATIONS

Population I stars are less massive, bluer and younger than Population II stars. They are found in the arms of galaxies, including our own, and specimens occur all along the Main Sequence and among the giants on the Hertzsprung-Russell diagram. They are metal-rich in comparison with Population II types. Population I is a comparatively modern type with stars built up of cosmic gas as it occurs in the arms of galaxies. Population I stars have circular velocities in the spiral planes of galaxies.

Population II stars extend from late A into the M class on the Main Sequence of the Hertzsprung-Russell diagram, but somewhat above the Main Sequence stream. They also occur among yellow and red giants, but there are no blue giants in Population II. Their atmospheres are deficient in metals; being the oldest stars known, they possibly began their lives when the galaxies were composed almost entirely of hydrogen. They are more usual in the nuclei of galaxies and in the haloes and globular clusters. Population II stars have more random orbits and higher velocities than Population I stars, and these facts underline the difference in age between the two types. Population II appear to be the fundamental population of the universe.

In our immediate neighbourhood the types are intermingled.

BINARY STARS

Binary stars having two components both in orbit around the common centre of gravity must be segregated from double stars, which may or may not have any physical connection. Double stars may appear as a pair merely because they happen to lie nearly in line of sight, and may actually be separated by great distances.

The separation of a binary star is measured in seconds of arc. If the distance and period of revolution are known, the total masses of the stars can be determined for the system. The individual masses can be inferred from their spectral types within limits. The position angle, or direction of an imaginary line from the bright component to the fainter one, is measured in degrees of arc with reference to the north point in the direction North, East, South, West, as seen in the telescope.

LIST OF BINARY STARS

Star	RA (1970) h m	Dec ° '	Magnitudes	Separa- tion (1971) "	PA deg (1971)	Period (years)
LONG PERIOD						
Lambda						
Cassiopeiae	00 30	+54 22	5·5 5·8	0·6	179	640
Alpha Piscium	02 00	+02 37	4·3 5·3	1·8	287	720
33 Orionis	05 30	+03 16	6·0 7·3	1·8	27	—
Epsilon ¹						
Lyrae	18 43	+39 39	5·4 6·5	2·7	357	1,200
Epsilon ²						
Lyrae	18 43	+39 36	5·1 5·3	2·2	88	600
Pi Aquilae	19 47	+11 44	6·0 6·8	1·4	110	—
Rho						
Cassiopeiae	23 57	+55 36	5·4 7·5	3·0	326	—
SHORT PERIOD						
Eta						
Cassiopeiae	00 47	+57 39	3·5 7·2	11·5	302	480
Gamma						
Andromedae						
AB	02 02	+42 12	2·1 5·4	9·8	64	—
Alpha Canis						
Majoris	06 44	−16 41	−1·4 8·5	11·2	66	50
Alpha						
Geminorum	07 33	+31 58	2·0 2·8	1·9	127	420
Gamma Leonis	10 18	+20 00	2·1 3·4	4·2	123	620
Xi Ursae						
Major AB	11 17	+31 42	4·3 4·8	3·0	123	60
Zeta Bootis	14 40	+13 52	4·5 4·5	1·2	307	125
Xi Bootis	14 50	+19 14	4·7 6·8	7·1	339	150
Zeta Herculis	16 40	+31 39	2·9 5·5	1·0	218	34
Alpha Herculis						
AB	17 13	+14 26	3·2 5·4	4·6	108	—
Tau Cygni	21 14	+37 54	3·8 6·4	1·0	181	50

The heading 'PA' in column six stands for position angle. The separations and position angles for short period binaries obviously change more rapidly than those for long period ones. The long period separations and position angles changing slowly make these stars suitable tests for the performance of telescopes.

Colours of binary stars are often striking. Some notable cases are listed below:

Eta Cassiopeiae	Yellow and purple
Gamma Andromedae	Yellow and blue
Phi Tauri	Red and bluish
Rho Orionis	Yellow and blue
Alpha Scorpii	Red and emerald green
Epsilon Boötis	Yellow and blue green
Alpha Herculis	Yellow and emerald
Gamma Leonis	Yellow and greenish
Beta Cygni	Gold and blue
Zeta Sagittae	Light green and blue
Epsilon Draconis	Yellow and blue
Beta Cephei	Light green and blue
Sigma Cassiopeiae	White and blue

It will be recalled that large stars use up their mass more quickly than smaller ones, and if binary systems are made of stars of the same age, the difference in colour today will indicate the difference in their respective development.

Orbits of binary stars are usually inclined to the line of sight, but some are nearly in the plane passing through Earth and therefore suffer eclipses. These eclipsing binaries are listed under Algol Type Eclipsing Variable Stars and under Beta Lyrae Variable Stars, both being extrinsic variables and the latter sometimes almost in rolling contact.

Spectroscopic Binary Stars are so called because, while they are too close together to be observed directly with a telescope, their spectra change both with the Doppler effect of their motions, and in the case of eclipsing specimens, the spectra change radically from time to time. Further complication occurs through reflection of one star from the surface of the other. Details of the orbits can be obtained by analysis of spectral changes. The periods range from some eight hours to several thousands of days, merging into those of visual binaries.

H

TRIPLE OR MULTIPLE STARS

Previously thought to be binaries, these are being segregated constantly. Additional components are detected by spectroscopic methods. Castor (Alpha Geminorum) is a case in point; visually double, each component is known to be a spectroscopic binary, while there is a third spectroscopic binary nearby, making six stars in all.

OBSERVATION OF BINARY STARS

Observation requires a telescope of 15cm (6in) diameter, or larger for the closer pairs. A micrometer is used for measuring the angle of separation in seconds of arc and the position angle in degrees. The projected orbit is usually an ellipse, and three good observations can be used to determine the actual orbit of the secondary star around the primary. More accurately, the problem is to determine the orbits of both primary and secondary stars around the common centre of gravity, and from these can be found the masses etc of the stars forming a binary system. (See section on stellar masses, densities and volumes.)

STAR CLUSTERS

Star Clusters can be divided into Open Clusters and Globular Clusters.

Open Clusters, such as the Pleiades, The Beehive in Cancer, or the Hyades, are beautiful objects as seen in binoculars. The Double Open Cluster in Perseus also falls in this class and is a most spectacular sight in a small telescope. The stars forming the Pleiades are blue or young type, while those in the Hyades are redder or old type stars. Telescopic clusters are numerous and are recorded in Messier's Catalogue, and are known by their numbers therein. The Pleiades are known in this way as M45, and the Praesepe or Beehive as M44.

Globular Clusters are reminiscent of balls of stars—an appearance due to their vast distance from us, but the stars are actually packed closer together than in the open clusters, although not so closely as appearances suggest. The globular clusters do not share in the general galactic rotation; they form a halo surrounding the Galaxy, but because of our position they appear more numerous in the southern constellations of Scorpio and Sagittarius. Globular Clusters contain RR Lyrae Stars, which enable their distances to be measured by the period of light variation and the mass-luminosity law. The brightest Globular Cluster to be seen in northern latitudes is M13, situated in Hercules. They are mostly faint and only about 100 are known; their stars are old Population II type.

The clusters listed during the following pages are worth observation.

LIST OF STAR CLUSTERS

The star clusters for this list have been selected to include those most conspicuous. Two types of clusters can be recognised: open (or galactic), and globular. Globulars appear as highly symmetrical agglomerations of very large numbers of stars, distributed throughout the galactic halo but concentrated toward the centre of the Galaxy. Their colour-magnitude diagrams are typical for the old stellar Population II. Open clusters appear usually as irregular aggregates of stars, sometimes barely distinguished from random fluctuations of the general field. They are confined to the galactic disk, with colour-magnitude diagrams typical for the stellar Population I of the normal stars of the solar neighbourhood.

The first table includes all well-defined open clusters with diameters greater than 40′ or integrated magnitudes brighter than 5·0, as well as the richest clusters and some of special interest. *NGC* indicates the serial number of the cluster in Dreyer's *New General Catalogue of Clusters and Nebulae*, *M*, its number in Messier's catalogue, α and δ denote right ascension and declination, *P*, the apparent integrated photographic magnitude according to Collinder (1931), *D*, the apparent diameter in minutes of arc according to Trumpler (1930) when possible, in one case from Collinder; *m*, the photographic magnitude of the fifth-brightest star according to Shapley (1933) when possible or from new data, in italics; *r*, the distance of the cluster in kpcs (1 kpc = 3,263 light-years), as a mean from the values given by Johnson, Hoag *et al.* (1961), and by Becker (1963/4), in a few cases from other sources, with values in italics from Trumpler; *Sp*, the earliest spectral type of cluster stars as determined from three-colour photometry, or from spectral types in italics. The spectral type also indicates the age of the cluster, expressed in millions of years, thus: O5 = 0·5; b0 = 5; b5 = 50; a0 = 300; a5 = 1,000; f0 = 3,000; f5 = 10,000.

The second table includes all globular clusters with a total apparent photographic magnitude brighter than 7·6. The first three columns are as in the first table, followed by *B*, the total photographic magnitude; *D*, the apparent diameter in minutes of arc containing 90 per cent of the stars, and in italics, total diameters from miscellaneous sources; *Sp*, the integrated spectral type; *m*, the mean blue magnitude of the 25 brightest stars (excluding the five brightest); *N*, the number of known variables; *r*, the distance in kpcs (absolute magnitude of RR Lyrae variables taken as $M_B = +0·5$); *V*, the radial velocity in km/sec. The data are taken from a compilation by Arp (1965); in case no data were available there, various other sources have been used, especially H. S. Hogg's Bibliography (1963).

OPEN CLUSTERS

NGC	α 1970 δ		*P*	*D*	*m*	*r*	*Sp*	*Remarks*
	h m	° ′						
188	00 41·0	+85 11	9·3	14	14·6	1·550	f5	oldest known
752	01 56·0	+37 32	6·6	45	9·6	0·380	f0	very large cluster
869	02 16·9	+57 01	4·3	30	9·5	2·260	b0	h Per*
884	02 20·3	+56 59	4·4	30	9·5	2·410	b0	*x* Per, M supergiants;
Perseus	03 20.0	+48 30	2·3	240	5·0	0·170	b3	moving cl, near Alpha Persei
Pleiades	03 45·3	+24 02	1·6	120	4·2	0·125	b7	M45, best known
Hyades	04 18·0	+15 34	0·8	400	*1·5*	0·040	a2	moving cl in Tau†
1912	05 26·6	+35 49	7·0	18	9·7	1·370	b8	

* NGC 869 and 884 form the Double Open Cluster in Perseus
† Basic for distance determination

NGC	α 1970 δ			P	D	m	r	Sp	Remarks
	h	m	° ′						
1976/80	05	33·9	−05 24	2·5	50	5·5	0·400	O5	Trapezium, very young-near Great Nebula in Orion
2099	05	50·4	+32 32	6·2	24	9·7	1·280	b8	M37
2168	06	07·0	+24 21	5·6	29	9·0	0·870	b5	M35
2232	06	25·0	−04 44	4·1	20	7·0	0·490	b3	bright star cluster
2244	06	30·8	+04 53	5·2	27	8·0	1·650	O5	Rosette, very young
2264	06	39·4	+09 55	4·1	30	8·0	0·730	O9	S Mon
2287	06	45·8	−20 42	5·0	32	8·8	0·670	b3	M41
2362	07	17·6	−24 53	3·8	7	9·4	1·530	b0	τ CMa
2422	07	34·2	−14 26	4·3	30	9·8	0·480	b4	
2437	07	40·4	−14 45	6·6	27	10·8	1·660	b3	M46
2451	07	44·3	−37 54	3·7	37	6·0	0·300	b5	Very large
2516	07	57·8	−60 49	3·3	50	10·1	0·370	b9	
2546	08	11·4	−37 33	5·0	45	7·0	0·740	b0	
2632	08	38·4	+20 06	3·9	90	7·5	0·158	a5	Praesepe, M44
IC2391	08	39·4	−52 57	2·6	45	3·5	0·150	b3	
IC2395	08	40·1	−48 05	4·6	20	10·1	0·900	b2	
2682	08	48·8	+11 56	7·4	18	10·8	0·830	f2	M67, old cl
3114	10	01·7	−59 58	4·5	37	7·0	0·850	b6	
IC2602	10	42·2	−64 14	1·6	65	6·0	0·160	b2	θ Car
Tr 16	10	44·0	−59 33	6·7	10	10·0	1·950	b0	η Car and Nebula
3532	11	05·1	−58 30	3·4	55	8·1	0·420	b9	
3766	11	34·7	−61 27	4·4	12	8·1	1·630	b0	
Coma	12	23·6	+26 16	2·9	300	5·5	0·080	a2	Very sparse cl
4755	12	51·8	−60 10	5·2	12	7·0	1·340	b3	κ Cru, jewel box'
6067	16	10·9	−54 08	6·5	16	10·9	2·100	b3	G and K supergiants
6231	16	51·9	−41 45	8·5	16	7·5	1·820	O5	O supergiants, WR-stars
Tr 24	16	54·9	−40 37	8·5	60	7·3	0·580	O5	
6405	17	38·1	−32 12	4·6	26	8·3	0·570	b4	M6
IC4665	17	45·2	+05 44	5·4	50	7·0	0·330	b5	
6475	17	51·9	−34 48	3·3	50	7·4	0·240	b8	M7
6494	17	55·1	−19 01	5·9	27	10·2	0·550	b9	M23
6523	18	01·3	−24 23	5·2	45	7·0	1·470	O5	M8, Lagoon neb and very young cl NGC6530
6611	18	17·2	−13 48	6·6	8	10·6	1·900	O5	M16, nebula
IC4725	18	29·9	−19 16	6·2	35	9·3	0·600	b3	M25, Cepheid, U Sgr
IC4756	18	37·8	+05 25	5·4	50	8·5	0·440	a3	
6705	18	49·5	−06 19	6·8	12·5	12·0	1·720	b8	M11, very rich cl
Mel 227	20	06·7	−79 25	5·2	60	9·0	0·240	b9	
IC1396	21	38·0	+57 22	5·1	60	8·5	0·730	O6	Tr 37
7790	23	56·9	+61	7·1	4·5	11·7	3·390	b4	C Ceph: CEa, CEb, CF Cas

IC=Index Catalogue

GLOBULAR CLUSTERS

NGC	M	α 1970 h m	δ ° ′	B	D	Sp	m	N	r	V	Remarks
104	47 Tuc	00 22·6	−72 14	4·35	44·0	G3	13·54	11	5·0	−24	Bright, resolvable
1851		05 13·0	−40 03	7·72:	11·5	F7	15·09	3	14·0	+309	
2808		09 11·3	−64 44	7·40	18·8	F8	13·01	4	9·1	+101	
5139	ω Cen	13 25·0	−47 09	4·50	65·4	F7	14·35	165	5·2	+230	Bright centre
5272	3	13 40·8	+28 32	6·86	9·3	F7	14·07	189	10·6	−153	
5904	5	15 17·0	+02 12	6·69	10·7	F6	13·21	97	8·1	+49	Bright stars well resolved
6121	4	16 21·8	−26 27	7·05	22·6	G0	13·85	43	4·3	+65	
6205	13	16 40·6	+36 31	6·43	12·9	F6	14·07	10	6·3	−241	Globular Cluster in Hercules
6218	12	16 45·6	−01 54	7·58	21·5	F8	14·17	1	7·4	−16	Bright, well resolved
6254	10	16 55·5	−04 04	7·26	16·2	G1	13·96	3	6·2	+71	Bright, well resolved
6341	92	17 16·2	+43 11	6·94	12·3	F1	12·71	16	7·9	−118	Bright
6397		17 38·4	−53 40	6·90	19·0	F5	13·45	3	2·9	+11	
6541		18 05·8	−43 45	7·50	23·2	F6	13·73	1	4·0	−148	
6656	22	18 34·5	−23 57	6·15	26·2	F7	14·32	24	3·0	−144	Bright, large
6723		18 57·6	−36 40	7·37	11·7	G4	13·36	19	7·4	−3	Large, resolvable
6752		19 08·2	−60 02	6·80	41·9	F6	13·68	1	5·3	−39	
6809	55	19 38·2	−31 00	6·72	21·1	F5		6	6·0	+170	
7078	15	21 28·6	+12 02	6·96	9·4	F2	14·44	103	10·5	−107	Bright, resolvable
7089	2	21 31·9	−00 58	6·94	6·8	·F4	14·77	22	12·3	−5	Large

VARIABLE STARS

These are stars that vary in energy output, and not in position on the celestial sphere, as is sometimes supposed. They fall into three main classes, with numerous subdivisions, according to the nature and causes of their variation.

1. *Extrinsic Variables:* All eclipsing types, where one of a pair of stars, or both successively, are eclipsed either partly or wholly as seen from Earth. Of these Algol is the best known as the prototype of this class, while Beta Lyrae heads another type.

2. *Intrinsic Variables:* Stars that for one reason or another vary their output with some regularity. To this class belong the RR Lyrae pulsating and the Cepheid Variable pulsating types; the rate of pulsating is proportionate to luminosity. In this class are also included the Long Period, the Semi-regular and the Irregular types.

3. *Eruptive Variables:* Those stars that suffer variation in output by sudden outbursts of energy, such as the U Geminorum and Flare Stars. Young unstable stars often connected with nebular matter, such as the T Tauri and T Orionis types, are included here, as are also the fading R Coronae Borealis type as well as the Nova and Supernova types which erupt with such violent and impressive displays.

The following pages list and describe the main types of variable stars together with observing hints. Variable stars are designated in each constellation by the letters R to Z, then RR to RZ followed by SS to SZ, TT to TZ etc. After ZZ is reached we return to AA to AZ, BB to BZ etc ending with QZ. This system allows for 334 variable stars per constellation.

ALGOL TYPE ECLIPSING VARIABLES

Star	Magnitudes		Period (days)	Spectrum
	maximum	minimum		
Algol	2·20	3·47	2·86731	B8
Ry Aqr	8·80	10·11	1·96666	A3
R Ara	6·05p	6·97	4·42509	B9
Beta Aur	2·07	2·16	3·96007	A2 & A2
U Cep	6·74p	9·81	2·49290	B8 & gG2
VV Cep	6·62p	7·42	7,430 days	cM2ep & B0
Y Cyg	7·00	7·64	2·99633	O9 & O9
Z Her	7·20	7·91	3·99279	F2 & F2
TX Leo	5·70	5·80	2·44500	A0
Delta Lib	4·79p	5·89	2·32735	Als
RR Lyn	5·60	5·97	9·94500	A6s
U Oph	5·80	6·50	1·67735	B5n & B5n
EE Peg	7·01	7·54	5·25600	A0
AG Per	6·49	6·80	2·02873	B3 & B3
U Sag	6·36p	9·04	3·38061	B9 & G2
RS Sgr	6·00p	6·97	2·41570	B5
V356 Sgr	6·81p	7·92	8·89650	B8 & A1
V505 Sgr	6·50	7·31	1·18287	A2
Mu¹ Sco	3·00p	3·31	1·66427	B3 & B6
RZ Sct	7·70p	8·87	15·19016	B2
Lambda Tau	3·50	4·00	3·95295	B3
TX UMa	6·83	8·92	3·06371	B9 & gF2
Alpha Vir	1·21	1·30	4·01416	B3n
Z Vul	6·97	8·60	2·45492	B3n & A3
RS Vul	6·90	7·63	4·47766	B5 & A2

p Indicates photographic magnitude

Secondary minima caused by the partial eclipse of the companion star by the brighter component are not shown in the above list.

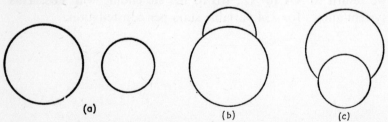

Fig 21   Algol (Beta Persei) eclipsing variables. The smaller component of spectral class B8 is the brighter of the two. (a) Maximum light is received from both stars. (b) Minimum light is when the brighter component is in eclipse by the fainter one. (c) Secondary minimum when the larger and fainter component is eclipsed by the smaller brighter one

BETA LYRAE TYPE VARIABLES

Eclipsing type stars but with tidal distortion of star bodies causing synchronisation of rotation and revolution.

Star	Magnitudes		Period (days)	Spectrum
	maximum	minimum		
Beta Lyr	3·40	4·31	12·9080	B8p
AN And	6·00	6·16	3·2196	A7s & A
S Ant	6·39	6·83	0·6483	A8 & A8
Sigma Aql	5·00	5·18	1·9502	B3 & B3
TT Aur	8·06p	9·02	1·3327	B3 & B3
SZ Cam	7·00p	7·27	2·6984	Bon
TU Cam	5·20	5·40	2·9333	A1
UW CMa	4·47	4·81	4·3934	O8 & O8
YY CMi	8·51	9·12	1·0740	F5
χ Car	8·05p	8·60	1·0826	A0 & A1
RX Cas	10·04pV	11·13	32·3166	gG3 & gA5e
AO Cas	5·80	6·01	3·5234	O8n & O8n
RR Cen	7·65p	8·11	0·6056	F2
SZ Cen	8·30	8·92	4·1079	A2
AH Cep	6·63	6·85	1·7746	B0 & B0
V Crt	9·52	10·21	0·7020	A6
u Her	4·60	5·14	2·0510	B3 & B3
RT Lac	8·80	9·61	5·0739	G9 & K1
VV Ori	5·10	5·44	1·4854	B2n & B8
Eta Ori	3·20	3·55	7·9892	B1
V Pup	4·53	5·14	1·4545	B1 & B3
V525 Sgr	8·52	9·22	0·7051	A2
Nu Sgr	4·26p	4·41	137·0042	B8p & F2p
V453 Sco	6·56	6·99	12·0042	Bose
AC Vel	8·53p	9·05	4·5622	B8

p Indicates photographic magnitudes
V Indicates variable magnitude

RR LYRAE TYPE VARIABLES

Named after RR Lyrae, many stars of this type occur in globular clusters and are sometimes therefore called 'Cluster Variables'. They are Population II type stars, and pulsate more rapidly than the Cepheid Variables. The light curves show a rapid rise to maximum followed by a slower decline. They are divided into four classes: short period stars with superimposed secondary periods; stars with almost sinusoidal light curves and small amplitudes; stars with periods between one-quarter and three-quarters of a day; stars with periods exceeding one day.

Star	Magnitude		Period (days)	Spectrum
	maximum	minimum		
SW And	9·30	10·31	0·4422	A3–F8
SW Aqr	10·64p	12·42	0·4593	A3
S Ara	10·20p	11·68	0·4519	A3–F5
RS Boo	9·71p	11·22	0·3773	B8–F0
RZ Cep	9·20p	9·80	0·3087	A0–A3
UY Cyg	10·40	11·40	0·5607	A5–F0
SU Dra	9·40p	10·40	0·6604	A2–A5
V Ind	9·22p	10·22	0·4796	A0–F2
RR Lyr	7·13p	8·03	0·5668	A2–F0
SS Tau	11·80	12·70	0·3699	A0–F3

CEPHEID VARIABLES

Named after Delta Cephei, these are pulsating stars whose period of pulsation is proportional to the luminosity of the star. As the star alternately expands and contracts, so the energy radiated varies with a regular period. The larger the mass, the longer is the period of pulsation, and the higher the luminosity. The period of pulsation is proportional to the square of the radius, and inversely proportional to the square root of the mass of the star.

Star	Magnitudes		Period (days)	Spectrum
	maximum	minimum		
U Aql	6·05	6·89	7·0238	G0–G6
Eta Aql	3·69	4·40	7·1766	F6–G4
SY Aur	8·80	9·50	10·1440	G0–G2
RU Cam	9·26	10·51	22·1725	K0–R2
TU Cas	7·50	8·72	2·1393	F5–G2
Delta Cep	3·78	4·63	5·3663	F5–G2
SU Cyg	6·37	7·08	3·8455	F0–G1
Beta Dor	4·50	5·71	9·8426	F2–F9
Zeta Gem	3·70	4·09	10·1535	F7–G3
Kappa Pav	4·81	5·68	9·0838	F5–G5
S Sag	5·80	7·00	8·3822	F6–G5
W Sgr	5·00p	6·39	7·5947	F2–G6
RV Sco	6·99	8·10	6·0613	F5–G5
ST Tau	8·48	9·61	4·0342	F5–G5
Alpha UMi	1·99	2·05	3·9696	cF7v

p Indicates photographic magnitude

RS Puppis is noteworthy as having an abnormally long period of 41·4 days and in being associated with interstellar matter, in four nearly concentric arcs, reflecting the star's radiation.

LONG-PERIOD VARIABLES

Sometimes called Mira Ceti Stars, these are a very numerous class of variable stars with periods extending over many days, but showing some irregularity. They are red stars, many being of spectral class M, and they exhibit large variations in light output. The curves indicate a shorter period of rise than decrease of light, and when near maximum the spectra often show bright emission lines of hydrogen. Due to their low temperature, broad absorption bands of titanium oxide and normal lines of neutral metals are seen in the spectra. At the commencement of an outburst, it appears that a shock wave is generated low in the star's atmosphere, and moves outwards imparting movement to the higher levels, where the density decreases rapidly and the velocity of the wavefront increases. The energy of the wave is rapidly dissipated as it travels over a large distance in matter of considerable rarity. The star then returns to lower brilliance, after which the cycle recommences with the outburst of a further emission of energy as a result of the increased temperature deep in the star's interior.

Despite the large variations in light output, there is evidence that the energy concerned is only a small part of the total emitted by the star. The infra-red radiation from this type of star has its maximum intensity after the visual maximum. This shows that the maximum energy radiated occurs later in the cycle, probably due to the lower contributions made at longer wavelengths by the titanium oxide absorption bands.

The large variations in visible light intensity make this class of variable star most suitable for amateur observation without recourse to photometric apparatus. The human eye can estimate variations of one tenth of a magnitude under good observing conditions, and as will be seen from the following list, this is much smaller than the variation of light from these stars between maximum and minimum brightness.

CHARACTERISTICS OF LONG-PERIOD VARIABLES

Period (days)	Proportionate number of stars in each group	Mean magnitude range
51– 75	8	1·1
76–100	8	1·5
101–125	10	1·8
126–150	16	3·3
151–175	19	3·1
176–200	23	4·1
201–225	46	4·5
226–250	53	4·0
251–275	51	4·8
276–300	48	4·8
301–325	47	4·8
326–350	49	4·8
351–375	38	4·3
376–400	37	4·5
401–425	21	5·4
426–450	16	5·3
451–475	7	5·8
476–500	9	4·6
501–525	3	5·4
526–550	1	9·4
551–575	3	7·2
576–600	1	3·2
601–625	1	6·5
626–650	—	—
651–675	1	0·6
676–700	1	1·4

LIST OF LONG-PERIOD VARIABLES

Star	Magnitude		Mean period (days)	Spectrum
	maximum	minimum		
R And	5·0	15·3	408·87	Se
T Aps	8·4	14·8	260·83	M3e
R Aqr	6·7	11·6	386·86	M7e + P + O
W Aql	7·2	14·0	489·28	Se
U Ara	9·2p	15·4	225·05	M4e
Z Car	9·6	15·1	382·64	M6e
S Cas	6·2	15·3	611·83	Se
T Cen	5·2	10·0	90·65	M0e
O Cet	1·0	10·2	331·48	M6e
V CrB	6·8	12·4	357·64	Ne
R Cyg	5·9	14·6	425·44	Se
Chi Cyg	2·3	14·3	406·66	Mpe
R Leo	4·4	11·6	313·13	M8e
T Oct	8·4	13·6	218·46	M2e
R Ori	8·5	13·4	378·52	Se
R Psc	7·0	14·8	343·69	M4e
R Sgr	6·6	13·3	268·83	M5e
RR Sco	5·0	12·2	279·45	M6e
R Tuc	8·7	15·2	285·84	M5e
R UMa	6·2	13·6	301·21	M4e
S UMa	7·1	12·9	225·62	Se
W Vel	9·5p	15·0	393·45	M7e
R Vir	6·2	12·6	145·35	M4e
S Vol	8·5	13·7	395·95	M0e
RU Vul	8·5	11·5	155·50	M3e

p Indicates photographic magnitude

SEMI-REGULAR VARIABLES

Mainly red stars and all of late spectral type, being giants or supergiants. They show long periods of completely irregular behaviour, including constant brightness. There may be a form of periodicity combined and obscured by irregular variations.

Star	Magnitude		Period (days)†		Spectrum
	maximum	minimum	primary	secondary	
SS And	10·0p	11·4	152·5	640	M6
BM Aqr	11·0p	11·9	60	550	M4
RX Boo	6·9	9·1	78	500	M8e
RS Cam	8·0	9·6	85	960	M5
ST Cam	9·0	12·1	195	2,100	N
RT Cnc	7·3	8·6	94·5	540	M5
Y CVn	5·2	6·6	158	2,100	N
VY Cas	9·0	10·2	100	620	M6
AD Cen	9·8p	11·4	62	2,800	M1e
RV Cyg	7·1	9·3	75	470	N
UW Her	7·5	8·6	81	195	M5
V Hya	6·0	12·5	532	6,500	N
S Lep	6·0	7·4	95	835	M6
W Ori	8·2p	12·4	200	2,300	N
V Pav	9·3p	11·2	225·5	3,735	N
S Per	7·2	12·2	810	916	cM3e
TT Per	9·3p	10·5	90	843	M5
Y Tau	6·8	9·2	241	1,750	N
Z UMa	6·6	9·1	198	1,560	M6e
ST UMa	6·4	7·5	81	583	M4

p Indicates photographic magnitude

† The period must not be regarded as a mean period (as in the case of long period variables); rather a cycle indicating that there does exist a form of periodicity

IRREGULAR VARIABLES

Most are cool red giant stars showing few emission lines in their spectra. The light amplitudes are small.

Star	Magnitude		Spectrum
	maximum	minimum	
U Ant	5·7	6·8	N
V Aps	10·5p	11·5	Mb
V Aql	6·7	8·2	N
V Ari	7·7p	8·3	R4
S Cae	9·7p	10·5	K
Rho Cas	4·1	6·2	cF8–M2
XY Cen	9·4p	10·4	M2
W CrA	11·3p	11·8	R3
SS CrB	10·0p	11·2	M5
R Crt	9·8p	10·4	M4
TZ Cyg	9·6	11·7	M7
RR Eri	9·0p	10·0	M5
TU Gem	11·2p	12·4	N
Pi^1 Gru	5·8	6·4	S
SX Lac	9·6p	10·4	K2
Z Lup	10·5p	11·6	N
X Lyr	8·8	9·5	M4
S Men	10·2p	11·5	Mb
Z Mon	9·0p	10·1	K5
X Nor	12·5p	13·5	N
RT Ori	8·1	8·9	N
T Per	8·3	9·3	cM1
W Pic	11·8p	13·2	N
S Sct	7·0	8·0	N
Y UMa	9·5p	11·2	M7

p Indicates photographic magnitude

Further small group known as Gamma Cassiopeiae Stars after the prototype: γ Cas Mag 2·25 normal brightness. Spectrum Be, possibly bright emission originating in shell, and in some cases even from rotating disk formed by ejection of material.

U GEMINORUM TYPE VARIABLES

Characterised by abrupt outbursts of light and slower declines to minimum. Some, including U Gem, have two types of maxima—long and short, with a tendency for the long maximum to be of greater brightness than the short one.

Star	Magnitudes		Period (days)	Remarks
	maximum	minimum		
VZ Aqr	11·8p	15·0	49	
UU Aql	11·0p	16·8	56	
SS Aur	10·5	14·5	54·1	Binary star
SS Cyg	8·1	12·1	50·4	Binary star
EY Cyg	11·4p	15·7	40·8	
U Gem	8·8	14·4	102·9	Binary star
VW Hyi	8·4p	13·4	35	
X Leo	12·0	15·1	22	
AY Lyr	12·6p	16·0	23	
CZ Ori	11·8p	16·2	38	
RU Peg	10·0	13·1	70	Binary star
UV Per	12·3	15·2	300	
UZ Ser	12·0	16·6	40	
SU UMa	11·1	14·5	16	
SW UMa	10·8p	16·2	1,000?	

p Indicates photographic magnitudes

FLARE STARS (UV CETI VARIABLES)

Red dwarfs, which are faint and require large apertures for observation. Changes in magnitude are only about a quarter of a magnitude in many cases.

Star	Magnitudes		Spectrum
	maximum	minimum	
UV Cet	5·9	12·9	dM5·5e
AD Leo	9·0	9·5	dM4e
WX UMa	13·1	14·8	dM5·5e

All magnitudes are photographic.

T TAURI TYPE VARIABLES

Very young stars rapidly forming into main sequence types, probably capable of providing evidence on the formation of planetary systems. Always associated with small nebulosities.

Star	Magnitudes		Spectrum
	maximum	*minimum*	
SU Aur	9·0	9·6	dG2
GM Aur	13·1p	13·9	dK5e
AN Ori	10·7	11·7	dK1e
GW Ori	10·1p	11·5	dK3e
GX Ori	14·0p	15·3	dK3e
T Tau	9·5	13·0	dG5e
RY Tau	8·6	11·0	dG0e
UX Tau	10·7p	13·4	dG5e
UZ Tau	11·7p	14·9	dG5e
AA Tau	13·7p	15·4	dM0e
BP Tau	10·7p	13·1	dG5e
CI Tau	14·4p	15·2	Ge
CW Tau	13·9p	15·1	dK5e

p Indicates photographic magnitudes

T ORIONIS TYPE VARIABLES

Stars in the process of formation and in such a situation that the highly irregular nature of their light variations are due to unstable fluctuations associated with the initial stages, and changes in the opacity of the surrounding gas, as it is forced away from these blue giants.

Star	Magnitudes		Spectrum
	maximum	*minimum*	
TY CrA	8·7	12·4	B2
T Ori	9·5	12·1	A0
UX Ori	8·9	10·6	A2e

R CORONAE BOREALIS TYPE VARIABLES

The only class of variable for which maximum light is the normal. Sudden fading without warning at irregular intervals makes constant observation necessary. No trace of periodicity exists, nor can a mean cycle be derived as for the semi-regulars.

Star	Magnitudes		Spectrum
	maximum	*minimum*	
S Aps	9·6	15·2	R3
R CrB	5·8	14·4	c G0ep
RY Sgr	6·0	14·0	cG0ep
SU Tau	9·5	16·0	cG0ep
RS Tel	9·3p	14·6	R8

Z CAMELOPARDALIS TYPE VARIABLES

A small class very similar to U Geminorum stars but exhibiting 'standstills', during which the star remains at almost constant brightness for an indefinite period. These 'standstills' occur one third of the way from maximum to minimum.

Typical stars are:

Star	Magnitudes		Period
	maximum	*minimum*	*(days)*
RX And	10·3	13·6	14·1
Z Cam	10·2	13·4	20·0
BS Cep	14·0	15·9	40·0
BP Cr Aus	13·9	15·6	13·5
AB Dra	12·0	15·8	12·0
AH Her	10·6	13·9	19·6
BI Ori	13·2	16·6	24·6
CN Ori	11·8	14·7	19·2
TZ Per	12·1	15·4	17·0
FO Per	13·8	16·2	11·3
BX Pup	13·8	15·8	18·0

RECURRENT NOVAE

Stars known to undergo more than one rapid outburst. Typical stars are:

Star	Magnitudes	
	maximum	*minimum*
T CrB	2·0	10·8
RS Oph	5·1	11·7
T Pyx	7·0	14·0
U Sco	8·8	17·6
WZ Sge	7·0	16·1

REMARKABLE NOVAE AND SUPERNOVAE

Constellation	Date	Magnitudes	
		maximum	minimum
Aquila	1899	5·5p	<15·6
	1918	−1·4	10·8
	1936	5·4	?
	1970	6·0	?
Ara	1910	6·0p	17·5
Auriga	1891	4·1p	15·8
Carina (Eta)	1843	−0·8	7·9
Cassiopeia	1572	−4·1	Tycho's star— supernova remnant
Corona Borealis (T)	1866	2·0	10·8
Cygnus	1600	3·0	?
	1876	3·0	15·2
	1920	2·0	15·4
Delphinus	1967	3·6	11·9?
Gemini	1903	4·8	16·5
	1912	3·5	14·7
Hercules	1934	1·3	15·4
	1960	3·0	Variable
	1963	2·9	—
Lacerta	1910	4·3p	14·4
	1936	2·1	15·6
	1950	6·0	?
Lyra	1919	6·5p	15·4
Monoceros	1918	5·2p	15·1
	1939	4·5p	16·0
Norma	1893	7·0p	<16·3
Ophiuchus	1604	−2·2	? Kepler's star— a supernova remnant
	1848	4·3	13·0
	1917	6·2p	<17·0
	1919	7·2p	<15·2
Perseus	1887	4·0p	<17·5
	1901	0·2	14·0
Pictor	1925	1·2p	13·6
Puppis	1942	0·4	?
Sagitta	1783	6·0	15·8
Sagittarius	1898	4·5p	16·5
	1936	4·3	15·2

Constellation	Date	Magnitudes	
		maximum	minimum
	1941	6·8p	<16·0
Serpens	1970	4·6	?
Taurus	1054	−6·0	Crab Nebula—a supernova remnant
	1927	6·0	?
Vulpecula	1670	2·7	<17·0
	1968	4·3	?

p Indicates photographic magnitudes

SUPERNOVAE AS RADIO SOURCES

Supernovae are of two types:

1 Those with masses similar to that of the Sun, they are older Population II type stars, deficient in hydrogen. Light curves have sharp maxima and fairly rapid decline.

2 Those with masses approaching some thirty times that of the Sun, and still probably associated with the parent gas cloud. Population I type stars exhibiting blue colour at maximum which lasts for a longer period than that of Type 1, they are comparatively rich in hydrogen.

Some Supernova Remnants are radio sources, such as the following:

The Crab Nebula (M1) in Taurus	Distance 6,000 light years
The Cygnus Loop	Distance 2,500 light years
Cassopeia A	Distance 10,000 light years
Kepler's Supernova	Distance 4,000 light years
Tycho's Supernova	Distance 1,000 light years
The Gum Nebula	Distance 1,500 light years, a multiple structure

Supernovae have also been observed in extra galactic objects, such as NGC 224, 1003, 4273, 4303, 4321, 4424, 4486, 4527, 4621, 4725, 5253 and 6946. These range from 6·4 to 14·4 apparent magnitude with absolute magnitudes −15·6 to −12·3.

VARIABLES ALWAYS OBSERVABLE WITH THE NAKED EYE

Alpha Orionis   Rho Persei
Beta Pegasi   Beta Persei (Algol)
Gamma Cassiopeiae   Delta Cephei
Beta Lyrae

VARIABLES ALWAYS OBSERVABLE WITH BINOCULARS

R Lyrae   R Scuti
Rho Cassiopeiae U Hydrae
W Cephei   X Cancri
W Cygni   Z Ursae Majoris
U Delphini   UU Aurigae
EU Delphini   P Cygni

LONG-PERIOD VARIABLES BRIGHT ENOUGH TO BE OBSERVED WITH BINOCULARS WHEN NEAR MAXIMUM

Omicron Ceti (Mira)   U Orionis
Chi Cygni   R Andromedae
R Leonis   R Cygni
Z Carinae   S Cassopeiae
R Hydrae   T Cephei
also the irregular variable star R Coronae Borealis

VARIABLES EASILY LOCATED WITH A TELE-SCOPE

U Cygni   S Ursae Majoris
W Lyrae   T Ursae Majoris
R Serpentis   R Draconis
SS Cygni   R Trianguli
R Vulpeculae   R Arietis

VARIABLES OBSERVABLE WITH THE NAKED EYE OVER ALL OR PART OF THEIR RANGES

Star	Magnitudes		Remarks
	maximum	minimum	
Eta Aquilae	3·70	4·50	Cepheid type*
Epsilon Aurigae	3·00	?	Eclipsing: period 27 years
Gamma Cassiopeiae	1·60	3·20	Irregular bursts*
Delta Cephei	3·50	4·40	Cepheid type*
Mu Cephei	3·70	5·70	Red irregular
Beta Ceti	2·02	Suspected short-lived rises	
Chi Cygni	2·30	14·30	Period 406·6 days*
Gamma Eridani	3·01	Considered variable, but now doubtful	
Eta Eridani	3·30	4·20	Period 231 days
Zeta Geminorum	3·70	4·09	Cepheid type*
Alpha Herculis	3·10	3·90	Red irregular
U Hydrae	4·50	6·00	Red irregular
Beta Leonis	2·14	Seems to have faded since Ptolemy's time	
R Leonis	4·40	11·60	Long-period type*
Delta Librae	4·80	5·90	Algol type*
Beta Lyrae	3·40	4·31	Eclipsing type*
Delta Orionis	2·20	2·35	Eclipsing type, small range
Epsilon Pegasi	2·31	Unconfirmed variation suspected	
Beta Persei (Algol)	2·20	3·47	Eclipsing type*
Rho Persei	3·20	3·80	Red irregular
Lambda Tauri	3·50	4·00	Algol type*
Delta Ursae Majoris	3·30	3·75	May be occasional falls

* Refer to appropriate variable star list for details

OBSERVATION

Stars that vary markedly in light output, like the long-period variables, can well be observed visually provided one uses a telescope large enough to provide a bright enough image when the star is at minimum brightness; sometimes if too faint to be easily seen, the variable is recorded as fainter than a known star in the field. The size of telescope available thus determines what stars may be observed visually.

Magnitude determinations of the variable are obtained by comparison with other stars of known brightness and either the fractional or the step method is employed. That is, the variable is noted as so many fractions of a magnitude fainter or brighter than the known star; or in the case of the step method, it is noted as so many steps fainter than a bright star that we can call A and so many steps brighter than a second star that we can call B which is preferably not more than half a magnitude fainter than A. Thus the record may read: A (2) V (3) B, meaning: Star A, then two steps to the variable, then three steps to star B. Knowing the magnitudes of stars A and B, the magnitude of the variable may be easily determined. Long series of observations can be valuable.

Photometers of various types may be employed but they all have their own problems, and the subject should be thoroughly read before attempting observation.

Photographic patrols of the sky can produce star images that can be used for photometry, and this method is largely used by professional observers, but this again is a specialised subject that requires study and practice before reliable results can be produced.

Both photometric and photographic methods are used for stars with little amplitude of light variation, while studies of the behaviour of spectra provide much information otherwise unobtainable.

NOTES

GALACTIC NEBULAE

Galactic nebulae are nebulae within the confines of our Galaxy. They fall into three classes: bright nebulae, dark nebulae and planetary nebulae. The word 'nebula' (plural nebulae) literally means a cloud, which is what a nebula looks like.

Bright Nebulae. These are subdivided into reflection and emission types.

Reflection bright nebulae consist of graphite grains, both pure and impure, with ice crystals; these reflect starlight and appear as irregular patches of luminous material. Radiation pressure is effective when the grains have a diameter of 10^{-5}cm or less, but in many cases the density of the cloud prevents scatter by gravitational attraction towards the centre of the cloud. The graphite is presumed to come from matter radiated by stars, while the ice crystals of small dimensions, with diameters proportionate to the wavelength of light, have developed from free hydrogen and oxygen in space.

Emission bright nebulae are composed of material ionised by the radiation from nearby very hot young stars. A star of W, O or B type can ionise hydrogen within a sphere of 500 light years radius. The return of the excited atoms to their normal state is accompanied by radiation in the visible range of the spectrum, so that emission nebulae become visible to the human eye. Regions of this kind are known as H-II Regions. An outstanding example is the Great Nebula in Orion (NGC1976, M42) which is in a region where star formation is still in progress, and is visually bright by emission from ionised hydrogen and oxygen.

The various kinds of reaction observed in the study of the radiation from emission bright nebulae arise from three causes:
1. Photo-ionisation and recombination producing complex spectra.
2. Electron collision mostly producing forbidden lines.
3. Flourescence of gas which emits radiation on return of electrons to their normal ground level.

Dark Nebulae. These do not differ from the bright types, except that they are not illuminated by stars near them. They are detectable because they cut off the light from stars lying behind them. A notable specimen occurs in the constellation of Cygnus, well seen by the naked eye as a dark patch devoid of stars. There are a number of others to be seen in the plane of our Galaxy (The Milky Way) and their actual diameters are between 1,000 and 100,000 astronomical units.

They were at one time known as 'Coalsacks'. The absorption effect on the spectrum of a star is well seen in Delta Orionis calcium lines.

Planetary Nebulae. These are probably ejected material left by a nova or supernova. The term 'planetary' refers only to their appearance in a telescope. They are not the remaining vestige of the nova itself; this would be the core of high-temperature material at 30,000 to 50,000°C. The planetary nebula is the remaining outer shell visible long after the outburst has taken place. In most cases the expansion is still apparent by the Doppler effect on the spectrum as light is received from the far, receding, side and from the near, approaching, side of the object. There is usually an unilluminated extension of the nebula outside the visible part.

CHEMICAL ABUNDANCES IN NEBULAE

Element	Planetary nebulae	Normal stars	Interstellar gas (nebulae)
Hydrogen	1,000,000	1,000,000	1,000,000
Helium	200,000	50,000/ 100,000	—
Carbon	165	90	—
Nitrogen	1,650	170	—
Oxygen	2,000	540	—
Flourine	6	(?) 2·7	—
Neon	320	590	—
Sodium	—	—	4·1
Sulphur	40	18	—
Chlorine	20	11	—
Argon	160	55	—
Potassium	—	0·13	0·4
Calcium	—	2·8	10·0
Titanium	—	0·1	0·2

Compounds of the above mentioned elements are occasionally found.

LIST OF GALACTIC NEBULAE

The following objects were selected from the brightest and largest of the various classes to illustrate the different types of interactions between stars and interstellar matter in our galaxy. *Emission regions* (HII) are excited by the strong ultraviolet flux of young, hot stars and are characterised by the lines of hydrogen in their spectra. *Reflection nebulae* (Ref) result from the diffusion of starlight by clouds of interstellar dust. At certain stages of their evolution stars become unstable and explode, shedding their outer layers into what becomes a *planetary nebula* (P1) or a *supernova remnant* (SN). Protostellar nebulae (PrS) are objects still poorly understood; they are somewhat similar to the reflection nebulae, but their associated stars, often variable, are very luminous infra-red stars which may be in the earliest stages of stellar evolution. Also included in the selection are four *extended complexes* (Comp) of special interest for their rich population of dark and bright nebulosities of various types. In the table S is the optical surface brightness in magnitude per square second of arc of representative regions of the nebula, and m* is the magnitude of the associated star.

NOTES

NGC	M	Con	h	m	°	′	Type	Size ′	S mag sq″	m *	Dist 10³ ly	Remarks
650/1	76	Per	01	40·3	+51	25	P1	1·5	20	17	15·0	
IC348		Per	03	42·6	+32	05	Ref	3·0	21	8	0·5	Nebular cluster
1435		Tau	03	45·7	+23	59	Ref	15·0	20	4	0·4	Merope nebula
1535		Eri	04	12·8	−12	49	P1	0·5	17	12		
1952	1	Tau	05	32·7	+22	05	SN	5·0	19	16v	4·0	'Crab' + pulsar
1976	42	Ori	05	33·8	−05	25	HII	30·0	18	4	1·5	Orion nebula
1999		Ori	05	35·0	−06	45	PrS	1·0		10v	1·5	
ζ Ori		Ori	05	39·3	−01	57	Comp	2°			1·5	Incl 'Horsehead'
2068	78	Ori	05	45·3	+00	02	Ref	5·0	20		1·5	
IC443		Gem	06	15·8	+22	36	SN	40·0			2·0	
2237		Mon	06	30·8	+04	53	HII	50·0	21	7	3·0	Rosette neb
2247		Mon	06	31·5	+10	20	PrS	2·0	20	9	3·0	
2261		Mon	06	37·5	+08	45	PrS	2·0		12v	4·0	Hubble's var neb
2392		Gem	07	27·4	+20	58	P1	0·3	18	10	10·0	Clown face neb
3587	97	UMa	11	13·0	+55	11	P1	3·0	21	13	12·0	Owl nebula
ρ Oph		Oph	16	23·8	−23	23	Comp	4°			0·5	Bright + dark nebula
θ Oph		Oph	17	20·1	−24	58	Comp	5°				Incl 'S' nebula
6514	20	Sgr	18	00·6	−23	02	HII	15·0	19		3·5	Trifid nebula
6523	8	Sgr	18	01·8	−24	23	HII	40·0	18		4·5	Lagoon nebula
6543		Dra	17	58·6	+66	37	P1	0·4	15	11	3·5	
6611	16	Ser	18	17·2	−13	48	HII	15·0	19	10	6·0	
6618	17	Sgr	18	19·1	−16	12	HII	20·0	19		3·0	Horseshoe neb
6720	57	Lyr	18	52·5	+33	00	P1	1·2	18	15	5·0	Ring nebula
6826		Cyg	19	44·1	+50	27	P1	0·7	16	10	3·5	
6853	27	Vul	19	58·2	+22	38	P1	7·0	20	13	3·5	Dumb-bell neb
6888		Cyg	20	11·2	+38	19	SN	15·0				
γ Cyg		Cyg	20	21·1	+40	10	Comp	6°				HII + dark neb
6960/95		Cyg	20	44·4	+30	36	SN	150·0			2·5	Cygnus loop
7000		Cyg	20	57·8	+44	12	HII	100·0	22		3·5	N America neb
7009		Aqr	21	02·5	−11	30	P1	0·5	16	12	3·0	Saturn nebula
7023		Cep	21	01·3	+68	03	Ref	5·0	21	7	1·3	
7027		Cyg	21	06·0	+42	07	P1	0·2	15	13		
7129		Cep	21	42·3	+65	57	Ref	3·0	21	10	2·5	Small cluster
7293		Aqr	22	28·0	−20	57	P1	13·0	22	13		Helix nebula
7662		And	23	24·5	+42	22	P1	0·3	16	12	4·0	

THE GALAXY

As seen from Earth, the Galaxy appears as a silvery arch spanning the sky. It is sometimes referred to as the Milky Way because of its appearance to the naked eye. On examination with even a small telescope or binoculars, it is seen to be composed of a great number of stars.

The Sun lies slightly North of the galactic plane, and about three-fifths of the radius from the centre (32,500 light years), which lies in the direction of Sagittarius.

The dimensions of the Galaxy have been measured by using Cepheid variable stars and spectroscopic parallax, and its diameter determined as 100,000 light years. Its thickness varies from about 7,000 to 20,000 light years; it is thicker at the centre than at the boundary, ie it is lenticular in section.

The mass of the Galaxy is about 100,000 million times that of the Sun. Two-thirds of the mass is in the nucleus, and one-third in or between the spiral arms.

Differential Rotation of the Galaxy causes the velocity of the stars about the galactic centre to increase by 16km/s (10 miles/s) relative to the Sun for every kiloparsec (3,261 light years) from the Sun towards the centre of the Galaxy. From the Sun outwards the velocity decreases at a similar rate. The Sun takes 224 million years to make one revolution around the centre of the Galaxy. This is the 'Cosmic Year'.

I 241

Stellar orbits in the Galaxy are of two main types: those of Population I stars lie in the plane of the Galaxy and the stars partake of the general revolution around the centre of the Galaxy. The orbits of Population II stars are more random and often are highly inclined to the galactic plane. These stars form a halo around the Galaxy, and are to be found in the globular clusters and between the arms of the Galaxy.

The gas, forming the nebulae, lies along the plane of the Galaxy. It has an overall movement away from the galactic centre similar to an explosion of matter from the nucleus. There is also a quantity of cosmic dust associated with the interstellar gas.

Chemical abundances for the interstellar gas are tabulated under the section of this book on galactic nebulae (p 237). It will be noted that hydrogen and calcium are predominant.

The composition of the Galaxy is of some 100,000 million stars of various types, including planetary nebulae, large amounts of hydrogen etc in the form of bright nebulae, together with interstellar dust that make up the bright and dark nebulae in irregular patches.

Magnetic fields have been detected in the interstellar matter, causing alignment of the dust and ice particles, which produces polarisation of the light coming to us from stars behind the clouds of interstellar matter.

The age of the Galaxy in its present form is thought to be about 10,000 million years, or perhaps more. The age of the Sun and Earth is considered to be about half this figure, or 5,000 million years. The Sun has therefore completed a number of revolutions around the galactic centre.

OTHER GALAXIES (External Galaxies)

CLASSIFICATION

Galaxies outside our own Milky Way Galaxy are classed as external galaxies, and are considered to be similar in nature to our own. Very large numbers of these have been photographed. They present various appearances, some variations being caused by the amount of tilt of their axes to the line of sight. Other variations in their appearances are due to intrinsic differences in their structure. Classification thus depends on at least two conditions: 1. The angle of tilt, noticeable in the case of the elliptical nebulae, which can be of disk appearance, with increasing angle of tilt making them appear elliptical and even cigar shaped. 2. Spiral nebulae, suffering the same apparent distortion in their individual appearances, but added to this there is an inherent difference between each type caused by the structural forms.

Elliptical nebulae of the E0 class present a full face view and appear disk shaped. Increase of apparent ellipticity is classified in steps to the E7 class, which are elongated. Following the E7 class we come to truly spiral nebulae, which in many cases are presented edge-on, and show extensions of their major axes in the form of rudimentary spiral arms at each extremity. Elliptical nebulae have no free hydrogen and are composed of old-type (Population I) stars. They show no structural details except that the nuclei appear more condensed than their outer portions.

243

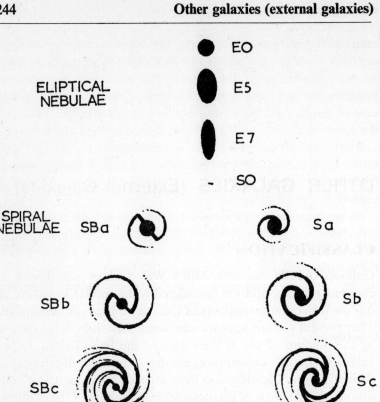

Fig 22   Classification of nebulae after Hubble's system

SO Nebulae have some characteristics of both elliptical and spiral types. They look like highly flattened nuclei of spiral nebulae that have started to develop spiral arms.

Spiral nebulae are subdivided into two main classes: normal spirals, and barred spirals.

Normal spirals show their spiral-arm structure when their planes are perpendicular to the line of sight. When presented edge-on they look like E7 type elliptical nebulae, except that they have a dark marking indicating the presence of absorbing material along their major axes. The spiral arms emerge tangentially from the nucleus at two diametrically opposite points. As we progress along the diagram we note that the nucleus becomes less in proportion to the mass of the arms until in the case of the Sc type the arms are clearly predominant. Similarly the rotation periods of the nebulae increase along the series.

Barred spirals are similar to normal spirals except that the nuclei have a bright bar across them. The spiral arms develop from the extremities of the bar and at right angles to it. Our own Galaxy is classed as SBb.

As we progress along the series from SBa to SBc, we find the arms become more predominant as in the case of normal spirals, while in the earliest type SBa the arms are long enough to make the nebula similar in appearance to the Greek letter theta, but in this case the nucleus is comparatively brighter than the arms.

Progression in the two series (S and SB) is indicated by the relative brightness of the nuclei and the arms, and the openness of the arms of the nebulae. In the very late types, the nuclei resemble globular clusters and show emission spectra. Bands of obscuring matter are found in the earlier types and are seen in silhouette when the nebulae are presented nearly edge-on.

Rotation of spiral nebulae normally follows the differential pattern expected in accordance with the gravitational laws of motion. There are exceptions. In M31 (Great Nebula in Andromeda), rotation increases from the centre to 96km/s (60 miles/s) at 200 parsecs radius, then decreases to zero at 500 parsecs and increases again to 96km/s (60 miles/s) at 1,200 parsecs radius. At 2 kiloparsecs the rotational speed is 192km/s (120 miles/s), at 4 kiloparsecs it is 322km/s (200 miles/s) and at 6 kiloparsecs it becomes 354km/s (220 miles/s). This is at variance with the star streaming velocity of the Galaxy. Similarly, in the case of M33 in Triangulum, the rotational velocity increases regularly from the nucleus outwards to 96–161km/s (60–100 miles/s) at 1 kiloparsec, and then decreases to 48–80km/s (30–

50 miles/s) at 2 kiloparsecs radius. It is suggested that these anomalies indicate the presence of strong magnetic fields.

Irregular nebulae must not be confused with galactic nebulae which are also irregular in shape. By irregular nebulae in the case of external galaxies we refer to those galaxies of irregular shape, which may at some long time hence become regular galaxies by condensation and rotation. Among the nearer members of this class are the Magellanic Clouds, or Nubeculae Major and Minor to give them their proper names. The Major has a definite spiral structure in its outer portions, and Population I stars are predominant, while it also contains an abundance of cosmic dust.

The Minor, on the other hand, appears to be dust free and is nearly transparent in this sense, but not really so. The stars are systematically bluer near the centre than at the edges. Their distances are in the region of 180,000 light years for the Major, and 150,000 light years for the Minor cloud.

Blue dwarf galaxies have emission line spectra, small diameter and very low luminosities.

Seyfert galaxies form a special class with relatively small, condensed nuclei and relatively inconspicuous spiral arms. They are frequently found to be radio sources.

N galaxies are similar to Seyfert galaxies, but more luminous.

Maffei objects are a class of two specimens discovered in 1968 by Maffei, invisible in blue light but conspicuous in red. Maffei 1 appears to be an elliptical (E3 or E4) and Maffei 2 spiral. They are only half a degree away from the plane of the Galaxy and are probably nearby galaxies dimmed by galactic dust clouds.

Abundance figures of the various classes of galaxies are as follows:

Type	Frequency (%)
EO–E7	17
Sa –SBa	19
Sb –SBb	25
SC–SBc	36
Irregular	2·5

Clustering of galaxies is observed despite their overall average equal spacing. Our own Galaxy has companions in space at comparatively small distances from us. M31 at 2 million light years is the nearest complete normal galaxy, but other specimens, as listed in the table on page 250, are much closer to us. It seems that in these clouds or families of galaxies the more central ones are of the elliptical types with spirals forming the periphery of the system. The clustering of galaxies is illustrated by Fig 23.

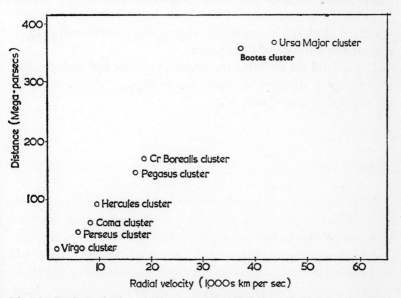

Fig 23   Radial velocity on the assumption that the red shift is an indication of distance and real velocity. Radial velocity is expressed at a rate of thousands of kilometres per second

Recessional velocity is suggested by the Doppler shift of the spectrum towards the red end. This shift is proportional to the distance of the individual galaxies from us. Some of the nearer specimens do not show this feature. The log of the shift is proportional to the apparent magnitude of each galaxy, ie the fainter the galaxy, the more shift is exhibited in the spectrum.

LIST OF EXTERNAL GALAXIES

Among the hundreds of thousands of systems far beyond our own Galaxy relatively few are readily seen in small telescopes. The first list contains the brightest galaxies. The first four columns give the catalogue numbers and position. In the column *Type*, *E* indicates elliptical, *I*, irregular, and *Sa*, *Sb*, *Sc*, spiral galaxies in which the arms are more open going from *a* to *c*. Roman numerals I, II, III, IV, and V refer to supergiant, bright giant, giant, subgiant and dwarf galaxies respectively, *p* means 'peculiar', *d* means dwarf. The remaining columns give the apparent photographic magnitude, the angular dimensions and the distance in millions of light-years.

The second list contains the nearest galaxies and includes the photographic distance modulus $(m - M)_{pg}$, and the absolute photographic magnitude, M_{pg}.

BRIGHTEST GALAXIES

NGC or name	M	α 1970 δ				Type	m_{pg}	Dimensions ′ ′	Distance millions of ly
		h	m	°	′				
55		00	13·5	−39	23	Sc or Ir	7·90	30×5	7·5
205		00	38·7	+41	32	E6p	8·89	12×6	2·1
221	32	00	41·1	+40	43	E2	9·06	3·4×2·9	2·1
224	31	00	41·1	+41	07	Sb I–II	4·33	163×42	2·1
247		00	45·6	−20	54	S IV	9·47	21×8·4	7·5
253		00	46·1	−25	27	Scp	7·00:	22×4·6	7·5
SMC		00	51·7	−72	59	Ir IV or IV–V	2·86	216×216	0·2
300		00	53·5	−37	51	Sc III–IV	8·66	22×16.5	7·5
598	33	01	32·2	+30	30	Sc II–III	6·19	61×42	2·4
Fornax		02	38·3	−34	39	dE	9·10:	50×35	0·4
LMC		05	23·8	−69	47	Ir or Sc III–IV	0·86	432×432	0·2
2403		07	33·9	+65	40	Sc III	8·80	22×12	6·5
2903		09	30·4	+21	39	Sb I–II	9·48	16×6·8	19·0
3031	81	09	53·1	+69	12	Sb I–II	7·85	25×12	6·5
3034	82	09	53·6	+69	50	Scp:	9·20	10×1·5	6·5
4258		12	17·5	+47	28	Sbp	8·90	19×7	14·0
4472	49	12	28·3	+08	09	E4	9·33	9·8×6·6	37·0
4594	104	12	38·3	−11	28	Sb	9·18	7·9×4·7	37·0
4736	94	12	49·5	+41	16	Sbp II:	8·91	13×12	14·0
4826	64	12	55·3	+21	51	?	9·27	10×3·8	12·0
4945		13	03·5	−49	19	Sb III	8·00	20×4	—
5055	63	13	14·4	+42	11	Sb II	9·26	8·0×3·0	14·0
5128		13	23·6	−42	51	E0p	7·87	23×20	—
5194	51	13	28·6	+47	21	Sc I	8·88	11×6·5	14·0
5236	83	13	35·4	−29	43	Sc I–II	7·00:	13×12	8·0:
5457	101	14	02·1	+54	29	Sc I	8·20	23×21	14·0
6822		19	43·2	−14	50	Ir IV–V	9·21	20×10	1·7

LMC=Large; SMC=Small Magellonic Cloud

LIST OF NEAREST GALAXIES

Name	NGC	α 1970 δ		m_{pg}	$(m-M)_{pg}$	M_{pg}	Type	Dist thous of ly
		h m	° ′					
M31	224	00 41·1	+41 07	4·33	24·65	−20·3	Sb I–II	2,100
Galaxy	—	—	—	-°	—	?	Sb or Sc	—
M33	598	01 32·2	+30 30	6·19	24·70	−18·5	Sc II–III	2,400
LMC		05 23·8	−69 47	0·86	18·65	−17·8	Ir or SBc III–IV	160
SMC		00 51·7	−72 59	2·86	19·05	−16·2	Ir IV or IV–V	190
NGC	205	00 38·7	+41 32	8·89	24·65	−15·8	E6p	2,100
M32	221	00 41·1	+40 43	9·06	24·65	−15·6	E2	2,100
NGC	6,822	19 43·2	−14 50	9·21	24·55	−15·3	Ir IV–V	1,700
NGC	185	00 37·2	+48 11	10·29	24·65	−14·4	E0	2,100
IC1613		01 03·5	+01 58	10·00	24·40	−14·4	Ir V	2,400
NGC	147	00 31·5	+48 11	10·57	24·65	−14·1	dE4	2,100
Fornax		02 38·3	−34 39	9·10:	20·60:	−12:	dE	430
Leo I		10 06·9	+12 27	11·27	21·80:	−10:	dE	750:
Sculptor		00 58·4	−33 52	10·50	19·70	− 9·2	dE	280:
Leo II		11 11·9	+22 19	12·85	21·80:	− 9:	dE	750:
Draco		17 19·7	+57 57	—	19·50	?	dE	260
Ursa Minor		15 08·4	+67 13	—	19·40	?	dE	250

LMC=Large Magellonic Cloud; SMC=Small Magellonic Cloud

NOTE

We must also add to the known objects two dense clouds of neutral hydrogen gas, isolated in intergalactic space within which formation of massive stars is proceeding. These tiny objects are situated at RA 09h 30m, Dec N 55° (in Ursa Major) and at RA 05h 53m, Dec N 03° (in Orion). They may be similar to Blue Dwarf galaxies.

LIST OF INTERESTING VISUAL OBJECTS

The reader will need a reliable star atlas in order to find the various objects mentioned in this book. The following list has been compiled for preliminary guidance from *Norton's Star Atlas* and *Reference Handbook*, which should be consulted, and in which a much more comprehensive list of interesting objects, together with a number of practical hints and information, will be found. M refers to *Messier's Catalogue* and NGC to the *New General Catalogue*.

ANDROMEDA	
Gamma	A magnificent binary, gold and blue
Gamma 2	Binary, widest in 1971, 0·6″
R	Long-period variable star
M31 (NGC 224)	The Great Nebula in Andromeda, visible to the naked eye
NGC 7662	Remarkably bright planetary nebula

AQUARIUS	
94	Relatively fixed double, yellowish and blue
R	Long-period variable star

AQUILA	
Pi	Binary with little change, separation 1·4″ a test for a 3in telescope
R	Long-period variable star
U	Cepheid-type variable star

ARIES	
30	Relatively fixed, white and blue
Epsilon	Binary, test for a 3in telescope
AURIGA	
Theta	Binary; test for 4in telescope
M38 (NGC 1912)	Striking loose cruciform cluster
M36 (NGC 1960)	Open cluster
M37 (NGC 2099)	Fine open cluster
BOOTES	
Epsilon	Binary, yellow and blue; test for 2in telescope
Delta	Binary, separation 105″ no change since 1822
R	Long-period variable star
CANCER	
Iota	Binary, yellow and blue. Separation 30·7″ no change
66	Binary, separation 4·6″ relatively fixed
R	Long-period variable star
M44 (NGC 2632)	'Praesepe' or 'Beehive' cluster, best seen with low power
M 67 (NGC 2682)	Circular open cluster of faint stars. Use low power
CANES VENATICI	
Alpha	Relatively fixed double, separation 19·7″
R	Long-period variable star
M 63 (NGC 5055)	Bright oval nebula, photographically spiral
M 51 (NGC 5194)	Larger of two nebulae nearly in contact
M 3 (NGC 5272)	Bright globular cluster
CANIS MAJOR	
Alpha	'Sirius', binary widest in 1975 at 11·5″
Mu	Binary, yellow and blue. Separation 3″ little change
Epsilon	Binary relatively fixed separation 7·7″
R	Algol-type variable star
M 41 (NGC 2287)	Open cluster of bright stars, just visible to naked eye
CAPRICORNUS	
Alpha	Alpha 1 and Alpha 2 form a naked eye pair, separation 376″
CARINA	
NGC 3372	The Keyhole Nebula

NGC 3532	Magnificent cluster
R	Long-period variable

CASSIOPEIA

Lambda	Close binary separation 0·6″ in 1971
Eta	Long-period binary, separation 11·5″ in 1971
Alpha	Irregular variable star
Gamma	Irregular variable star
NGC 457	Condensed cluster
NGC 7789	Between Rho and Sigma; large faint cluster
NGC 7243	Open irregular cluster, followed by beautiful field

CENTAURUS

Omega	A noble cluster, like a tailless comet

CEPHEUS

Kappa	Relatively fixed binary, separation 7·4″
Omicron	Binary, test for 2in telescope at separation 3·0″
T	Long-period variable
V	Long-period variable
Delta	Type star of Cepheid variable class
Mu	Irregular variable star

CETUS

Gamma	Binary with little movement, separation 3·0″
Omicron	Long-period variable star
M 77 (NGC 1068)	Small round faint nebula

COMA BERENICES

24	Binary, yellow and greenish-white, relatively fixed
M 88 (NGC 4501)	Long bright nebula. Many nebulae in this region
M 64 (NGC 4826)	Black eye nebula, visible in large telescopes

CORONA BOREALIS

Eta	Close binary
Zeta	Binary with little change, beautiful object
S	Long-period variable star
R	Long-period variable star with long periods of standstills
T	Recurrent nova period $\approx$ 80 years

CRUX

NGC 4755	Surrounding Kappa, brilliant cluster

CYGNUS

Beta	Binary, yellow and blue. Fine object in small telescope
Delta	Long-period binary, test for 4in telescope
49	Binary, yellow and blue
SU	Short-period variable, mags 6·2 to 7·0
Chi	Long-period variable star, Mira type
X	Short-period variable, mags 5·9 to 7·0
W	Long-period variable star
M 39 (NGC 7092)	Large open cluster of bright stars

DELPHINUS

Gamma	Binary, yellow and emerald

DORADO

NGC 2070	The Great Looped Nebula round 30 Doradus, large and bright
Nub Maj	Nubecula Major containing many interesting objects

DRACO

Pulkova 123	Fine wide double at RA 13h 25m Dec N 65°. (Epoch 1950) Yellow and blue
Psi	Wide bright binary, yellow and lilac
NGC 6543	Planetary nebula, bright and bluish

ERIDANUS

32	Binary, topaz and green

GEMINI

Lambda	Relatively fixed double at 9·9″ separation; test for 3in telescope
Delta	Binary with primary star yellow
Alpha	Castor. Separation 1971: 1·9″
Kappa	Relatively fixed at 6·8″ separation
Eta	Long-period variable
Zeta	Cepheid variable
R	Long-period variable star
M 35 (NGC 2168)	Fine bright open cluster
NGC 2392	Oval planetary nebula, central star 9·5 mag

HERCULES

Alpha	{ Alpha A is an irregular variable star { Binary, orange and green. Separation 1971: 4·6″
Delta	Double with diminishing separation
90	Binary, gold and blue
S	Long-period variable

M 13 (NGC 6205)	The Great Globular Cluster in Hercules, just visible to the naked eye
M 92 (NGC 6341)	Globular cluster fainter than M 13

HYDRA	
U	Irregular variable star
R	Long-period variable star
W	Long-period variable star
NGC 3242	Planetary nebula, pale blue

LEO	
3	Binary, light test for 4in telescope
R	Long-period variable star
Gamma	Binary, separation 4·2″ in 1971

LIBRA	
Mu	Binary, test for a 2½in telescope at 1·8″ separation
Delta	Algol-type eclipsing binary

LYRA	
Alpha	'Vega' optical double mags 0·2 and 10·5: separation 56·4″ increasing
Beta	Type star of Beta Lyrae eclipsing variables
M 57 (NGC 6720)	Ring nebula. Distance 1,410 light years

MONOCEROS	
NGC 2244	Beautiful open cluster visible to naked eye

NORMA	
NGC 6067	Large rich cluster

OPHIUCHUS	
39	Binary, orange and blue
U	Algol-type, eclipsing variable
Y	Cepheid-type variable star
M 19 (NGC 6273)	Fine globular cluster, but low for northern observers

ORION	
Beta	'Rigel'; secondary star is bluish. Test for 2in telescope
33	Binary, separation 1·8″ in 1971
Theta	'The Trapezium'. Mags 6·0, 7·0, 7·5 and 8·0
Sigma	Group. Mags 4·0, 10·0, 7·5 and 7·0, striking colours
Alpha	'Betelgeuse'. Irregular variable star, ruddy
U	Long-period variable star

M 42 (NGC 1976)	The Great Nebula in Orion, visible to the naked eye
PAVO NGC 6752	Large bright globular cluster
PEGASUS 32	Wide binary, separation 72″, with 11 mag comes near B
37	Binary with orbit in line of sight
Beta	Irregular variable star
PERSEUS Eta	Binary, yellow and blue
Beta	'Algol'-type star of eclipsing variable star class
NGC 869 and 884	These two objects form the Double Open Cluster in Perseus, fine objects visible to the naked eye
PUPPIS M 46 (NGC 2437)	Cluster of small stars, on its northern edge is the irregular planetary ring nebula NGC 2438
NGC 2440	Bright planetary nebula
SAGITTARIUS W	Cepheid-type variable star
Y	Cepheid-type variable star
M8 (NGC 6523)	'Lagoon Nebula', visible to the naked eye
M 17 (NGC 6618)	'The Omega or Horseshoe Nebula'
M 22 (NGC 6656)	Large bright globular cluster
SCORPIO Alpha	'Antares', binary red and green, separation 3·0″
M 80 (NGC 6093)	Bright condensed globular cluster
M 4 (NGC 6121)	Easily resolved cluster
SCUTUM M11 (NGC 6705)	Grand fan-shaped cluster
SERPENS R	Long-period variable star
M 5 (NGC 5904)	Fine globular cluster
TAURUS Alpha	'Aldebaran', binary with distance increasing from proper motion of primary star
Lambda	Algol-type eclipsing binary
NGC 1435	Faint nebula near Merope in the Pleiades

M 1 (NGC 1952)	'The Crab Nebula' remnant of Nova of 1054. Distance 6,000 light years
TRIANGULUM M 33 (NGC 598) R	Very large faint, ill-defined, nebula Long-period variable star
TRIANGULUM AUSTRALE NGC 6025	Bright open cluster
TUCANA Beta NGC 104 NGC 362 Nub Mi	Binary, superb object 47 Tucanae. Most glorious cluster Globular cluster Nubecula Minor
URSA MAJOR R M 81 (NGC 3031) M 82 (NGC 3034 Xi Zeta M 97 (NGC 3587)	Long-period variable star Bright spiral nebula with faint arms Spiral seen almost edge on, near M 81 Binary, widening to 2·9″ in 1980 'Mizar' naked eye binary with 'Alcor' 'The Owl Nebula', large faint planetary nebula
URSA MINOR Alpha	'The Pole Star' or 'Polaris'. Binary, easy with a 2½in telescope, secondary is bluish
VIRGO Gamma Theta R S	Splendid binary, separation 4·5″ in 1971 Binary, test for a 3in telescope, there is a 10th magnitude star at 71″ distance Long-period variable star Long-period variable star
VULPECULA T M 27 (NGC 6853)	Cepheid-type variable star 'The Dumbell Nebula'. Planetary Nebula

MESSIER'S CATALOGUE OF DIFFUSE OBJECTS

This table lists the 103 objects in Messier's original catalogue. The columns contain: Messier's number (M), the number in Dreyer's New General Catalogue (NGC), the constellation, the 1970 position, the integrated visual magnitude (m$_v$), and the class of object. OC means open cluster, GC, globular cluster, PN, planetary nebula, DN, diffuse nebula, and G, galaxy. The type of galaxy is also indicated.

M	NGC	Con	α 1970 δ		mv	Type	M	NGC	Con	α 1970 δ		mv	Type
1	1952	Tau	5 32.7	+22 01	11.30	DN	56	6779	Lyr	19 15.4	+30 07	8.33	GC
2	7089	Aqr	21 31.9	—00 57	6.27	GC	57	6720	Lyr	18 52.5	+33 00	9.00	PN
3	5272	CVn	13 40.8	+28 32	6.22	GC	58	4579	Vir	12 36.2	+11 59	9.90	G–SBb
4	6121	Sco	16 21.8	—26 26	6.07	GC	59	4621	Vir	12 40.5	+11 50	10.30	G–E
5	5904	Ser	15 17.0	+02 13	5.99	GC	60	4649	Vir	12 42.1	+11 44	9.30	G–E
6	6405	Sco	17 38.1	—32 11	6.00	OC	61	4303	Vir	12 20.3	+04 39	9.70	G–Sc
7	6475	Sco	17 51.9	—34 48	5.00	OC	62	6266	Sco	16 59.3	—30 04	7.20	GC
8	6523	Sgr	18 01.8	—24 23		DN	63	5055	CVn	13 14.4	+42 11	8.80	G–Sb
9	6333	Oph	17 17.5	—18 29	7.58	GC	64	4826	Com	12 55.2	+21 51	8.70	G–Sb
10	6254	Oph	16 55.5	—04 04	6.40	GC	65	3623	Leo	11 17.3	+13 16	9.60	G–Sa
11	6705	Sct	18 49.5	—06 19	6.00	OC	66	3627	Leo	11 18.6	+13 10	9.20	G–Sb
12	6218	Oph	16 45.6	—01 54	6.74	GC	67	2682	Cnc	8 49.5	+11 56	7.00	OC
13	6205	Her	16 40.6	+36 31	5.78	GC	68	4590	Hya	12 37.8	—26 35	8.04	GC
14	6402	Oph	17 36.0	—03 14	7.82	GC	69	6637	Sgr	18 29.4	—32 23	7.70	GC
15	7078	Peg	21 28.6	+12 02	6.29	GC	70	6681	Sgr	18 41.3	—32 19	8.20	GC
16	6611	Ser	18 17.2	—13 48	7.00	OC	71	6838	Sge	19 52.4	+18 42	6.90	GC
17	6618	Sgr	18 19.1	—16 12	7.00	DN	72	6981	Aqr	20 51.8	—12 41	9.15	GC
18	6613	Sgr	18 18.2	—17 09	7.00	OC	73	6994	Aqr	20 57.3	—12 46		OC
19	6273	Oph	17 00.7	—26 13	6.94	GC	74	628	Psc	1 35.1	+15 38	9.50	G–Sc
20	6514	Sgr	18 00.6	—23 02		DN	75	6864	Sgr	20 04.3	—22 01	8.31	GC
21	6531	Sgr	18 02.8	—22 30	7.00	OC	76	650	Per	1 40.3	+51 25	11.40	PN
22	6656	Sgr	18 34.6	—23 56	5.22	GC	77	1068	Cet	2 41.1	—00 07	9.01	G–S
23	6494	Sgr	17 55.1	—19 00	6.00	OC	78	2068	Ori	5 45.3	+00 02		DN
24	6603	Sgr	18 16.7	—18 27	6.00	OC	79	1904	Lep	5 22.9	—24 33	7.30	GC
25	4725*	Sgr	18 29.9	—19 16	6.00	OC	80	6093	Sco	16 15.2	—22 55	7.17	GC
26	6694	Sct	18 43.6	—09 26	9.00	OC	81	3031	UMa	9 53.4	+69 12	6.90	G–Sb
27	6853	Vul	19 58.4	+22 38	8.20	PN	82	3034	UMa	9 53.6	+69 50	8.70	G–Irr
28	6626	Sgr	18 22.6	—24 52	7.07	GC	83	5236	Hya	13 35.3	—29 43	7.50	G–Sc
29	6913	Cyg	20 22.9	+38 25	8.00	OC	84	4374	Vir	12 23.6	+13 03	9.80	G–E
30	7099	Cap	21 38.6	—23 18	7.63	GC	85	4382	Com	12 23.8	+18 21	9.50	G–SO
31	224	And	0 41.1	+41 06	3.70	G–Sb	86	4406	Vir	12 24.6	+13 06	9.80	G–E
32	221	And	0 41.1	+40 42	8.50	G–E	87	4486	Vir	12 29.2	+12 33	9.30	G–Ep
33	598	Tri	1 32.2	+30 30	5.90	G–Sc	88	4501	Com	12 30.4	+14 35	9.70	G–Sb
34	1039	Per	2 40.1	+42 40	6.00	OC	89	4552	Vir	12 34.1	+12 43	10.30	G–E
35	2168	Gem	6 07.0	+24 21	6.00	OC	90	4569	Vir	12 35.3	+13 19	9.70	G–Sb
36	1960	Aur	5 34.3	+34 05	6.00	OC	91						M58?
37	2099	Aur	5 50.4	+32 33	6.00	OC	92	6341	Her	17 16.2	+43 11	6.33	GC
38	1912	Aur	5 26.6	+35 48	6.00	OC	93	2447	Pup	7 43.2	—23 48	6.00	OC
39	7092	Cyg	21 31.1	+48 18	6.00	OC	94	4736	CVn	12 49.6	+41 17	8.10	G–Sb
40	—	UMa	—	—		2 stars	95	3351	Leo	10 42.3	+11 52	9.90	G–SBb
41	2287	CMa	6 45.8	—20 42	6.00	OC	96	3368	Leo	10 45.1	+11 59	9.40	G–Sa
42	1976	Ori	5 33.9	—05 24		DN	97	3587	UMa	11 13.1	+55 11	11.10	PN
43	1982	Ori	5 34.1	—05 18		DN	98	4192	Com	12 12.2	+15 04	10.40	G–Sb
44	2632	Cnc	8 38.2	+20 06	4.00	OC	99	4254	Com	12 17.3	+14 35	9.90	G–Sc
45	—	Tau	3 45.7	+24 01	2.00	OC	100	4321	Com	12 21.4	+15 59	9.60	G–Sc
46	2437	Pup	7 40.4	—14 45	7.00	OC	101	5457	UMa	14 02.1	+54 30	8.10	G–Sc
47	2422	Pup	7 35.1	—14 26	5.00	OC	102	—	—	—	—		M101?
48	2548	Hya	8 12.0	—05 41	6.00	OC	103	581	Cas	1 31.2	+60 32	7.00	OC
49	4472	Vir	12 28.3	+08 10	8.90	G–E							
50	2323	Mon	7 01.5	—08 18	7.00	OC							
51	5194	CVn	13 28.6	+47 21	8.40	G–Sc							
52	7654	Cas	23 22.9	+61 26	7.00	OC							
53	5024	Com	13 11.5	+18 20	7.70	GC							
54	6715	Sgr	18 53.2	—30 31	7.70	GC							
55	6809	Sgr	19 38.1	—31 01	6.09	GC							

* Index Catalogue Number.

RADIO ASTRONOMY

Radio astronomy is the study of the heavens by radiation at radio frequencies, as opposed to visual astronomy at visible light frequencies. Radio is not interfered with by weather and cloud conditions as is optical astronomy, but at longer wavelengths the conditions of the ionosphere are important.

Radio astronomy is roughly divided into two types: 1. Radar —pulses transmitted and returned to the sending station by reflection from some other body. 2. Radio emissions—originating in some other source and received by suitable apparatus on Earth.

RADAR

Radar can be used in the observation of the Sun, Moon and planets. Electromagnetic waves travelling at the speed of light take only 2·4s to make the double journey to the Moon and back again. The returning signals show fading in concert with the lateral movement of the lunar surface due to libration. Because the centre of the disk is nearer Earth, a radar pulse takes longer to return from the limb than from the centre of the disk by some $11\frac{1}{2}$ milliseconds. By using radar reflection from the Moon, the distance can be accurately measured from various transmitters at different points on the Earth's surface. The results can be compared, and the distances of the transmitters from the axis of the Moon's distance can be found; the shape of the Earth can be determined accordingly.

The Sun, Mercury, Venus, Mars and the asteroid Icarus have all been contacted by radar, and measurements of the rotation periods of Mercury and Venus depend on these observations. Radar measurements of the distance of Venus have provided a method of measuring the scale of the solar system and determining the length of the astronomical unit.

RADIO EMISSIONS

The Sun. Radio observation of the Sun is informative and at longer wavelengths the solar corona plays a dominant part and becomes the only detected part of the Sun. The longer the wavelength, the more oval the Sun appears, and this is because a progressively greater part of the radiation is from the corona. Much information on the structure of the corona is obtained by observations of the occultation of the Crab Nebula (M1), the remains of the supernova of AD 1054, as they occur from time to time. Both the Sun and the M1 are radio emitters. Radio traces are detected emitted by solar 'hot spots', or flares, and by absorption, cooler prominences lying over the more active photosphere.

Jupiter emits at radio frequencies which seem to be controlled by Io's position in its orbit.

The Galaxy presents quite a different picture at radio frequencies from that obtained visually. Sagittarius A (the nucleus of the Galaxy) is a complex area. Cassiopeia A is the shell of a supernova known as Tycho's Star, observed at maximum in AD 1572, while Kepler's Nova of 1604 is also a radio object. The Great Nebula in Orion (M42) is a radio object as well as being a visual one. It is rich in HII with OH emission. The Northern Spur is the invisible shell of an old supernova. Cygnus X is a spiral arm of the Galaxy. Pulsars are also galactic objects and are dealt with on pages 261–2.

Galactic and extra-galactic objects are differentiated as follows:

Near objects	Distant objects
In galactic plane, intense radiation	Weak radiation
Diameters 20′ and more	Small diameters, less than 20′ of arc

The observable sphere is of greater radius at radio frequencies than in the visual range. Radio waves can penetrate intergalactic and interstellar dust clouds, whereas visual waves cannot.

PULSARS

Pulsars are radio objects, although one has been identified optically in the Crab Nebula (M1) in Taurus. In all, some sixty are known.

Characteristic is the precise periodicity of their bursts of radiation varying between 0·033 and 3·75s in various specimens. Intervals between pulses vary with age. Many are observed to be gradually slowing down.

Preference for the galactic plane shows them to be members of our Galaxy, and correcting for Doppler shift, we find their distances less than 1 kiloparsec.

Diameters are of the order of 15 to 5,000km and they are most probably neutron stars with rapid rotation and a magnetic axis inclined to the axis of rotation. Contraction to this small dimension is concurrent with compression of the magnetic field, but the radiating sphere is suspected to be larger than the main body of the pulsar. They are thought to be supernova remnants.

Radiation is directional and fan shaped and is observed with frequencies between 500 and 20 MHz.

Phases of emission are characterised by several different periodicities. In addition to the main pulses, there are sub-pulses which, over a long series, are seen to march or drift through the intervals between the main pulses. These sub-pulses are attributed to plasma cloud concentrations or areas similar to sunspots. Some Pulsars also show 'jump periods', which are attributed to 'starquakes' in the outer crust, producing sudden emissions.

Nulls, or periods of no radiation, are observed of the order of 1–10 pulses missing from the steady bursts, over a large range of frequencies.

Dispersion in arrival time of each pulse is introduced by electrons in interstellar space, high frequency radiation arriving first.

Variation in the periods between emissions with age of the 'Pulsar' suggest a lifetime of some 10 million years.

EXTRA-GALACTIC SOURCES

Extra-galactic sources include the Andromeda Nebula (M31), from which 90 per cent of the radiation comes from the halo, whose radius is 6,000 light years.

Cygnus A is a strongly emitting radio galaxy with a double source; Virgo A (M87) is an EO galaxy with a spur jet attached; 3C295 is a galaxy 4,500,000 light years away; 3C353 is a double source, probably a galaxy; 3C446 is a quasar; 3C273 is the nearest and strongest quasar known; N and Seyfert galaxies are frequently found to be radio sources. (Note that 3C refers to the *Third Cambridge Catalogue*, the remaining figures being the Catalogue numbers.)

Quasars are probably extra-galactic objects and are dealt with on page 264.

WAVELENGTHS AND FREQUENCIES

Radiation is observed over a range of frequencies tabulated below in relation to wavelengths for ease of reference.

Frequency	Wavelengths	Specimen
100 KHz	3,000m	Radio 2, BBC, Long wave
300	1,000	
1 MHz	300	Radio 4, BBC, Medium wave
3	100	
10	30	Short wave
		Russian Satellites
30	10	BBC 1 Television
		3·7 metres is used for sky
		mapping
100	3	
300	1	BAA Radio Telescope +
1 GHz	30cm	
		21cm natural hydrogen
3	10	Radar as used in war, 1939
10	3	
30	1	
100	3mm	

* BAA Telescopes refers to instruments used by the British Astronomical Association.

QUASARS

Quasars, or quasi-stellar objects, are starlike objects with the following additional characteristics:
1. Starlike objects with identification as radio objects.
2. They have variable light output.
3. They have large ultra-violet to violet excess.
4. They have broad emission lines.
5. They have large Doppler shifts of the spectrum.

Their output of energy is proportionate to 10 million million Suns; their masses are of the order of 20 million million Suns. Linear dimensions seem to be below 172 parsecs diameter. Emission is often from two opposite sources, from photo-ionisation.

Quasars may evolve into radio galaxies, although revision of their masses might show them to be galactic objects; indeed they may be collapsed galaxies.

Absorption lines are shown by a small proportion of quasars, suggesting a cooler shell.

The red shift may be gravitational, with a limit of 1·95 corresponding to the Schwarzchild solution, arising from the infall velocity of emitting gas inside the absorbing region. However, the consensus of opinion is that the red shift is a Doppler effect, implying great distance (up to 7×10^9 light years) and an energy output equal to that of one hundred galaxies.

Their variable behaviour might arise from stellar collisions within a cluster of stars, changing the centre of mass velocity, and causing changes in brightness.

LIST OF RADIO TELESCOPES

The following lists are not exhaustive, but indicate typical types of radio telescopes of large dimensions.

STEERABLE BOWLS

Diameter (ft)	Location
1,000	Arecibo, Puerta Rica
400	Projected for Jodrell Bank, Cheshire
328	Effelsberg, Western Germany
260	Ohio State University, USA
250	Jodrell Bank, Cheshire, England
210	Parkes Observatory, New South Wales
130	Owens Valley, California, USA
120	Haystack and Danville, USA

FIXED ARRAYS

Cambridge, England
Mills Cross, Australia
Westerbork, Holland
Pulkova, Leningrad, USSR
Jodrell Bank, Cheshire, England
Lake Baikal, Siberia; 125 acre, three-dimensional solar radio-telescope projected in 1971.

LIST OF RADIO SOURCES

Although several thousand radio sources have been catalogued most of them are only observable with the largest radio telescopes. This list contains the few strong sources which could be detected with amateur radio telescopes as well as representative examples of astronomical objects which emit radio waves.

Name	α (1970) δ			Remarks
	h	m	° ′	
Tycho's supernova	00	24·0	+63 58	Remnant of supernova of 1572
M 31	00	41·0	+41 06	Closest normal spiral galaxy
IC 1795, W3	02	23·1	+61 58	Multiple HII region, OH emission
PKS 0237–23	02	38·7	−23 17	Quasar with large red shift, $Z = 2·2$
NGC 1275, 3C 84	03	17·8	+41 24	Seyfert galaxy, radio variable
Fornax A	03	21·2	−37 17	10th mag, SO galaxy
CP 0328	03	30·5	+54 27	Pulsar, period $= 0·7145$sec, H abs'n
Crab neb, M 1	05	32·6	+22 00	Remnant of supernova of 1054
NP 0527	05	32·6	+22 00	Radio, optical and X-ray pulsar
V 371 Orionis	05	32·2	+01 54	Red dwarf, radio and optical flare star
Orion neb, M 42	05	33·8	−05 24	HII region, OH emission, IR source
IC 443	06	15·5	+22 36	Supernova remnant (date unknown)
Rosette nebula	06	30·4	+04 53	HII region
YV CMa	07	21·8	−20 41	Optical var IR source, OH, H_2O emission
3C 273	12	27·5	+02 13	Nearest, strongest quasar
Virgo A, M 87	12	29·3	+12 33	EO galaxy with jet
Centaurus A	13	23·6	−42 52	NGC 5128 peculiar galaxy
3C 295	14	10·3	+52 21	21st mag galaxy, 4,500,000 light years
Scorpio X-1	16	18·2	−15 34	X-ray, radio optical variable
3C 353	17	19·0	−00 57	Double source, probably galaxy
Kepler's supernova	17	27·0	−21 16	Remnant of supernova of 1604
Galactic nucleus	17	43·7	−28 56	Complex region OH, NH_3 em, H_2CO abs'n
Omega nebula, M 17	18	18·7	−16 10	HII region, double structure
W 49	19	08·9	+09 04	HII region supernova remnant, OH emission
CP 1919	19	20·4	+21 49	First pulsar discovered, $P = 1·337$sec
Cygnus A	19	58·4	+40 39	Strong radio galaxy, double source
Cygnus X	20	21·5	+40 17	Complex region
NML Cygnus	20	45·4	+40 00	Infra-red source, OH emission
Cygnus loop	20	51·0	+29 34	Supernova remnant (Network nebula)
NGC 7000, N America nebula	20	54·0	+43 57	Radio shape resembles photographs
3C 446	22	24·2	−05 07	Quasar, optical mag and spectrum var
Cassiopeia A	23	22·0	+58 39	Strongest source, supernova remnant
Sun				Continuous emission and bursts
Moon				Thermal source only
Jupiter				Radio bursts controlled by Io

NOTES

GAMMA RAY, X-RAY, AND INFRA-RED ASTRONOMY

GAMMA RAY ASTRONOMY

Because these short-wave radiations are absorbed by the upper layers of the Earth's atmosphere, recourse has to be made to rockets etc for their study.

Gamma rays are detected in Czernkov showers of some 3° diameter. The showers are dipole with detectable cross currents.

The Crab Nebula in Taurus (M1) is a strong source.

X-RAY ASTRONOMY

Like gamma rays, X-rays are absorbed by the upper layers of the atmosphere and study of them is similarly hindered.

Most sources are near the centre of the Galaxy and within 3° of its plane. Some show rapid variations in flux.

Radiation of solar flares polarises X-ray radiation.

The Crab Nebula in Taurus (M1) is a strong source, as is also the X1 in Scorpio. Kepler's Nova of 1604 is a source of X-ray radiation, but neither Cassiopeia A nor Cygnus A exhibit this form of radiation. X-ray novae have been observed. A cosmological background of diffuse X-rays has been suggested.

INFRA-RED ASTRONOMY

Infra-red solar radiation was observed by Sir William Herschel, but the major developments are of recent years. Various forms of detectors are in use including those using silicon, lead sulphide, indium antimonide etc, all of which are very sensitive to the wavelengths for which they are designed.

The Sun, Moon and several planets as well as stars have been observed to advantage, especially where the surface temperature is below 3,000°K. Some non-thermal sources also give rise to infra-red radiation, possibly through synchrotron radiation.

NOTES

ACKNOWLEDGEMENTS

Grateful acknowledgements are made to the following: The Council of the British Astronomical Association for permission to reproduce material from their *Handbook*; The Editor of *Sky and Telescope* for permission to use the table of precession; Mrs J. P. Merrilees for the drawing of a sunspot; W. M. Baxter, Director of the Solar Section of the British Astronomical Association, for details of sunspot activity; A. Mulligan for the list of total eclipses of the Sun 1954–2000; C. A. Cross, Miss P. A. Cullen, R. J. Livesey and Patrick Moore for the lunar maps; Dr A Dollfus for permission to reproduce the map of Mercury; J. Meeus for his list of occultations, lists of transits of Mercury, Inferior Conjunctions of Venus, oppositions of Mars 1971 to 1999, and passages of Saturn's rings through both the Earth and the Sun; the late M. B. B. Heath for lists of elongations of Mercury and Venus; S. W. Milbourn, Director of the Comet Section of the British Astronomical Association, for valuable assistance in compiling the list of periodic comets; H. G. Miles for the list of principal meteor showers; Dr Donald A. MacRae and the Royal Astronomical Society of Canada for the list of Brightest Stars; C. E. Worley of the US Naval Observatory, Washington, and the Royal Astronomical Society of Canada for selections from his list of binary stars; Dr Th. Schmidt-Kaler of the Ruhr-Universitat, Bochum, Germany, and the Royal Astronomical Society of Canada for the list of Star Clusters, to which the author has added some descriptive notes; J. S. Glasby, of the Variable

Star Section of the British Astronomical Association, for permission to reproduce the lists of Variable Stars in his excellent book on the subject; René Racine and the Royal Astronomical Society of Canada for permission to reproduce the list of galactic nebulae; S. van den Bergh and the Royal Astronomical Society of Canada for the list of external galaxies; the Royal Astronomical Society of Canada for the reproduction of *Messier's Catalogue*; J. Galt of the Dominion Radio Astrophysical Observatory, Penticton, and the Royal Astronomical Society of Canada, for the list of radio sources; J. R. Smith, Director of the Radio Section of the British Astronomical Association, for the table of frequencies and wavelengths; K. E. Chilton of the Royal Astronomical Society of Canada for his kind assistance in supplying information; E. A. Beet for helpful suggestions; Patrick Moore for his most valuable suggestions and permission to use much of the information contained in many of his excellent books.